MW00668622

# **FREE** Study Skills Videos/DVD Offer

Dear Customer,

Thank you for your purchase from Mometrix! We consider it an honor and a privilege that you have purchased our product and we want to ensure your satisfaction.

As part of our ongoing effort to meet the needs of test takers, we have developed a set of Study Skills Videos that we would like to give you for <u>FREE</u>. These videos cover our *best practices* for getting ready for your exam, from how to use our study materials to how to best prepare for the day of the test.

All that we ask is that you email us with feedback that would describe your experience so far with our product. Good, bad, or indifferent, we want to know what you think!

To get your FREE Study Skills Videos, you can use the **QR code** below, or send us an **email** at studyvideos@mometrix.com with *FREE VIDEOS* in the subject line and the following information in the body of the email:

- The name of the product you purchased.
- Your product rating on a scale of 1-5, with 5 being the highest rating.
- Your feedback. It can be long, short, or anything in between. We just want to know your impressions and experience so far with our product. (Good feedback might include how our study material met your needs and ways we might be able to make it even better. You could highlight features that you found helpful or features that you think we should add.)

If you have any questions or concerns, please don't hesitate to contact me directly.

Thanks again!

Sincerely,

Jay Willis
Vice President
jay.willis@mometrix.com
1-800-673-8175

SCAN HERE

# ISEE

## Upper Level Prep Book 2023 and 2024

## 3 Full-Length Practice Tests

ISEE Exam Secrets Study Guide with Video Tutorials

**2nd Edition**

Copyright © 2023 by Mometrix Media LLC

All rights reserved. This product, or parts thereof, may not be reproduced, stored in a retrieval system, or transmitted in any form or by any means—electronic, mechanical, photocopy, recording, scanning, or other—except for brief quotations in critical reviews or articles, without the prior written permission of the publisher.

Written and edited by Mometrix Test Prep

Printed in the United States of America

This paper meets the requirements of ANSI/NISO Z39.48-1992 (Permanence of Paper).

Mometrix offers volume discount pricing to institutions. For more information or a price quote, please contact our sales department at sales@mometrix.com or 888-248-1219.

Mometrix Media LLC is not affiliated with or endorsed by any official testing organization. All organizational and test names are trademarks of their respective owners.

Paperback
ISBN 13: 978-1-5167-2224-2
ISBN 10: 1-5167-2224-8

# Dear Future Exam Success Story

First of all, **THANK YOU** for purchasing Mometrix study materials!

Second, congratulations! You are one of the few determined test-takers who are committed to doing whatever it takes to excel on your exam. **You have come to the right place.** We developed these study materials with one goal in mind: to deliver you the information you need in a format that's concise and easy to use.

In addition to optimizing your guide for the content of the test, we've outlined our recommended steps for breaking down the preparation process into small, attainable goals so you can make sure you stay on track.

We've also analyzed the entire test-taking process, identifying the most common pitfalls and showing how you can overcome them and be ready for any curveball the test throws you.

Standardized testing is one of the biggest obstacles on your road to success, which only increases the importance of doing well in the high-pressure, high-stakes environment of test day. Your results on this test could have a significant impact on your future, and this guide provides the information and practical advice to help you achieve your full potential on test day.

### Your success is our success

**We would love to hear from you!** If you would like to share the story of your exam success or if you have any questions or comments in regard to our products, please contact us at **800-673-8175** or **support@mometrix.com**.

Thanks again for your business and we wish you continued success!

Sincerely,
The Mometrix Test Preparation Team

Copyright © 2023 by Mometrix Media LLC. All rights reserved.
Written and edited by the Mometrix Exam Secrets Test Prep Team
Printed in the United States of America

# TABLE OF CONTENTS

# Introduction

**Thank you for purchasing this resource!** You have made the choice to prepare yourself for a test that could have a huge impact on your future, and this guide is designed to help you be fully ready for test day. Obviously, it's important to have a solid understanding of the test material, but you also need to be prepared for the unique environment and stressors of the test, so that you can perform to the best of your abilities.

For this purpose, the first section that appears in this guide is the **Secret Keys**. We've devoted countless hours to meticulously researching what works and what doesn't, and we've boiled down our findings to the five most impactful steps you can take to improve your performance on the test. We start at the beginning with study planning and move through the preparation process, all the way to the testing strategies that will help you get the most out of what you know when you're finally sitting in front of the test.

We recommend that you start preparing for your test as far in advance as possible. However, if you've bought this guide as a last-minute study resource and only have a few days before your test, we recommend that you skip over the first two Secret Keys since they address a long-term study plan.

If you struggle with **test anxiety**, we strongly encourage you to check out our recommendations for how you can overcome it. Test anxiety is a formidable foe, but it can be beaten, and we want to make sure you have the tools you need to defeat it.

1

Copyright © Mometrix Media. You have been licensed one copy of this document for personal use only. Any other reproduction or redistribution is strictly prohibited. All rights reserved. This content is provided for test preparation purposes only and does not imply an endorsement by Mometrix of any particular political, scientific, or religious point of view.

# Secret Key #1 – Plan Big, Study Small

There's a lot riding on your performance. If you want to ace this test, you're going to need to keep your skills sharp and the material fresh in your mind. You need a plan that lets you review everything you need to know while still fitting in your schedule. We'll break this strategy down into three categories.

## Information Organization

Start with the information you already have: the official test outline. From this, you can make a complete list of all the concepts you need to cover before the test. Organize these concepts into groups that can be studied together, and create a list of any related vocabulary you need to learn so you can brush up on any difficult terms. You'll want to keep this vocabulary list handy once you actually start studying since you may need to add to it along the way.

## Time Management

Once you have your set of study concepts, decide how to spread them out over the time you have left before the test. Break your study plan into small, clear goals so you have a manageable task for each day and know exactly what you're doing. Then just focus on one small step at a time. When you manage your time this way, you don't need to spend hours at a time studying. Studying a small block of content for a short period each day helps you retain information better and avoid stressing over how much you have left to do. You can relax knowing that you have a plan to cover everything in time. In order for this strategy to be effective though, you have to start studying early and stick to your schedule. Avoid the exhaustion and futility that comes from last-minute cramming!

## Study Environment

The environment you study in has a big impact on your learning. Studying in a coffee shop, while probably more enjoyable, is not likely to be as fruitful as studying in a quiet room. It's important to keep distractions to a minimum. You're only planning to study for a short block of time, so make the most of it. Don't pause to check your phone or get up to find a snack. It's also important to **avoid multitasking**. Research has consistently shown that multitasking will make your studying dramatically less effective. Your study area should also be comfortable and well-lit so you don't have the distraction of straining your eyes or sitting on an uncomfortable chair.

 The time of day you study is also important. You want to be rested and alert. Don't wait until just before bedtime. Study when you'll be most likely to comprehend and remember. Even better, if you know what time of day your test will be, set that time aside for study. That way your brain will be used to working on that subject at that specific time and you'll have a better chance of recalling information.

Finally, it can be helpful to team up with others who are studying for the same test. Your actual studying should be done in as isolated an environment as possible, but the work of organizing the information and setting up the study plan can be divided up. In between study sessions, you can discuss with your teammates the concepts that you're all studying and quiz each other on the details. Just be sure that your teammates are as serious about the test as you are. If you find that your study time is being replaced with social time, you might need to find a new team.

2

Copyright © Mometrix Media. You have been licensed one copy of this document for personal use only. Any other reproduction or redistribution is strictly prohibited. All rights reserved.
This content is provided for test preparation purposes only and does not imply an endorsement by Mometrix of any particular political, scientific, or religious point of view.

# Secret Key #2 – Make Your Studying Count

You're devoting a lot of time and effort to preparing for this test, so you want to be absolutely certain it will pay off. This means doing more than just reading the content and hoping you can remember it on test day. It's important to make every minute of study count. There are two main areas you can focus on to make your studying count.

## Retention

It doesn't matter how much time you study if you can't remember the material. You need to make sure you are retaining the concepts. To check your retention of the information you're learning, try recalling it at later times with minimal prompting. Try carrying around flashcards and glance at one or two from time to time or ask a friend who's also studying for the test to quiz you.

To enhance your retention, look for ways to put the information into practice so that you can apply it rather than simply recalling it. If you're using the information in practical ways, it will be much easier to remember. Similarly, it helps to solidify a concept in your mind if you're not only reading it to yourself but also explaining it to someone else. Ask a friend to let you teach them about a concept you're a little shaky on (or speak aloud to an imaginary audience if necessary). As you try to summarize, define, give examples, and answer your friend's questions, you'll understand the concepts better and they will stay with you longer. Finally, step back for a big picture view and ask yourself how each piece of information fits with the whole subject. When you link the different concepts together and see them working together as a whole, it's easier to remember the individual components.

Finally, practice showing your work on any multi-step problems, even if you're just studying. Writing out each step you take to solve a problem will help solidify the process in your mind, and you'll be more likely to remember it during the test.

## Modality

*Modality* simply refers to the means or method by which you study. Choosing a study modality that fits your own individual learning style is crucial. No two people learn best in exactly the same way, so it's important to know your strengths and use them to your advantage.

For example, if you learn best by visualization, focus on visualizing a concept in your mind and draw an image or a diagram. Try color-coding your notes, illustrating them, or creating symbols that will trigger your mind to recall a learned concept. If you learn best by hearing or discussing information, find a study partner who learns the same way or read aloud to yourself. Think about how to put the information in your own words. Imagine that you are giving a lecture on the topic and record yourself so you can listen to it later.

For any learning style, flashcards can be helpful. Organize the information so you can take advantage of spare moments to review. Underline key words or phrases. Use different colors for different categories. Mnemonic devices (such as creating a short list in which every item starts with the same letter) can also help with retention. Find what works best for you and use it to store the information in your mind most effectively and easily.

3

Copyright © Mometrix Media. You have been licensed one copy of this document for personal use only. Any other reproduction or redistribution is strictly prohibited. All rights reserved.
This content is provided for test preparation purposes only and does not imply an endorsement by Mometrix of any particular political, scientific, or religious point of view.

# Secret Key #3 – Practice the Right Way

Your success on test day depends not only on how many hours you put into preparing, but also on whether you prepared the right way. It's good to check along the way to see if your studying is paying off. One of the most effective ways to do this is by taking practice tests to evaluate your progress. Practice tests are useful because they show exactly where you need to improve. Every time you take a practice test, pay special attention to these three groups of questions:

- The questions you got wrong
- The questions you had to guess on, even if you guessed right
- The questions you found difficult or slow to work through

This will show you exactly what your weak areas are, and where you need to devote more study time. Ask yourself why each of these questions gave you trouble. Was it because you didn't understand the material? Was it because you didn't remember the vocabulary? Do you need more repetitions on this type of question to build speed and confidence? Dig into those questions and figure out how you can strengthen your weak areas as you go back to review the material.

 Additionally, many practice tests have a section explaining the answer choices. It can be tempting to read the explanation and think that you now have a good understanding of the concept. However, an explanation likely only covers part of the question's broader context. Even if the explanation makes perfect sense, **go back and investigate** every concept related to the question until you're positive you have a thorough understanding.

As you go along, keep in mind that the practice test is just that: practice. Memorizing these questions and answers will not be very helpful on the actual test because it is unlikely to have any of the same exact questions. If you only know the right answers to the sample questions, you won't be prepared for the real thing. **Study the concepts** until you understand them fully, and then you'll be able to answer any question that shows up on the test.

It's important to wait on the practice tests until you're ready. If you take a test on your first day of study, you may be overwhelmed by the amount of material covered and how much you need to learn. Work up to it gradually.

On test day, you'll need to be prepared for answering questions, managing your time, and using the test-taking strategies you've learned. It's a lot to balance, like a mental marathon that will have a big impact on your future. Like training for a marathon, you'll need to start slowly and work your way up. When test day arrives, you'll be ready.

Start with the strategies you've read in the first two Secret Keys—plan your course and study in the way that works best for you. If you have time, consider using multiple study resources to get different approaches to the same concepts. It can be helpful to see difficult concepts from more than one angle. Then find a good source for practice tests. Many times, the test website will suggest potential study resources or provide sample tests.

Copyright © Mometrix Media. You have been licensed one copy of this document for personal use only. Any other reproduction or redistribution is strictly prohibited. All rights reserved.
This content is provided for test preparation purposes only and does not imply an endorsement by Mometrix of any particular political, scientific, or religious point of view.

# Practice Test Strategy

If you're able to find at least three practice tests, we recommend this strategy:

## Untimed and Open-Book Practice

Take the first test with no time constraints and with your notes and study guide handy. Take your time and focus on applying the strategies you've learned.

## Timed and Open-Book Practice

Take the second practice test open-book as well, but set a timer and practice pacing yourself to finish in time.

## Timed and Closed-Book Practice

Take any other practice tests as if it were test day. Set a timer and put away your study materials. Sit at a table or desk in a quiet room, imagine yourself at the testing center, and answer questions as quickly and accurately as possible.

Keep repeating timed and closed-book tests on a regular basis until you run out of practice tests or it's time for the actual test. Your mind will be ready for the schedule and stress of test day, and you'll be able to focus on recalling the material you've learned.

5

Copyright © Mometrix Media. You have been licensed one copy of this document for personal use only. Any other reproduction or redistribution is strictly prohibited. All rights reserved.
This content is provided for test preparation purposes only and does not imply an endorsement by Mometrix of any particular political, scientific, or religious point of view.

# Secret Key #4 – Pace Yourself

Once you're fully prepared for the material on the test, your biggest challenge on test day will be managing your time. Just knowing that the clock is ticking can make you panic even if you have plenty of time left. Work on pacing yourself so you can build confidence against the time constraints of the exam. Pacing is a difficult skill to master, especially in a high-pressure environment, so **practice is vital**.

Set time expectations for your pace based on how much time is available. For example, if a section has 60 questions and the time limit is 30 minutes, you know you have to average 30 seconds or less per question in order to answer them all. Although 30 seconds is the hard limit, set 25 seconds per question as your goal, so you reserve extra time to spend on harder questions. When you budget extra time for the harder questions, you no longer have any reason to stress when those questions take longer to answer.

Don't let this time expectation distract you from working through the test at a calm, steady pace, but keep it in mind so you don't spend too much time on any one question. Recognize that taking extra time on one question you don't understand may keep you from answering two that you do understand later in the test. If your time limit for a question is up and you're still not sure of the answer, mark it and move on, and come back to it later if the time and the test format allow. If the testing format doesn't allow you to return to earlier questions, just make an educated guess; then put it out of your mind and move on.

On the easier questions, be careful not to rush. It may seem wise to hurry through them so you have more time for the challenging ones, but it's not worth missing one if you know the concept and just didn't take the time to read the question fully. Work efficiently but make sure you understand the question and have looked at all of the answer choices, since more than one may seem right at first.

Even if you're paying attention to the time, you may find yourself a little behind at some point. You should speed up to get back on track, but do so wisely. Don't panic; just take a few seconds less on each question until you're caught up. Don't guess without thinking, but do look through the answer choices and eliminate any you know are wrong. If you can get down to two choices, it is often worthwhile to guess from those. Once you've chosen an answer, move on and don't dwell on any that you skipped or had to hurry through. If a question was taking too long, chances are it was one of the harder ones, so you weren't as likely to get it right anyway.

On the other hand, if you find yourself getting ahead of schedule, it may be beneficial to slow down a little. The more quickly you work, the more likely you are to make a careless mistake that will affect your score. You've budgeted time for each question, so don't be afraid to spend that time. Practice an efficient but careful pace to get the most out of the time you have.

Copyright © Mometrix Media. You have been licensed one copy of this document for personal use only. Any other reproduction or redistribution is strictly prohibited. All rights reserved. This content is provided for test preparation purposes only and does not imply an endorsement by Mometrix of any particular political, scientific, or religious point of view.

# Secret Key #5 – Have a Plan for Guessing

When you're taking the test, you may find yourself stuck on a question. Some of the answer choices seem better than others, but you don't see the one answer choice that is obviously correct. What do you do?

The scenario described above is very common, yet most test takers have not effectively prepared for it. Developing and practicing a plan for guessing may be one of the single most effective uses of your time as you get ready for the exam.

In developing your plan for guessing, there are three questions to address:

- When should you start the guessing process?
- How should you narrow down the choices?
- Which answer should you choose?

## When to Start the Guessing Process

Unless your plan for guessing is to select C every time (which, despite its merits, is not what we recommend), you need to leave yourself enough time to apply your answer elimination strategies. Since you have a limited amount of time for each question, that means that if you're going to give yourself the best shot at guessing correctly, you have to decide quickly whether or not you will guess.

Of course, the best-case scenario is that you don't have to guess at all, so first, see if you can answer the question based on your knowledge of the subject and basic reasoning skills. Focus on the key words in the question and try to jog your memory of related topics. Give yourself a chance to bring the knowledge to mind, but once you realize that you don't have (or you can't access) the knowledge you need to answer the question, it's time to start the guessing process.

It's almost always better to start the guessing process too early than too late. It only takes a few seconds to remember something and answer the question from knowledge. Carefully eliminating wrong answer choices takes longer. Plus, going through the process of eliminating answer choices can actually help jog your memory.

**Summary**: Start the guessing process as soon as you decide that you can't answer the question based on your knowledge.

7

Copyright © Mometrix Media. You have been licensed one copy of this document for personal use only. Any other reproduction or redistribution is strictly prohibited. All rights reserved.
This content is provided for test preparation purposes only and does not imply an endorsement by Mometrix of any particular political, scientific, or religious point of view.

# How to Narrow Down the Choices

The next chapter in this book (**Test-Taking Strategies**) includes a wide range of strategies for how to approach questions and how to look for answer choices to eliminate. You will definitely want to read those carefully, practice them, and figure out which ones work best for you. Here though, we're going to address a mindset rather than a particular strategy.

Your odds of guessing an answer correctly depend on how many options you are choosing from.

| Number of options left | 5 | 4 | 3 | 2 | 1 |
|---|---|---|---|---|---|
| Odds of guessing correctly | 20% | 25% | 33% | 50% | 100% |

You can see from this chart just how valuable it is to be able to eliminate incorrect answers and make an educated guess, but there are two things that many test takers do that cause them to miss out on the benefits of guessing:

- Accidentally eliminating the correct answer
- Selecting an answer based on an impression

We'll look at the first one here, and the second one in the next section.

To avoid accidentally eliminating the correct answer, we recommend a thought exercise called **the $5 challenge**. In this challenge, you only eliminate an answer choice from contention if you are willing to bet $5 on it being wrong. Why $5? Five dollars is a small but not insignificant amount of money. It's an amount you could afford to lose but wouldn't want to throw away. And while losing

$5 once might not hurt too much, doing it twenty times will set you back $100. In the same way, each small decision you make—eliminating a choice here, guessing on a question there—won't by itself impact your score very much, but when you put them all together, they can make a big difference. By holding each answer choice elimination decision to a higher standard, you can reduce the risk of accidentally eliminating the correct answer.

The $5 challenge can also be applied in a positive sense: If you are willing to bet $5 that an answer choice *is* correct, go ahead and mark it as correct.

**Summary**: Only eliminate an answer choice if you are willing to bet $5 that it is wrong.

8

Copyright © Mometrix Media. You have been licensed one copy of this document for personal use only. Any other reproduction or redistribution is strictly prohibited. All rights reserved. This content is provided for test preparation purposes only and does not imply an endorsement by Mometrix of any particular political, scientific, or religious point of view.

# Which Answer to Choose

You're taking the test. You've run into a hard question and decided you'll have to guess. You've eliminated all the answer choices you're willing to bet $5 on. Now you have to pick an answer. Why do we even need to talk about this? Why can't you just pick whichever one you feel like when the time comes?

The answer to these questions is that if you don't come into the test with a plan, you'll rely on your impression to select an answer choice, and if you do that, you risk falling into a trap. The test writers know that everyone who takes their test will be guessing on some of the questions, so they intentionally write wrong answer choices to seem plausible. You still have to pick an answer though, and if the wrong answer choices are designed to look right, how can you ever be sure that you're not falling for their trap? The best solution we've found to this dilemma is to take the decision out of your hands entirely. Here is the process we recommend:

**Once you've eliminated any choices that you are confident (willing to bet $5) are wrong, select the first remaining choice as your answer.**

Whether you choose to select the first remaining choice, the second, or the last, the important thing is that you use some preselected standard. Using this approach guarantees that you will not be enticed into selecting an answer choice that looks right, because you are not basing your decision on how the answer choices look.

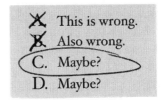

This is not meant to make you question your knowledge. Instead, it is to help you recognize the difference between your knowledge and your impressions. There's a huge difference between thinking an answer is right because of what you know, and thinking an answer is right because it looks or sounds like it should be right.

**Summary**: To ensure that your selection is appropriately random, make a predetermined selection from among all answer choices you have not eliminated.

Copyright © Mometrix Media. You have been licensed one copy of this document for personal use only. Any other reproduction or redistribution is strictly prohibited. All rights reserved.
This content is provided for test preparation purposes only and does not imply an endorsement by Mometrix of any particular political, scientific, or religious point of view.

# Test-Taking Strategies

This section contains a list of test-taking strategies that you may find helpful as you work through the test. By taking what you know and applying logical thought, you can maximize your chances of answering any question correctly!

It is very important to realize that every question is different and every person is different: no single strategy will work on every question, and no single strategy will work for every person. That's why we've included all of them here, so you can try them out and determine which ones work best for different types of questions and which ones work best for you.

## Question Strategies

### ☑ READ CAREFULLY

Read the question and the answer choices carefully. Don't miss the question because you misread the terms. You have plenty of time to read each question thoroughly and make sure you understand what is being asked. Yet a happy medium must be attained, so don't waste too much time. You must read carefully and efficiently.

### ☑ CONTEXTUAL CLUES

Look for contextual clues. If the question includes a word you are not familiar with, look at the immediate context for some indication of what the word might mean. Contextual clues can often give you all the information you need to decipher the meaning of an unfamiliar word. Even if you can't determine the meaning, you may be able to narrow down the possibilities enough to make a solid guess at the answer to the question.

### ☑ PREFIXES

If you're having trouble with a word in the question or answer choices, try dissecting it. Take advantage of every clue that the word might include. Prefixes can be a huge help. Usually, they allow you to determine a basic meaning. *Pre-* means before, *post-* means after, *pro-* is positive, *de-* is negative. From prefixes, you can get an idea of the general meaning of the word and try to put it into context.

### ☑ HEDGE WORDS

Watch out for critical hedge words, such as *likely, may, can, sometimes, often, almost, mostly, usually, generally, rarely,* and *sometimes*. Question writers insert these hedge phrases to cover every possibility. Often an answer choice will be wrong simply because it leaves no room for exception. Be on guard for answer choices that have definitive words such as *exactly* and *always*.

### ☑ SWITCHBACK WORDS

Stay alert for *switchbacks*. These are the words and phrases frequently used to alert you to shifts in thought. The most common switchback words are *but, although,* and *however*. Others include *nevertheless, on the other hand, even though, while, in spite of, despite,* and *regardless of*. Switchback words are important to catch because they can change the direction of the question or an answer choice.

Copyright © Mometrix Media. You have been licensed one copy of this document for personal use only. Any other reproduction or redistribution is strictly prohibited. All rights reserved.
This content is provided for test preparation purposes only and does not imply an endorsement by Mometrix of any particular political, scientific, or religious point of view.

## ⊘ Face Value

When in doubt, use common sense. Accept the situation in the problem at face value. Don't read too much into it. These problems will not require you to make wild assumptions. If you have to go beyond creativity and warp time or space in order to have an answer choice fit the question, then you should move on and consider the other answer choices. These are normal problems rooted in reality. The applicable relationship or explanation may not be readily apparent, but it is there for you to figure out. Use your common sense to interpret anything that isn't clear.

# Answer Choice Strategies

## ⊘ Answer Selection

The most thorough way to pick an answer choice is to identify and eliminate wrong answers until only one is left, then confirm it is the correct answer. Sometimes an answer choice may immediately seem right, but be careful. The test writers will usually put more than one reasonable answer choice on each question, so take a second to read all of them and make sure that the other choices are not equally obvious. As long as you have time left, it is better to read every answer choice than to pick the first one that looks right without checking the others.

## ⊘ Answer Choice Families

An answer choice family consists of two (in rare cases, three) answer choices that are very similar in construction and cannot all be true at the same time. If you see two answer choices that are direct opposites or parallels, one of them is usually the correct answer. For instance, if one answer choice says that quantity $x$ increases and another either says that quantity $x$ decreases (opposite) or says that quantity $y$ increases (parallel), then those answer choices would fall into the same family. An answer choice that doesn't match the construction of the answer choice family is more likely to be incorrect. Most questions will not have answer choice families, but when they do appear, you should be prepared to recognize them.

## ⊘ Eliminate Answers

Eliminate answer choices as soon as you realize they are wrong, but make sure you consider all possibilities. If you are eliminating answer choices and realize that the last one you are left with is also wrong, don't panic. Start over and consider each choice again. There may be something you missed the first time that you will realize on the second pass.

## ⊘ Avoid Fact Traps

Don't be distracted by an answer choice that is factually true but doesn't answer the question. You are looking for the choice that answers the question. Stay focused on what the question is asking for so you don't accidentally pick an answer that is true but incorrect. Always go back to the question and make sure the answer choice you've selected actually answers the question and is not merely a true statement.

## ⊘ Extreme Statements

In general, you should avoid answers that put forth extreme actions as standard practice or proclaim controversial ideas as established fact. An answer choice that states the "process should be used in certain situations, if..." is much more likely to be correct than one that states the "process should be discontinued completely." The first is a calm rational statement and doesn't even make a definitive, uncompromising stance, using a hedge word *if* to provide wiggle room, whereas the second choice is far more extreme.

Copyright © Mometrix Media. You have been licensed one copy of this document for personal use only. Any other reproduction or redistribution is strictly prohibited. All rights reserved.
This content is provided for test preparation purposes only and does not imply an endorsement by Mometrix of any particular political, scientific, or religious point of view.

### ⊘ BENCHMARK

As you read through the answer choices and you come across one that seems to answer the question well, mentally select that answer choice. This is not your final answer, but it's the one that will help you evaluate the other answer choices. The one that you selected is your benchmark or standard for judging each of the other answer choices. Every other answer choice must be compared to your benchmark. That choice is correct until proven otherwise by another answer choice beating it. If you find a better answer, then that one becomes your new benchmark. Once you've decided that no other choice answers the question as well as your benchmark, you have your final answer.

### ⊘ PREDICT THE ANSWER

Before you even start looking at the answer choices, it is often best to try to predict the answer. When you come up with the answer on your own, it is easier to avoid distractions and traps because you will know exactly what to look for. The right answer choice is unlikely to be word-for-word what you came up with, but it should be a close match. Even if you are confident that you have the right answer, you should still take the time to read each option before moving on.

## General Strategies

### ⊘ TOUGH QUESTIONS

If you are stumped on a problem or it appears too hard or too difficult, don't waste time. Move on! Remember though, if you can quickly check for obviously incorrect answer choices, your chances of guessing correctly are greatly improved. Before you completely give up, at least try to knock out a couple of possible answers. Eliminate what you can and then guess at the remaining answer choices before moving on.

### ⊘ CHECK YOUR WORK

Since you will probably not know every term listed and the answer to every question, it is important that you get credit for the ones that you do know. Don't miss any questions through careless mistakes. If at all possible, try to take a second to look back over your answer selection and make sure you've selected the correct answer choice and haven't made a costly careless mistake (such as marking an answer choice that you didn't mean to mark). This quick double check should more than pay for itself in caught mistakes for the time it costs.

### ⊘ PACE YOURSELF

It's easy to be overwhelmed when you're looking at a page full of questions; your mind is confused and full of random thoughts, and the clock is ticking down faster than you would like. Calm down and maintain the pace that you have set for yourself. Especially as you get down to the last few minutes of the test, don't let the small numbers on the clock make you panic. As long as you are on track by monitoring your pace, you are guaranteed to have time for each question.

### ⊘ DON'T RUSH

It is very easy to make errors when you are in a hurry. Maintaining a fast pace in answering questions is pointless if it makes you miss questions that you would have gotten right otherwise. Test writers like to include distracting information and wrong answers that seem right. Taking a little extra time to avoid careless mistakes can make all the difference in your test score. Find a pace that allows you to be confident in the answers that you select.

Copyright © Mometrix Media. You have been licensed one copy of this document for personal use only. Any other reproduction or redistribution is strictly prohibited. All rights reserved.
This content is provided for test preparation purposes only and does not imply an endorsement by Mometrix of any particular political, scientific, or religious point of view.

## ⊘ KEEP MOVING

Panicking will not help you pass the test, so do your best to stay calm and keep moving. Taking deep breaths and going through the answer elimination steps you practiced can help to break through a stress barrier and keep your pace.

# Final Notes

The combination of a solid foundation of content knowledge and the confidence that comes from practicing your plan for applying that knowledge is the key to maximizing your performance on test day. As your foundation of content knowledge is built up and strengthened, you'll find that the strategies included in this chapter become more and more effective in helping you quickly sift through the distractions and traps of the test to isolate the correct answer.

Now that you're preparing to move forward into the test content chapters of this book, be sure to keep your goal in mind. As you read, think about how you will be able to apply this information on the test. If you've already seen sample questions for the test and you have an idea of the question format and style, try to come up with questions of your own that you can answer based on what you're reading. This will give you valuable practice applying your knowledge in the same ways you can expect to on test day.

**Good luck and good studying!**

Copyright © Mometrix Media. You have been licensed one copy of this document for personal use only. Any other reproduction or redistribution is strictly prohibited. All rights reserved. This content is provided for test preparation purposes only and does not imply an endorsement by Mometrix of any particular political, scientific, or religious point of view.

14

Copyright © Mometrix Media. You have been licensed one copy of this document for personal use only. Any other reproduction or redistribution is strictly prohibited. All rights reserved.
This content is provided for test preparation purposes only and does not imply an endorsement by Mometrix of any particular political, scientific, or religious point of view.

# Verbal Reasoning

## Synonyms

As part of your exam, you need to understand how words connect to each other. When you understand how words relate to each other, you will discover more in a passage. This is explained by understanding **synonyms** (e.g., words that mean the same thing) and **antonyms** (e.g., words that mean the opposite of one another). As an example, *dry* and *arid* are synonyms, and *dry* and *wet* are antonyms. There are many pairs of words in English that can be considered synonyms, despite having slightly different definitions. For instance, the words *friendly* and *collegial* can both be used to describe a warm interpersonal relationship, and one would be correct to call them **synonyms**. However, *collegial* (kin to *colleague*) is often used in reference to professional or academic relationships, and *friendly* has no such connotation. If the difference between two words is too great, then they should not be called synonyms. *Hot* and *warm* are not synonyms because their meanings are too distinct. A good way to determine whether two words are synonyms is to substitute one word for the other word and verify that the meaning of the sentence has not changed. Substituting *warm* for *hot* in a sentence would convey a different meaning. Although warm and hot may seem close in meaning, warm generally means that the temperature is moderate, and hot generally means that the temperature is excessively high.

> **Review Video: What Are Synonyms and Antonyms?**
> Visit mometrix.com/academy and enter code: 105612
>
> **Review Video: Synonyms**
> Visit mometrix.com/academy and enter code: 355036

### SYNONYM EXAMPLES

For the Synonyms section, you will have one word and four choices for a synonym of that word. Before you look at the choices, try to think of a few words that could be a synonym for your question. Then, check the choices for a synonym of the question. Some words may seem close to the question, but you are looking for the best choice of a synonym. So, don't let your first reaction be your final decision.

### EXAMPLE 1

**Insatiable**:

A. Compensated

B. Content

C. Fulfilled

D. Unsatisfied

Copyright © Mometrix Media. You have been licensed one copy of this document for personal use only. Any other reproduction or redistribution is strictly prohibited. All rights reserved.
This content is provided for test preparation purposes only and does not imply an endorsement by Mometrix of any particular political, scientific, or religious point of view.

## EXAMPLE 2
**Adherent:**

A. Antagonist

B. Disciple

C. Piquant

D. Zealot

## EXAMPLE 3
**Protrude:**

A. Contract

B. Evocative

C. Secede

D. Swell

## EXAMPLE 4
**Unkempt:**

A. Disorder

B. Flaunt

C. Volatile

D. Unblemished

*Answers*

Example 1: D, Unsatisfied

Example 2: B, Disciple

Example 3: D, Swell

Example 4: A, Disorder

# Sentence Completion

On your exam and in everyday life, you will be introduced to unfamiliar words. Most of the time, the definition of an unknown word can be learned from context clues. Context refers to how a word or phrase is used in a sentence. Understanding the context can help you decide which word or phrase

16

Copyright © Mometrix Media. You have been licensed one copy of this document for personal use only. Any other reproduction or redistribution is strictly prohibited. All rights reserved.
This content is provided for test preparation purposes only and does not imply an endorsement by Mometrix of any particular political, scientific, or religious point of view.

should go in the blank. There are different contextual clues such as definition, description, example, comparison, and contrast. The following are examples:

- Definition: the unknown word is clearly defined by the previous words.
  - "When he was painting, his instrument was a __." (paintbrush)
- Description: the unknown word is described by the previous words.
  - "I was hot, tired, and thirsty; I was __." (dehydrated)
- Example: the unknown word is part of a series of examples.
  - "Water, soda, and __ were the offered beverages." (coffee)
- Comparison: the unknown word is compared to another word.
  - "Barney is agreeable and happy like his __ parents." (positive)
- Contrast: the unknown word is contrasted with another word.
  - "I prefer cold weather to __ conditions." (hot)

## SENTENCE COMPLETION EXAMPLES

The second type of question in the Verbal Reasoning section asks you to read a sentence with a missing word and fill in the blank with the appropriate word. Also, some questions will ask you to read part of a sentence, and you will need to decide how to finish the sentence. In the same way with the Synonyms section, you should read the question and think of a few possible ways to complete the sentence. Then, look over your choices and select the best choice.

## EXAMPLE 1

Determine how to complete this sentence:

As a man of questionable morals, Evan had such a reputation for _____ that Sarah gave _____ to nothing that he told her.

To fill in the blanks, you need to look at the context of the sentence. In this example, Evan, a man who has little respect or poor character, is trying to tell something to Sarah. So, Sarah should be cautious with anything that Evan explains to her. You know that Evan is a man of questionable morals. So, you need to think of a synonym for questionable morals that will be logical in the sentence. If Evan has a reputation for being duplicitous (i.e., lacking truthfulness) or hypocritical, then Sarah should not give credence (i.e., belief) or certainty to anything that Evan explains to her.

## EXAMPLE 2

Determine how to complete this sentence:

When property is limited and the population is constantly growing, real estate _____ typically _____ over time.

1. values ... increase

In this example, you read of restrictions on availability of real estate with a growing demand for housing. When there is a high demand for a product and the product is not widely available, the product can become very expensive. So, you would look over your answer choices and decide on a combination that relates to increasing demand for a limited resource which leads to an increase in the resource's value or price.

Copyright © Mometrix Media. You have been licensed one copy of this document for personal use only. Any other reproduction or redistribution is strictly prohibited. All rights reserved.
This content is provided for test preparation purposes only and does not imply an endorsement by Mometrix of any particular political, scientific, or religious point of view.

### EXAMPLE 3

Determine how to complete this sentence:

He was modest about his accomplishments and did not _____ a promotion to higher levels of responsibility.

In this example, we have a gentleman who has the opportunity to acquire more responsibility with a higher position in his company. However, he has been modest about his skills and efforts that he has performed in the past. So, you will want to look over your answer choices for something that has a connection to plans or strategy.

Copyright © Mometrix Media. You have been licensed one copy of this document for personal use only. Any other reproduction or redistribution is strictly prohibited. All rights reserved.
This content is provided for test preparation purposes only and does not imply an endorsement by Mometrix of any particular political, scientific, or religious point of view.

# Mathematics

## Numbers and Operations

### CLASSIFYING NUMBERS

There are several different kinds of numbers. When you learn to count as a child, you typically start with *Natural Numbers*. These are sometimes called "counting numbers" and begin with 1, 2, 3 ... etc. *Whole Numbers* include all natural numbers as well as 0. *Integers* include all whole numbers as well as their associated negative values (...-2, -1, 0, 1, 2...). Fractions with an integer in the numerator and a non-zero integer in the denominator are called *Rational Numbers*. Numbers such as π, that are non-terminating and non-repeating and cannot be expressed as a fraction, are considered *Irrational Numbers*. Any number that contains the imaginary number $i$, where $i^2 = -1$ and $i = \sqrt{-1}$, is referred to as a *Complex Number*. All natural numbers, whole numbers, integers, rational numbers, and irrational numbers are *Real Numbers*; complex numbers are not real numbers.

Aside from the number 1, all natural numbers can either be classified as prime or composite. *Prime Numbers* are natural numbers greater than 1 whose only factors are 1 and itself. On the other hand, *Composite Numbers* are natural numbers greater than 1 that are not prime numbers. 1 is a special case in that it is neither a prime number nor composite number. According to the *Fundamental Theorem of Arithmetic*, every composite number can be uniquely written as the product of prime numbers.

Numbers are the basic building blocks of mathematics. Specific features of numbers are identified by the following terms:

Integers – The set of positive and negative numbers, including zero. Integers do not include fractions $\left(\frac{1}{3}\right)$, decimals (0.56), or mixed numbers $\left(7\frac{3}{4}\right)$.

Even number – Any integer that can be divided by 2 without leaving a remainder. For example: 2, 4, 6, 8, and so on.

Odd number – Any integer that cannot be divided evenly by 2. For example: 3, 5, 7, 9, and so on.

Decimal number – a number that uses a decimal point to show the part of the number that is less than one. Example: 1.234.

Decimal point – a symbol used to separate the ones place from the tenths place in decimals or dollars from cents in currency.

Decimal place – the position of a number to the right of the decimal point. In the decimal 0.123, the 1 is in the first place to the right of the decimal point, indicating tenths; the 2 is in the second place, indicating hundredths; and the 3 is in the third place, indicating thousandths.

The decimal, or base 10, system is a number system that uses ten different digits (0, 1, 2, 3, 4, 5, 6, 7, 8, 9). An example of a number system that uses something other than ten digits is the binary, or

Copyright © Mometrix Media. You have been licensed one copy of this document for personal use only. Any other reproduction or redistribution is strictly prohibited. All rights reserved. This content is provided for test preparation purposes only and does not imply an endorsement by Mometrix of any particular political, scientific, or religious point of view.

base 2, number system, used by computers, which uses only the numbers 0 and 1. It is thought that the decimal system originated because people had only their 10 fingers for counting.

> **Review Video: Classification of Numbers**
> Visit mometrix.com/academy and enter code: 461071

## OPERATIONS

There are four basic mathematical operations:

Addition increases the value of one quantity by the value of another quantity. Example: 2 + 4 = 6; 8 + 9 = 17. The result is called the sum. With addition, the order does not matter. 4 + 2 = 2 + 4.

Subtraction is the opposite operation to addition; it decreases the value of one quantity by the value of another quantity. Example: 6 – 4 = 2; 17 – 8 = 9. The result is called the difference. Note that with subtraction, the order does matter. 6 – 4 ≠ 4 – 6.

Multiplication can be thought of as repeated addition. One number tells how many times to add the other number to itself. Example: 3 × 2 (three times two) = 2 + 2 + 2 = 6. With multiplication, the order does not matter. 2 × 3 (or 3 + 3) = 3 × 2 (or 2 + 2 + 2).

Division is the opposite operation to multiplication; one number tells us how many parts to divide the other number into. Example: 20 ÷ 4 = 5; if 20 is split into 4 equal parts, each part is 5. With division, the order of the numbers does matter. 20 ÷ 4 ≠ 4 ÷ 20.

## WORKING WITH POSITIVE & NEGATIVE NUMBERS

A precursor to working with negative numbers is understanding what **absolute values** are. A number's absolute value is simply the distance away from zero a number is on the number line. The absolute value of a number is always positive and is written $|x|$.

When adding signed numbers, if the signs are the same simply add the absolute values of the addends and apply the original sign to the sum. For example, $(+4) + (+8) = +12$ and $(-4) + (-8) = -12$. When the original signs are different, take the absolute values of the addends and subtract the smaller value from the larger value, then apply the original sign of the larger value to the difference. For instance, $(+4) + (-8) = -4$ and $(-4) + (+8) = +4$.

For subtracting signed numbers, change the sign of the number after the minus symbol and then follow the same rules used for addition. For example, $(+4) - (+8) = (+4) + (-8) = -4$.

If the signs are the same the product is positive when multiplying signed numbers. For example, $(+4) \times (+8) = +32$ and $(-4) \times (-8) = +32$. If the signs are opposite, the product is negative. For example, $(+4) \times (-8) = -32$ and $(-4) \times (+8) = -32$. When more than two factors are multiplied together, the sign of the product is determined by how many negative factors are present. If there are an odd number of negative factors then the product is negative, whereas an even number of negative factors indicates a positive product. For instance, $(+4) \times (-8) \times (-2) = +64$ and $(-4) \times (-8) \times (-2) = -64$.

The rules for dividing signed numbers are similar to multiplying signed numbers. If the dividend and divisor have the same sign, the quotient is positive. If the dividend and divisor have opposite signs, the quotient is negative. For example, $(-4) \div (+8) = -0.5$.

Copyright © Mometrix Media. You have been licensed one copy of this document for personal use only. Any other reproduction or redistribution is strictly prohibited. All rights reserved. This content is provided for test preparation purposes only and does not imply an endorsement by Mometrix of any particular political, scientific, or religious point of view.

## EXPONENTS AND PARENTHESES

An exponent is a superscript number placed next to another number at the top right. It indicates how many times the base number is to be multiplied by itself. Exponents provide a shorthand way to write what would be a longer mathematical expression. Example: $a^2 = a \times a$; $2^4 = 2 \times 2 \times 2 \times 2$. A number with an exponent of 2 is said to be "squared," while a number with an exponent of 3 is said to be "cubed." The value of a number raised to an exponent is called its power. So, $8^4$ is read as "8 to the 4th power," or "8 raised to the power of 4." A negative exponent is the same as the reciprocal of a positive exponent. Example: $a^{-2} = 1/a^2$.

Parentheses are used to designate which operations should be done first when there are multiple operations. Example: $4 - (2 + 1) = 1$; the parentheses tell us that we must add 2 and 1, and then subtract the sum from 4, rather than subtracting 2 from 4 and then adding 1 (this would give us an answer of 3).

## ORDER OF OPERATIONS

The **order of operations** is a set of rules that dictates the order in which we must perform each operation in an expression so that we will evaluate it accurately. If we have an expression that includes multiple different operations, the order of operations tells us which operations to do first. The most common mnemonic for the order of operations is **PEMDAS**, or "Please Excuse My Dear Aunt Sally." PEMDAS stands for parentheses, exponents, multiplication, division, addition, and subtraction. It is important to understand that multiplication and division have equal precedence, as do addition and subtraction, so those pairs of operations are simply worked from left to right in order.

Example: Evaluate the expression $5 + 20 \div 4 \times (2 + 3)^2 - 6$ using the correct order of operations.

- **P:** Perform the operations inside the parentheses: $(2 + 3) = 5$
- **E:** Simplify the exponents: $(5)^2 = 5 \times 5 = 25$
  - The expression now looks like this: $5 + 20 \div 4 \times 25 - 6$
- **MD:** Perform multiplication and division from left to right: $20 \div 4 = 5$; then $5 \times 25 = 125$
  - The expression now looks like this: $5 + 125 - 6$
- **AS:** Perform addition and subtraction from left to right: $5 + 125 = 130$; then $130 - 6 = 124$

> **Review Video: Order of Operations**
> Visit mometrix.com/academy and enter code: 259675

## LAWS OF EXPONENTS

The laws of exponents are as follows:

1. Any number to the power of 1 is equal to itself: $a^1 = a$.
2. The number 1 raised to any power is equal to 1: $1^n = 1$.
3. Any number raised to the power of 0 is equal to 1: $a^0 = 1$.
4. Add exponents to multiply powers of the same base number: $a^n \times a^m = a^{n+m}$.
5. Subtract exponents to divide powers of the same number; that is $a^n \div a^m = a^{n-m}$.
6. Multiply exponents to raise a power to a power: $(a^n)^m = a^{n \times m}$.
7. If multiplied or divided numbers inside parentheses are collectively raised to a power, this is the same as each individual term being raised to that power: $(a \times b)^n = a^n \times b^n$; $(a \div b)^n = a^n \div b^n$.

21

Copyright © Mometrix Media. You have been licensed one copy of this document for personal use only. Any other reproduction or redistribution is strictly prohibited. All rights reserved. This content is provided for test preparation purposes only and does not imply an endorsement by Mometrix of any particular political, scientific, or religious point of view.

Note: Exponents do not have to be integers. Fractional or decimal exponents follow all the rules above as well. Example: $5^{\frac{1}{4}} \times 5^{\frac{3}{4}} = 5^{\frac{1}{4}+\frac{3}{4}} = 5^1 = 5$.

**Review Video: Properties of Exponents**
Visit mometrix.com/academy and enter code: 532558

## ROOTS AND SQUARE ROOTS

A root, such as a square root, is another way of writing a fractional exponent. Instead of using a superscript, roots use the radical symbol ($\sqrt{\phantom{x}}$) to indicate the operation. A radical will have a number underneath the bar, and may sometimes have a number in the upper left: $\sqrt[n]{a}$, read as "the nth root of a." The relationship between radical notation and exponent notation can be described by this equation: $\sqrt[n]{a} = a^{1/n}$. The two special cases of n = 2 and n = 3 are called square roots and cube roots. If there is no number to the upper left, it is understood to be a square root (n = 2). Nearly all of the roots you encounter will be square roots. A square root is the same as a number raised to the one-half power. When we say that a is the square root of b (a = $\sqrt{b}$), we mean that a multiplied by itself equals b: (a × a = b).

A perfect square is a number that has an integer for its square root. There are 10 perfect squares from 1 to 100: 1, 4, 9, 16, 25, 36, 49, 64, 81, 100 (the squares of integers 1 through 10).

## FACTORS AND MULTIPLES

Factors are numbers that are multiplied together to obtain a product. For example, in the equation 2 × 3 = 6, the numbers 2 and 3 are factors. A prime number has only two factors (1 and itself), but other numbers can have many factors.

**Review Video: Factors**
Visit mometrix.com/academy and enter code: 920086

A common factor is a number that divides exactly into two or more other numbers. For example, the factors of 12 are 1, 2, 3, 4, 6, and 12, while the factors of 15 are 1, 3, 5, and 15. The common factors of 12 and 15 are 1 and 3. A prime factor is also a prime number. Therefore, the prime factors of 12 are 2 and 3. For 15, the prime factors are 3 and 5.

The greatest common factor (GCF) is the largest number that is a factor of two or more numbers. For example, the factors of 15 are 1, 3, 5, and 15; the factors of 35 are 1, 5, 7, and 35. Therefore, the greatest common factor of 15 and 35 is 5.

The least common multiple (LCM) is the smallest number that is a multiple of two or more numbers. For example, the multiples of 3 include 3, 6, 9, 12, 15, etc.; the multiples of 5 include 5, 10, 15, 20, etc. Therefore, the least common multiple of 3 and 5 is 15.

**Review Video: Multiples**
Visit mometrix.com/academy and enter code: 626738

## FRACTIONS

A fraction is a number that is expressed as one integer written above another integer, with a dividing line between them ($\frac{x}{y}$). It represents the quotient of the two numbers "x divided by y." It can also be thought of as x out of y equal parts.

22

Copyright © Mometrix Media. You have been licensed one copy of this document for personal use only. Any other reproduction or redistribution is strictly prohibited. All rights reserved.
This content is provided for test preparation purposes only and does not imply an endorsement by Mometrix of any particular political, scientific, or religious point of view.

The top number of a fraction is called the numerator, and it represents the number of parts under consideration. The 1 in $\frac{1}{4}$ means that 1 part out of the whole is being considered in the calculation. The bottom number of a fraction is called the denominator, and it represents the total number of equal parts. The 4 in $\frac{1}{4}$ means that the whole consists of 4 equal parts. A fraction cannot have a denominator of zero; this is referred to as "undefined."

Fractions can be manipulated by multiplying or dividing (but not adding or subtracting) both the numerator and denominator by the same number, without changing the value of the fraction. If you divide both numbers by a common factor, you are reducing or simplifying the fraction. Two fractions that have the same value, but are expressed differently are known as equivalent fractions. For example, $\frac{2}{10}, \frac{3}{15}, \frac{4}{20}$, and $\frac{5}{25}$ are all equivalent fractions. They can also all be reduced or simplified to $\frac{1}{5}$.

When two fractions are manipulated so that they have the same denominator, this is known as finding a common denominator. The number chosen to be that common denominator should be the least common multiple of the two original denominators. Example: $\frac{3}{4}$ and $\frac{5}{6}$; the least common multiple of 4 and 6 is 12. Manipulating to achieve the common denominator: $\frac{3}{4} = \frac{9}{12}; \frac{5}{6} = \frac{10}{12}$.

If two fractions have a common denominator, they can be added or subtracted simply by adding or subtracting the two numerators and retaining the same denominator. Example: $\frac{1}{2} + \frac{1}{4} = \frac{2}{4} + \frac{1}{4} = \frac{3}{4}$. If the two fractions do not already have the same denominator, one or both of them must be manipulated to achieve a common denominator before they can be added or subtracted.

Two fractions can be multiplied by multiplying the two numerators to find the new numerator and the two denominators to find the new denominator. Example: $\frac{1}{3} \times \frac{2}{3} = \frac{1 \times 2}{3 \times 3} = \frac{2}{9}$.

Two fractions can be divided flipping the numerator and denominator of the second fraction and then proceeding as though it were a multiplication. Example: $\frac{2}{3} \div \frac{3}{4} = \frac{2}{3} \times \frac{4}{3} = \frac{8}{9}$.

A fraction whose denominator is greater than its numerator is known as a proper fraction, while a fraction whose numerator is greater than its denominator is known as an improper fraction. Proper fractions have values less than one and improper fractions have values greater than one.

A mixed number is a number that contains both an integer and a fraction. Any improper fraction can be rewritten as a mixed number. Example: $\frac{8}{3} = \frac{6}{3} + \frac{2}{3} = 2 + \frac{2}{3} = 2\frac{2}{3}$. Similarly, any mixed number can be rewritten as an improper fraction. Example: $1\frac{3}{5} = 1 + \frac{3}{5} = \frac{5}{5} + \frac{3}{5} = \frac{8}{5}$.

A fraction that contains a fraction in the numerator, denominator, or both is called a *Complex Fraction*. These can be solved in a number of ways; with the simplest being by following the order of operations as stated earlier. For example, $\frac{\left(\frac{4}{7}\right)}{\left(\frac{5}{8}\right)} = \frac{0.571}{0.625} = 0.914$. Another way to solve

Copyright © Mometrix Media. You have been licensed one copy of this document for personal use only. Any other reproduction or redistribution is strictly prohibited. All rights reserved. This content is provided for test preparation purposes only and does not imply an endorsement by Mometrix of any particular political, scientific, or religious point of view.

this problem is to multiply the fraction in the numerator by the reciprocal of the fraction in the denominator. For example, $\dfrac{\left(\frac{4}{7}\right)}{\left(\frac{5}{8}\right)} = \frac{4}{7} \times \frac{8}{5} = \frac{32}{35} = 0.914$.

**Review Video: Overview of Fractions**
Visit mometrix.com/academy and enter code: 262335

## PERCENTAGES

Percentages can be thought of as fractions that are based on a whole of 100; that is, one whole is equal to 100%. The word percent means "per hundred." Fractions can be expressed as percents by finding equivalent fractions with a denomination of 100. Example: $\frac{7}{10} = \frac{70}{100} = 70\%$; $\frac{1}{4} = \frac{25}{100} = 25\%$.

To express a percentage as a fraction, divide the percentage number by 100 and reduce the fraction to its simplest possible terms. Example: $60\% = \frac{60}{100} = \frac{3}{5}$; $96\% = \frac{96}{100} = \frac{24}{25}$.

Converting decimals to percentages and percentages to decimals is as simple as moving the decimal point. To convert from a decimal to a percent, move the decimal point two places to the right. To convert from a percent to a decimal, move it two places to the left. Example: 0.23 = 23%; 5.34 = 534%; 0.007 = 0.7%; 700% = 7.00; 86% = 0.86; 0.15% = 0.0015.

It may be helpful to remember that the percentage number will always be larger than the equivalent decimal number.

A percentage problem can be presented three main ways: (1) Find what percentage of some number another number is. Example: What percentage of 40 is 8? (2) Find what number is some percentage of a given number. Example: What number is 20% of 40? (3) Find what number another number is a given percentage of. Example: What number is 8 20% of? The three components in all of these cases are the same: a whole (W), a part (P), and a percentage (%). These are related by the equation: P = W × %. This is the form of the equation you would use to solve problems of type (2). To solve types (1) and (3), you would use these two forms: % = P/W and W = P/%.

The thing that frequently makes percentage problems difficult is that they are most often also word problems, so a large part of solving them is figuring out which quantities are what. Example: In a school cafeteria, 7 students choose pizza, 9 choose hamburgers, and 4 choose tacos. Find the percentage that chooses tacos. To find the whole, you must first add all of the parts: 7 + 9 + 4 = 20. The percentage can then be found by dividing the part by the whole (% = P/W): $\frac{4}{20} = \frac{20}{100} = 20\%$.

## RATIOS

A ratio is a comparison of two quantities in a particular order. Example: If there are 14 computers in a lab, and the class has 20 students, there is a student to computer ratio of 20 to 14, commonly written as 20:14.

Two more comparisons used frequently in algebra are ratios and proportions. A *Ratio* is a comparison of two quantities, expressed in a number of different ways. Ratios can be listed as "a to

Copyright © Mometrix Media. You have been licensed one copy of this document for personal use only. Any other reproduction or redistribution is strictly prohibited. All rights reserved. This content is provided for test preparation purposes only and does not imply an endorsement by Mometrix of any particular political, scientific, or religious point of view.

b", "a:b", or "a/b". Examples of ratios are miles per hour (miles/hour), meters per second (meters/second), miles per gallon (miles/gallon), etc.

**Review Video: Ratios**
Visit mometrix.com/academy and enter code: 996914

## PROPORTIONS AND CROSS PRODUCTS

A proportion is a relationship between two quantities that dictates how one changes when the other changes. A direct proportion describes a relationship in which a quantity increases by a set amount for every increase in the other quantity, or decreases by that same amount for every decrease in the other quantity. Example: For every 1 sheet cake, 18 people can be served cake. The number of sheet cakes, and the number of people that can be served from them is directly proportional.

A statement of two equal ratios is a *Proportion*, such as $\frac{m}{b} = \frac{w}{z}$. If Fred travels 2 miles in 1 hour and Jane travels 4 miles in 2 hours, their speeds are said to be proportional because $\frac{2}{1} = \frac{4}{2}$. In a proportion, the product of the numerator of the first ratio and the denominator of the second ratio is equal to the product of the denominator of the first ratio and the numerator of the second ratio. Using the previous example, we see that $m \times z = b \times w$, thus $2 \times 2 = 1 \times 4$.

**Review Video: Proportions**
Visit mometrix.com/academy and enter code: 505355

An **inverse proportion** is a relationship in which an increase in one quantity is accompanied by a decrease in the other, or vice versa. Example: the time required for a car trip decreases as the speed increases, and increases as the speed decreases, so the time required is inversely proportional to the speed of the car.

## SCIENTIFIC NOTATION

Scientific notation is a way of writing long numbers in a shorter form. The form $a \times 10^n$ is used in scientific notation. This form means that $a$ is greater than or equal to 1 but less than 10. Also, $n$ is the number of places the decimal must move to get from the original number to $a$.

Example: The number 230,400,000 is long to write. To see this value in scientific notation, place a decimal point between the first and second numbers. This includes all digits through the last non-zero digit ($a = 2.304$).

To find the correct power of 10, count the number of places the decimal point had to move ($n = 8$). The number is positive if the decimal moved to the left. Thus, the number is negative if it moved to the right. So, 230,400,000 can be written as $2.304 \times 10^8$.

Now, let's look at the number 0.00002304. We have the same value for $a$. However, this time the decimal moved 5 places to the right ($n = -5$). So, 0.00002304 can be written as $2.304 \times 10^{-5}$. This notation makes it easy to compare very large or very small numbers. By comparing exponents, you can see that $3.28 \times 10^4$ is smaller than $1.51 \times 10^5$ because 4 is less than 5.

## ADDITION AND SUBTRACTION

To add and subtract numbers in scientific notation, you need the numbers to have the same power of 10. Next, you can add the constants. Then, you can use the power of 10 with the result.

Copyright © Mometrix Media. You have been licensed one copy of this document for personal use only. Any other reproduction or redistribution is strictly prohibited. All rights reserved. This content is provided for test preparation purposes only and does not imply an endorsement by Mometrix of any particular political, scientific, or religious point of view.

If the constant is greater than 10 or less than 1, you need to move the decimal place. For constants less than 1, the decimal is moved to the right. For constants greater than 10, the decimal is moved to the left. Also, the power of 10 needs to change as you move the decimal place.

## EXAMPLE 1

In the problem $(4.8 \times 10^4) + (2.2 \times 10^4)$, the numbers have the same power of 10. So, add 4.8 and 2.2. So, you have 7 as the result. Now, the number can be written as $(7 \times 10^4)$.

## EXAMPLE 2

In the problem $(3.1 \times 10^8) - (2.4 \times 10^8)$, the numbers have the same power of 10. So, subtract 3.1 and 2.4, and you'll have 0.7 as the result. Remember that you cannot have a constant that is less than 1. So, you need to move the decimal place one time to the right: $(7 \times 10^8)$. Also, the power of 10 has to change. Now, the number can be written as $(7 \times 10^{-1})$.

The power of 10 is -1 because we moved the decimal place one time to the right. Now you have $(7 \times 10^{-1}) \times 10^8$. The reason is that we still have the power of 10 as 8. Now, you can add the -1 to the +8 for an answer of $(7 \times 10^7)$.

## EXAMPLE 3

In the problem $(5.3 \times 10^6) + (2.7 \times 10^7)$, the numbers do not have the same power of 10. So, you need one of the terms to have the same power. So, take $(5.3 \times 10^6)$ and change it to $(0.53 \times 10^7)$. Now, you can add 0.53 and 2.7. So, the number can be written as $(3.23 \times 10^7)$.

## MULTIPLICATION

In the problem $(2.4 \times 10^3) \times (5.7 \times 10^5)$, you need to multiply 2.4 and 5.7. Then, you need to add the powers of 10 which are 3 and 5 for this example. So, you have $(13.68 \times 10^8)$. Remember that this cannot be an answer for scientific notation. The 13.68 for a constant is higher than 10. So, move the decimal to the left one time and change the exponent. Now, you have $(1.368 \times 10^9)$ as the answer.

## DIVISION

In the problem $(5.6 \times 10^6) \div (2.3 \times 10^2)$, you need to divide 5.6 and 2.3. Then, you need to subtract the powers of 10 which are 6 and 2 for this example. So, you have $(2.43 \times 10^4)$.

## MATRICES
### MATRIX BASICS

A **matrix** (plural: matrices) is a rectangular array of numbers or variables, often called **elements**, which are arranged in columns and rows. A matrix is generally represented by a capital letter, with its elements represented by the corresponding lowercase letter with two subscripts indicating the row and column of the element. For example, $n_{ab}$ represents the element in row $a$ column $b$ of matrix $N$.

$$N = \begin{bmatrix} n_{11} & n_{12} & n_{13} \\ n_{21} & n_{22} & n_{23} \end{bmatrix}$$

A matrix can be described in terms of the number of rows and columns it contains in the format $a \times b$, where $a$ is the number of rows and $b$ is the number of columns. The matrix shown above is a $2 \times 3$ matrix. Any $a \times b$ matrix where $a = b$ is a square matrix.

Copyright © Mometrix Media. You have been licensed one copy of this document for personal use only. Any other reproduction or redistribution is strictly prohibited. All rights reserved. This content is provided for test preparation purposes only and does not imply an endorsement by Mometrix of any particular political, scientific, or religious point of view.

## ADDITION AND SUBTRACTION WITH MATRICES

There are two categories of basic operations with regard to matrices: operations between a matrix and a scalar, and operations between two matrices.

### SCALAR OPERATIONS

A scalar being added to a matrix is treated as though it were being added to each element of the matrix:

$$M + 4 = \begin{bmatrix} m_{11} + 4 & m_{12} + 4 \\ m_{21} + 4 & m_{22} + 4 \end{bmatrix}$$

The same is true for the other three operations. Subtraction:

$$M - 4 = \begin{bmatrix} m_{11} - 4 & m_{12} - 4 \\ m_{21} - 4 & m_{22} - 4 \end{bmatrix}$$

### MATRIX ADDITION AND SUBTRACTION

All four of the basic operations can be used with operations between matrices (although division is usually discarded in favor of multiplication by the inverse), but there are restrictions on the situations in which they can be used. Matrices that meet all the qualifications for a given operation are called **conformable matrices**. However, conformability is specific to the operation; two matrices that are conformable for addition are not necessarily conformable for multiplication.

For two matrices to be conformable for addition or subtraction, they must be of the same dimension; otherwise the operation is not defined. If matrix $M$ is a $3 \times 2$ matrix and matrix $N$ is a $2 \times 3$ matrix, the operations $M + N$ and $M - N$ are meaningless. If matrices $M$ and $N$ are the same size, the operation is as simple as adding or subtracting all of the corresponding elements:

$$\begin{bmatrix} m_{11} & m_{12} \\ m_{21} & m_{22} \end{bmatrix} + \begin{bmatrix} n_{11} & n_{12} \\ n_{21} & n_{22} \end{bmatrix} = \begin{bmatrix} m_{11} + n_{11} & m_{12} + n_{12} \\ m_{21} + n_{21} & m_{22} + n_{22} \end{bmatrix}$$

$$\begin{bmatrix} m_{11} & m_{12} \\ m_{21} & m_{22} \end{bmatrix} - \begin{bmatrix} n_{11} & n_{12} \\ n_{21} & n_{22} \end{bmatrix} = \begin{bmatrix} m_{11} - n_{11} & m_{12} - n_{12} \\ m_{21} - n_{21} & m_{22} - n_{22} \end{bmatrix}$$

The result of addition or subtraction is a matrix of the same dimension as the two original matrices involved in the operation.

### PERMUTATION AND COMBINATION

When trying to calculate the probability of an event using the (desired outcomes)/(total outcomes formula), you may frequently find that there are too many outcomes to individually count them.

Permutation and combination formulas offer a shortcut to counting outcomes. The primary distinction between permutations and combinations is that permutations take into account order, while combinations do not. To calculate the number of possible groupings, there are two necessary parameters: the number of items available for selection and the number to be selected. The number of permutations of $r$ items given a set of $n$ items can be calculated as $_nP_r = \frac{n!}{(n-r)!}$. The number of combinations of $r$ items given a set of $n$ items can be calculated as $_nC_r = \frac{n!}{r!(n-r)!}$ or $_nC_r = \frac{_nP_r}{r!}$.

### EXAMPLE 1

Liz plays a game where she draws 6 cards from a deck of 52. How many combinations of cards can she draw?

Copyright © Mometrix Media. You have been licensed one copy of this document for personal use only. Any other reproduction or redistribution is strictly prohibited. All rights reserved. This content is provided for test preparation purposes only and does not imply an endorsement by Mometrix of any particular political, scientific, or religious point of view.

To determine the number of combinations of 6 cards from a deck of 52, evaluate:

$$\frac{52!}{(52-6)!\,6!} = \frac{52 \cdot 51 \cdot 50 \cdot 49 \cdot 48 \cdot 47 \cdot 46!}{46!\,6!} =$$

$$\frac{52 \cdot 51 \cdot 50 \cdot 49 \cdot 48 \cdot 47}{6 \cdot 5 \cdot 4 \cdot 3 \cdot 2 \cdot 1} = \frac{13 \cdot 17 \cdot 10 \cdot 49 \cdot 4 \cdot 47}{1}$$

$$= 20358520$$

There are 20,358,520 combinations of cards that she can draw.

## Example 2

Write the formula to compute the combination of r objects from a group of n objects. Twenty students are running for four class representative positions. Determine how many different combinations of four students can be selected from the twenty?

To determine the number of combinations of $r$ objects from a total of $n$ objects, use the formula: $_nC_r = \frac{n!}{(n-r)!\,r!}$

To determine the number of combinations of 4 students from 20, evaluate:

$$\frac{20!}{(20-4)!\,4!} = \frac{20 \cdot 19 \cdot 18 \cdot 17 \cdot 16!}{16!\,4!} =$$

$$\frac{20 \cdot 19 \cdot 18 \cdot 17}{4 \cdot 3 \cdot 2 \cdot 1} = \frac{5 \cdot 19 \cdot 3 \cdot 17}{1} = 4845$$

There are 4845 possible combinations of 4 students.

## Factorials

The factorial is a function that can be performed on any non-negative integer. It is represented by the ! sign written after the integer on which it is being performed. The factorial of an integer is the product of all positive integers less than or equal to the number. For example, 4! (read "4 factorial") is calculated as $4 \times 3 \times 2 \times 1 = 24$.

Since 0 is not itself a positive integer, nor does it have any positive integers less than it, 0! cannot be calculated using this method. Instead, 0! is defined by convention to equal 1. This makes sense if you consider the pattern of descending factorials:

$$5! = 120$$

$$4! = \frac{5!}{5} = 24$$

$$3! = \frac{4!}{4} = 6$$

$$2! = \frac{3!}{3} = 2$$

$$1! = \frac{2!}{2} = 1$$

Copyright © Mometrix Media. You have been licensed one copy of this document for personal use only. Any other reproduction or redistribution is strictly prohibited. All rights reserved. This content is provided for test preparation purposes only and does not imply an endorsement by Mometrix of any particular political, scientific, or religious point of view.

$$0! = \frac{1!}{1} = 1$$

# Algebra

## POLYNOMIAL ALGEBRA

Equations are made up of monomials and polynomials. A *Monomial* is a single variable or product of constants and variables, such as $x$, $2x$, or $\frac{2}{x}$. There will never be addition or subtraction symbols in a monomial. Like monomials have like variables, but they may have different coefficients. *Polynomials* are algebraic expressions which use addition and subtraction to combine two or more monomials. Two terms make a binomial; three terms make a trinomial; etc... The *Degree of a Monomial* is the sum of the exponents of the variables. The *Degree of a Polynomial* is the highest degree of any individual term.

## ADD POLYNOMIALS

To add polynomials, you need to add like terms. These terms have the same variable part. An example is $4x^2$ and $3x^2$ have $x^2$ terms. To find the sum of like terms, find the sum of the coefficients. Then, keep the same variable part. You can use the distributive property to distribute the plus sign to each term of the polynomial. For example:

$(4x^2 - 5x + 7) + (3x^2 + 2x + 1) =$

$(4x^2 - 5x + 7) + 3x^2 + 2x + 1 =$

$(4x^2 + 3x^2) + (-5x + 2x) + (7 + 1) =$

$7x^2 - 3x + 8$

## SUBTRACT POLYNOMIALS

To subtract polynomials, you need to subtract like terms. To find the difference of like terms, find the difference of the coefficients. Then, keep the same variable part. You can use the distributive property to distribute the minus sign to each term of the polynomial. For example:

$(-2x^2 - x + 5) - (3x^2 - 4x + 1) =$

$(-2x^2 - x + 5) - 3x^2 + 4x - 1 =$

$(-2x^2 - 3x^2) + (-x + 4x) + (5 - 1) =$

$-5x^2 + 3x + 4$

## MULTIPLY POLYNOMIALS

To multiply two binomials, follow the *FOIL* method. FOIL stands for:

- First: Multiply the first term of each binomial
- Outer: Multiply the outer terms of each binomial
- Inner: Multiply the inner terms of each binomial
- Last: Multiply the last term of each binomial

Using FOIL $(Ax + By)(Cx + Dy) = ACx^2 + ADxy + BCxy + BDy^2$.

Copyright © Mometrix Media. You have been licensed one copy of this document for personal use only. Any other reproduction or redistribution is strictly prohibited. All rights reserved.
This content is provided for test preparation purposes only and does not imply an endorsement by Mometrix of any particular political, scientific, or religious point of view.

Example: $(3x + 6)(4x - 2)$

First: $3x \times 4x = 12x^2$

Outer: $3x \times -2 = -6x$ | Current Expression: $12x^2 - 6x$

Inner: $6 \times 4x = 24x$ | Current Expression: $12x^2 - 6x + 24x$

Last: $6 \times -2 = -12$ | Final Expression: $12x^2 - 6x + 24x - 12$

Now, combine like terms. For this example, that is $-6x + 24x$. Then, the expression looks like: $12x^2 + 18x - 12$. Each number is a multiple of 6. So, the expression becomes $6(2x^2 + 3x - 2)$, and the polynomial has been expanded.

## DIVIDE POLYNOMIALS

To divide polynomials, start with placing the terms of each polynomial in order of one variable. You may put them in ascending or descending order. Also, be consistent with both polynomials. To get the first term of the quotient, divide the first term of the dividend by the first term of the divisor. Next, multiply the first term of the quotient by the entire divisor. Then, subtract that product from the dividend and repeat for the following terms.

You want to end with a remainder of zero or a remainder with a degree that is less than the degree of the divisor. If the quotient has a remainder, write the answer as a mixed expression in the form: $\text{quotient} + \dfrac{\text{remainder}}{\text{divisor}}$.

Example: Divide $4x^5 + 3x^2 - x$ by $x$

$$\frac{4x^5}{x} + \frac{3x^2}{x} - \frac{x}{x} = 4x^4 + 3x - 1$$

Below are patterns of some special products to remember: *perfect trinomial squares*, the *difference between two squares*, the *sum and difference of two cubes*, and *perfect cubes*.

- Perfect Trinomial Squares: $x^2 + 2xy + y^2 = (x + y)^2$ or $x^2 - 2xy + y^2 = (x - y)^2$
- Difference between Two Squares: $x^2 - y^2 = (x + y)(x - y)$
- Sum of Two Cubes: $x^3 + y^3 = (x + y)(x^2 - xy + y^2)$
  Note: the second factor is NOT the same as a perfect trinomial square. So, do not try to factor it further.
- Difference between Two Cubes: $x^3 - y^3 = (x - y)(x^2 + xy + y^2)$
  Again, the second factor is NOT the same as a perfect trinomial square.
- Perfect Cubes: $x^3 + 3x^2y + 3xy^2 + y^3 = (x + y)^3$ and $x^3 - 3x^2y + 3xy^2 - y^3 = (x - y)^3$

## FACTOR A POLYNOMIAL

1. Check for a common monomial factor.
2. Factor out the greatest common monomial factor
3. Look for patterns of special products: differences of two squares, the sum or difference of two cubes for binomial factors, or perfect trinomial squares for trinomial factors.

*Example*

Solve the equation $2x^2 - 5x - 12 = 0$ by factoring.

Copyright © Mometrix Media. You have been licensed one copy of this document for personal use only. Any other reproduction or redistribution is strictly prohibited. All rights reserved. This content is provided for test preparation purposes only and does not imply an endorsement by Mometrix of any particular political, scientific, or religious point of view.

The expression $2x^2 - 5x - 12$ splits into two factors of the form $(2x + a)(x + b)$. To find $a$ and $b$, you must find two factors of -12 that sum to -5 after one of them is doubled.

-12 can be factored in the following ways: 1 and -12 | 2 and -6 | 3 and -4 |

4 and -3 | 6 and -2 | 12 and -1.

Of these factors, only 3 and -4 will sum to -5 after we double one of them. Since -4 is the factor that must be doubled, it should go in position $b$, where it will be multiplied by $2x$ when the FOIL method is used. The factored expression is $(2x + 3)(x - 4)$. So, you are left with $(2x + 3)(x - 4) = 0$.

By the zero product property, each value of $x$ that will make one of the factors equal zero is a solution to this equation. The first factor equals zero when $x = -1.5$, and the second factor equals zero when x = 4. So, those are the solutions.

Note: The factor may be a trinomial but not a perfect trinomial square. So, look for a factorable form: $x^2 + (a + b)x + ab = (x + a)(x + b)$

or $(ac)x^2 + (ad + bc)x + bd = (ax + b)(cx + d)$

Some factors may have four terms. So, look for groups to factor. After you have found the factors, write the original polynomial as the product of all the factors. Make sure that all of the polynomial factors are prime. Monomial factors may be prime or composite. Check your work by multiplying the factors to make sure you get the original polynomial.

> **Review Video: Polynomials**
> Visit mometrix.com/academy and enter code: 305005

## INEQUALITIES

In algebra and higher areas of math, you will work with problems that do not equal each other. The statement comparing such expressions with symbols such as < (less than) or > (greater than) is called an *Inequality*.

One way to remember these symbols is to see that the sign for "less than" looks like an *L* for *Less*. *The terms less than or equal to, at most*, or *no more than* are for the symbol ≤. Also, the terms *greater than or equal to, at least*, and *no less than* are for the symbol ≥.

### GRAPHING AND SOLVING INEQUALITIES

Solving inequalities can be done with the same rules as for solving equations. However, when multiplying or dividing by a negative number, the direction of the inequality sign must be flipped or reversed.

*Example 1*

An example of an inequality is $7x > 5$. To solve for $x$, divide both sides by 7, and the solution is $x > \frac{5}{7}$. Graphs of the solution set of inequalities are given on a number line. Open circles are used to show that an expression approaches a number. However, the open circle points out that it is not equal to that number.

*Example 2*

Graph $10 > -2x + 4$.

Copyright © Mometrix Media. You have been licensed one copy of this document for personal use only. Any other reproduction or redistribution is strictly prohibited. All rights reserved.
This content is provided for test preparation purposes only and does not imply an endorsement by Mometrix of any particular political, scientific, or religious point of view.

In order to graph the inequality $10 > -2x + 4$, you need to solve for $x$. The opposite of addition is subtraction. So, subtract 4 from both sides. This gives you $6 > -2x$.

Next, the opposite of multiplication is division. So, divide both sides by $-2$. Don't forget to flip the inequality symbol because you are dividing by a negative number. Now, you have $-3 < x$. You can rewrite this as $x > -3$.

To graph an inequality, you make a number line. Then, put a circle around the value that is being compared to $x$. If you are graphing a *greater than* or *less than* inequality, the circle remains open. This stands for all of the values except $-3$. If the inequality is *greater than or equal to* or *less than or equal to*, you draw a closed circle around the value. This would stand for all of the values including the number.

Finally, look over the values that the solution stands for. Then, shade the number line in the needed direction. This example calls for graphing all of the values greater than $-3$. This is all of the numbers to the right of $-3$. So, you shade this area on the number line.

## OTHER INEQUALITIES

*Conditional Inequalities* are those with certain values for the variable that will make the condition true. So, other values for the variable where the condition will be false. *Absolute Inequalities* can have any real number as the value for the variable to make the condition true. So, there is no real number value for the variable that will make the condition false.

*Double Inequalities* are when two inequality statements are part of the same variable expression. An example of this is $-c < ax + b < c$.

## SOLVING QUADRATIC EQUATIONS

The *Quadratic Formula* is used to solve quadratic equations when other methods are more difficult. To use the quadratic formula to solve a quadratic equation, begin by rewriting the equation in standard form $ax^2 + bx + c = 0$, where $a$, $b$, and $c$ are coefficients. Once you have identified the values of the coefficients, substitute those values into the quadratic formula $= \frac{-b \pm \sqrt{b^2 - 4ac}}{2a}$. Evaluate the equation and simplify the expression. Again, check each root by substituting into the original equation. In the quadratic formula, the portion of the formula under the radical ($b^2 - 4ac$) is called the *Discriminant*. If the discriminant is zero, there is only one root: zero. If the discriminant is positive, there are two different real roots. If the discriminant is negative, there are no real roots.

To solve a quadratic equation by *Factoring*, begin by rewriting the equation in standard form, if necessary. Factor the side with the variable then set each of the factors equal to zero and solve the resulting linear equations. Check your answers by substituting the roots you found into the original equation. If, when writing the equation in standard form, you have an equation in the form $x^2 + c = 0$ or $x^2 - c = 0$, set $x^2 = -c$ or $x^2 = c$ and take the square root of $c$. If $c = 0$, the only real root is zero. If $c$ is positive, there are two real roots—the positive and negative square root values. If $c$ is negative, there are no real roots because you cannot take the square root of a negative number.

To solve a quadratic equation by *Completing the Square*, rewrite the equation so that all terms containing the variable are on the left side of the equal sign, and all the constants are on the right side of the equal sign. Make sure the coefficient of the squared term is 1. If there is a coefficient with the squared term, divide each term on both sides of the equal side by that number. Next, work with the coefficient of the single-variable term. Square half of this coefficient, and add that value to both sides. Now you can factor the left side (the side containing the variable) as the square of a binomial.

Copyright © Mometrix Media. You have been licensed one copy of this document for personal use only. Any other reproduction or redistribution is strictly prohibited. All rights reserved.
This content is provided for test preparation purposes only and does not imply an endorsement by Mometrix of any particular political, scientific, or religious point of view.

$x^2 + 2ax + a^2 = C \Rightarrow (x + a)^2 = C$, where $x$ is the variable, and $a$ and $C$ are constants. Take the square root of both sides and solve for the variable. Substitute the value of the variable in the original problem to check your work.

In order to solve a *Radical Equation*, begin by isolating the radical term on one side of the equation, and move all other terms to the other side of the equation. Look at the index of the radicand. Remember, if no number is given, the index is 2, meaning square root. Raise both sides of the equation to the power equal to the index of the radical. Solve the resulting equation as you would a normal polynomial equation. When you have found the roots, you must check them in the original problem to eliminate extraneous roots.

| **Review Video: Using the Quadratic Formula** |
| Visit mometrix.com/academy and enter code: 163102 |

Copyright © Mometrix Media. You have been licensed one copy of this document for personal use only. Any other reproduction or redistribution is strictly prohibited. All rights reserved. This content is provided for test preparation purposes only and does not imply an endorsement by Mometrix of any particular political, scientific, or religious point of view.

# Geometry

## LINES AND PLANES

A point is a fixed location in space; has no size or dimensions; commonly represented by a dot.

A line is a set of points that extends infinitely in two opposite directions. It has length, but no width or depth. A line can be defined by any two distinct points that it contains. A line segment is a portion of a line that has definite endpoints. A ray is a portion of a line that extends from a single point on that line in one direction along the line. It has a definite beginning, but no ending.

A **plane** is a two-dimensional flat surface defined by three non-collinear points. A plane extends an infinite distance in all directions in those two dimensions. It contains an infinite number of points, parallel lines and segments, intersecting lines and segments, as well as parallel or intersecting rays. A plane will never contain a three-dimensional figure or skew lines, which are lines that don't intersect and are not parallel. Two given planes are either parallel or they intersect at a line. A plane may intersect a circular conic surface to form **conic sections**, such as a parabola, hyperbola, circle or ellipse.

| Review Video: **Lines and Planes** |
| :-: |
| Visit mometrix.com/academy and enter code: 554267 |

Perpendicular lines are lines that intersect at right angles. They are represented by the symbol ⊥. The shortest distance from a line to a point not on the line is a perpendicular segment from the point to the line.

Parallel lines are lines in the same plane that have no points in common and never meet. It is possible for lines to be in different planes, have no points in common, and never meet, but they are not parallel because they are in different planes.

A bisector is a line or line segment that divides another line segment into two equal lengths. A perpendicular bisector of a line segment is composed of points that are equidistant from the endpoints of the segment it is dividing.

Intersecting lines are lines that have exactly one point in common. Concurrent lines are multiple lines that intersect at a single point.

A transversal is a line that intersects at least two other lines, which may or may not be parallel to one another. A transversal that intersects parallel lines is a common occurrence in geometry.

## COORDINATE PLANE

When algebraic functions and equations are shown graphically, they are usually shown on a *Cartesian Coordinate Plane*. The Cartesian coordinate plane consists of two number lines placed

Copyright © Mometrix Media. You have been licensed one copy of this document for personal use only. Any other reproduction or redistribution is strictly prohibited. All rights reserved.
This content is provided for test preparation purposes only and does not imply an endorsement by Mometrix of any particular political, scientific, or religious point of view.

perpendicular to each other, and intersecting at the zero point, also known as the origin. The horizontal number line is known as the x-axis, with positive values to the right of the origin, and negative values to the left of the origin. The vertical number line is known as the y-axis, with positive values above the origin, and negative values below the origin.

Any point on the plane can be identified by an ordered pair in the form (x,y), called coordinates. The x-value of the coordinate is called the abscissa, and the y-value of the coordinate is called the ordinate. The two number lines divide the plane into four quadrants: I, II, III, and IV.

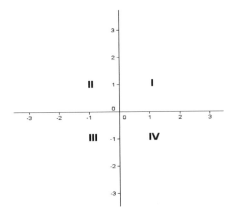

Before learning the different forms equations can be written in, it is important to understand some terminology. A ratio of the change in the vertical distance to the change in horizontal distance is called the *Slope*. On a graph with two points, $(x_1, y_1)$ and $(x_2, y_2)$, the slope is represented by the formula $= \frac{y_2 - y_1}{x_2 - x_1}$; $x_1 \neq x_2$. If the value of the slope is positive, the line slopes upward from left to right. If the value of the slope is negative, the line slopes downward from left to right. If the y-coordinates are the same for both points, the slope is 0 and the line is a *Horizontal Line*. If the x-coordinates are the same for both points, there is no slope and the line is a *Vertical Line*. Two or more lines that have equal slopes are *Parallel Lines*. *Perpendicular Lines* have slopes that are negative reciprocals of each other, such as $\frac{a}{b}$ and $\frac{-b}{a}$.

As mentioned previously, equations can be written many ways. Below is a list of the many forms equations can take.

- Standard Form: $Ax + By = C$; the slope is $\frac{-A}{B}$ and the y-intercept is $\frac{C}{B}$
- *Slope Intercept Form*: $y = mx + b$, where $m$ is the slope and $b$ is the y-intercept
- Point-Slope Form: $y - y_1 = m(x - x_1)$, where m is the slope and $(x_1, y_1)$ is a point on the line
- Two-Point Form: $\frac{y - y_1}{x - x_1} = \frac{y_2 - y_1}{x_2 - x_1}$, where $(x_1, y_1)$ and $(x_2, y_2)$ are two points on the given line
- *Intercept Form*: $\frac{x}{x_1} + \frac{y}{y_1} = 1$, where $(x_1, 0)$ is the point at which a line intersects the x-axis, and $(0, y_1)$ is the point at which the same line intersects the y-axis

Equations can also be written as $ax + b = 0$, where $a \neq 0$. These are referred to as *One Variable Linear Equations*. A solution to an equation is called a *Root*. In the case where we have the equation $5x + 10 = 0$, if we solve for x we get a solution of $x = -2$. In other words, the root of the equation is -2. This is found by first subtracting 10 from both sides, which gives $5x = -10$. Next, simply divide both sides by the coefficient of the variable, in this case 5, to get $x = -2$. This can be checked by plugging -2 back into the original equation $(5)(-2) + 10 = -10 + 10 = 0$.

Copyright © Mometrix Media. You have been licensed one copy of this document for personal use only. Any other reproduction or redistribution is strictly prohibited. All rights reserved. This content is provided for test preparation purposes only and does not imply an endorsement by Mometrix of any particular political, scientific, or religious point of view.

The *Solution Set* is the set of all solutions of an equation. In our example, the solution set would simply be -2. If there were more solutions (there usually are in multivariable equations) then they would also be included in the solution set. When an equation has no true solutions, this is referred to as an *Empty Set*. Equations with identical solution sets are *Equivalent Equations*. An *Identity* is a term whose value or determinant is equal to 1.

**Review Video: Linear Equations Basics**
Visit mometrix.com/academy and enter code: 793005

## CALCULATIONS USING POINTS

Sometimes you need to perform calculations using only points on a graph as input data. Using points, you can determine what the midpoint and distance are. If you know the equation for a line you can calculate the distance between the line and the point.

To find the *Midpoint* of two points $(x_1, y_1)$ and $(x_2, y_2)$, average the x-coordinates to get the x-coordinate of the midpoint, and average the y-coordinates to get the y-coordinate of the midpoint. The formula is midpoint $= \left(\frac{x_1+x_2}{2}, \frac{y_1+y_2}{2}\right)$.

The *Distance* between two points is the same as the length of the hypotenuse of a right triangle with the two given points as endpoints, and the two sides of the right triangle parallel to the x-axis and y-axis, respectively. The length of the segment parallel to the x-axis is the difference between the x-coordinates of the two points. The length of the segment parallel to the y-axis is the difference between the y-coordinates of the two points. Use the Pythagorean Theorem $a^2 + b^2 = c^2$ or $c = \sqrt{a^2 + b^2}$ to find the distance. The formula is: distance $= \sqrt{(x_2 - x_1)^2 + (y_2 - y_1)^2}$.

When a line is in the format $Ax + By + C = 0$, where $A$, $B$, and $C$ are coefficients, you can use a point $(x_1, y_1)$ not on the line and apply the formula $d = \frac{|Ax_1+By_1+C|}{\sqrt{A^2+B^2}}$ to find the distance between the line and the point $(x_1, y_1)$.

**Review Video: Calculations Using Points on a Graph**
Visit mometrix.com/academy and enter code: 883228

## TRANSFORMATION

- Rotation: An object is rotated, or turned, between 0 and 360 degrees, around a fixed point. The size and shape of the object are unchanged.
- Reflection: An object is reflected, or flipped, across a line, so that the original object and reflected object are the same distance from the line of reflection. The size and shape of the object are unchanged.
- Translation: An object is translated, or shifted, horizontally and/or vertically to a new location. The orientation, size, and shape of the object are unchanged.

Copyright © Mometrix Media. You have been licensed one copy of this document for personal use only. Any other reproduction or redistribution is strictly prohibited. All rights reserved. This content is provided for test preparation purposes only and does not imply an endorsement by Mometrix of any particular political, scientific, or religious point of view.

## ROTATION

A line segment begins at (1, 4) and ends at (5, 4). Draw the line segment and rotate the line segment 90º about the point (3, 4).

The point about which the line segment is being rotated is on the line segment. This point should be on both the original and rotated line. The point (3, 4) is the center of the original line segment, and should still be the center of the rotated line segment. The dashed line is the rotated line segment.

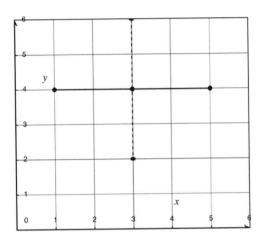

## REFLECTION

*Example 1*: To create a congruent rectangle by reflecting, first draw a line of reflection. The line can be next to or on the figure. Then draw the image reflected across this line.

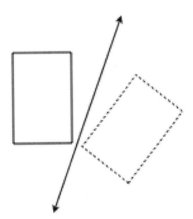

Copyright © Mometrix Media. You have been licensed one copy of this document for personal use only. Any other reproduction or redistribution is strictly prohibited. All rights reserved.
This content is provided for test preparation purposes only and does not imply an endorsement by Mometrix of any particular political, scientific, or religious point of view.

*Example 2*: A line segment begins at (1, 5) and ends at (5, 4). Draw the line segment, then reflect the line segment across the line $y = 3$.

To reflect a segment, consider folding a piece of paper at the line of reflection. The new image should line up exactly with the old image when the paper is folded. The dashed line is the reflected line segment.

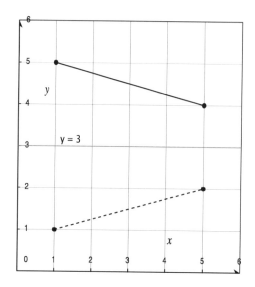

## TRANSLATION

*Example 1:* A line segment on an x-y grid starts at (3, 2) and ends at (4, 1). Draw the line segment, and translate the segment up 2 units and left 2 units.

The solid line segment is the original line segment, and the dashed line is the translated line segment. The y-coordinate of each point has increased by 2, because the points moved two units away from 0. The x-coordinate of each point has decreased by 2, because the points moved two units closer to 0.

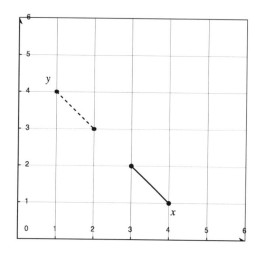

Copyright © Mometrix Media. You have been licensed one copy of this document for personal use only. Any other reproduction or redistribution is strictly prohibited. All rights reserved.
This content is provided for test preparation purposes only and does not imply an endorsement by Mometrix of any particular political, scientific, or religious point of view.

*Example 2:* Identify a transformation that could have been performed on the solid triangle to result in the dashed triangle.

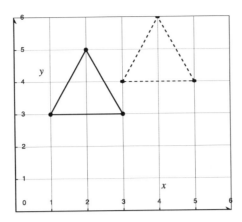

The transformed triangle has the same orientation as the original triangle. It has been shifted up one unit and two units to the right. Because the orientation of the figure has not changed, and its new position can be described using shifts up and to the right, the figure was translated.

## ANGLES

An angle is formed when two lines or line segments meet at a common point. It may be a common starting point for a pair of segments or rays, or it may be the intersection of lines. Angles are represented by the symbol ∠.

The vertex is the point at which two segments or rays meet to form an angle. If the angle is formed by intersecting rays, lines, and/or line segments, the vertex is the point at which four angles are formed. The pairs of angles opposite one another are called vertical angles, and their measures are equal.

An acute angle is an angle with a degree measure less than 90°.

A right angle is an angle with a degree measure of exactly 90°.

An obtuse angle is an angle with a degree measure greater than 90° but less than 180°.

A straight angle is an angle with a degree measure of exactly 180°. This is also a semicircle.

A reflex angle is an angle with a degree measure greater than 180° but less than 360°.

A **full angle** is an angle with a degree measure of exactly 360°. This is also a circle.

> **Review Video: <u>Angles</u>**
> Visit mometrix.com/academy and enter code: 264624

Two angles whose sum is exactly 90° are said to be complementary. The two angles may or may not be adjacent. In a right triangle, the two acute angles are complementary.

Two angles whose sum is exactly 180° are said to be supplementary. The two angles may or may not be adjacent. Two intersecting lines always form two pairs of supplementary angles. Adjacent supplementary angles will always form a straight line.

Copyright © Mometrix Media. You have been licensed one copy of this document for personal use only. Any other reproduction or redistribution is strictly prohibited. All rights reserved. This content is provided for test preparation purposes only and does not imply an endorsement by Mometrix of any particular political, scientific, or religious point of view.

Two angles that have the same vertex and share a side are said to be adjacent. Vertical angles are not adjacent because they share a vertex but no common side.

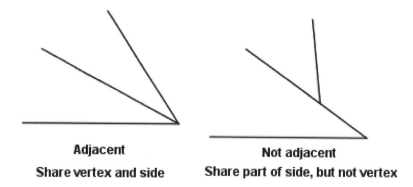

**Adjacent**

**Share vertex and side**

**Not adjacent**

**Share part of side, but not vertex**

When two parallel lines are cut by a transversal, the angles that are between the two parallel lines are interior angles. In the diagram below, angles 3, 4, 5, and 6 are interior angles.

When two parallel lines are cut by a transversal, the angles that are outside the parallel lines are exterior angles. In the diagram below, angles 1, 2, 7, and 8 are exterior angles.

When two parallel lines are cut by a transversal, the angles that are in the same position relative to the transversal and a parallel line are corresponding angles. The diagram below has four pairs of corresponding angles: angles 1 and 5; angles 2 and 6; angles 3 and 7; and angles 4 and 8. Corresponding angles formed by parallel lines are congruent.

When two parallel lines are cut by a transversal, the two interior angles that are on opposite sides of the transversal are called alternate interior angles. In the diagram below, there are two pairs of alternate interior angles: angles 3 and 6, and angles 4 and 5. Alternate interior angles formed by parallel lines are congruent.

When two parallel lines are cut by a transversal, the two exterior angles that are on opposite sides of the transversal are called alternate exterior angles. In the diagram below, there are two pairs of alternate exterior angles: angles 1 and 8, and angles 2 and 7. Alternate exterior angles formed by parallel lines are congruent.

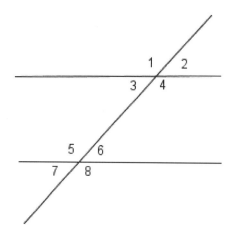

**40**

Copyright © Mometrix Media. You have been licensed one copy of this document for personal use only. Any other reproduction or redistribution is strictly prohibited. All rights reserved.
This content is provided for test preparation purposes only and does not imply an endorsement by Mometrix of any particular political, scientific, or religious point of view.

When two lines intersect, four angles are formed. The non-adjacent angles at this vertex are called vertical angles. Vertical angles are congruent. In the diagram, $\angle ABD \cong \angle CBE$ and $\angle ABC \cong \angle DBE$.

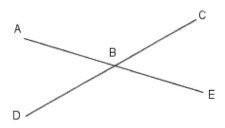

## TRIANGLES

An equilateral triangle is a triangle with three congruent sides. An equilateral triangle will also have three congruent angles, each 60°. All equilateral triangles are also acute triangles.

An isosceles triangle is a triangle with two congruent sides. An isosceles triangle will also have two congruent angles opposite the two congruent sides.

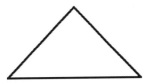

A scalene triangle is a triangle with no congruent sides. A scalene triangle will also have three angles of different measures. The angle with the largest measure is opposite the longest side, and the angle with the smallest measure is opposite the shortest side.

An acute triangle is a triangle whose three angles are all less than 90°. If two of the angles are equal, the acute triangle is also an isosceles triangle. If the three angles are all equal, the acute triangle is also an equilateral triangle.

A right triangle is a triangle with exactly one angle equal to 90°. All right triangles follow the Pythagorean Theorem. A right triangle can never be acute or obtuse.

An obtuse triangle is a triangle with exactly one angle greater than 90°. The other two angles may or may not be equal. If the two remaining angles are equal, the obtuse triangle is also an isosceles triangle.

Copyright © Mometrix Media. You have been licensed one copy of this document for personal use only. Any other reproduction or redistribution is strictly prohibited. All rights reserved.
This content is provided for test preparation purposes only and does not imply an endorsement by Mometrix of any particular political, scientific, or religious point of view.

## TRIANGLE TERMINOLOGY

Altitude of a Triangle: A line segment drawn from one vertex perpendicular to the opposite side. In the diagram below, $\overline{BE}$, $\overline{AD}$, and $\overline{CF}$ are altitudes. The three altitudes in a triangle are always concurrent.

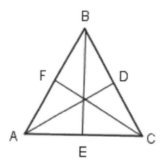

Height of a Triangle: The length of the altitude, although the two terms are often used interchangeably.

Orthocenter of a Triangle: The point of concurrency of the altitudes of a triangle. Note that in an obtuse triangle, the orthocenter will be outside the triangle, and in a right triangle, the orthocenter is the vertex of the right angle.

Median of a Triangle: A line segment drawn from one vertex to the midpoint of the opposite side. This is not the same as the altitude, except the altitude to the base of an isosceles triangle and all three altitudes of an equilateral triangle.

Centroid of a Triangle: The point of concurrency of the medians of a triangle. This is the same point as the orthocenter only in an equilateral triangle. Unlike the orthocenter, the centroid is always inside the triangle. The centroid can also be considered the exact center of the triangle. Any shape triangle can be perfectly balanced on a tip placed at the centroid. The centroid is also the point that is two-thirds the distance from the vertex to the opposite side.

> **Review Video: Incenter, Circumcenter, Orthocenter, and Centroid**
> Visit mometrix.com/academy and enter code: 598260

## GENERAL RULES FOR TRIANGLES

The Triangle Inequality Theorem states that the sum of the measures of any two sides of a triangle is always greater than the measure of the third side. If the sum of the measures of two sides were equal to the third side, a triangle would be impossible because the two sides would lie flat across the third side and there would be no vertex. If the sum of the measures of two of the sides was less than the third side, a closed figure would be impossible because the two shortest sides would never meet.

The sum of the measures of the interior angles of a triangle is always 180°. Therefore, a triangle can never have more than one angle greater than or equal to 90°.

In any triangle, the angles opposite congruent sides are congruent, and the sides opposite congruent angles are congruent. The largest angle is always opposite the longest side, and the smallest angle is always opposite the shortest side.

Copyright © Mometrix Media. You have been licensed one copy of this document for personal use only. Any other reproduction or redistribution is strictly prohibited. All rights reserved. This content is provided for test preparation purposes only and does not imply an endorsement by Mometrix of any particular political, scientific, or religious point of view.

The line segment that joins the midpoints of any two sides of a triangle is always parallel to the third side and exactly half the length of the third side.

## TRIGONOMETRIC RATIOS OF RIGHT TRIANGLES

$$\sin A = \frac{\text{opposite side}}{\text{hypotenuse}} = \frac{a}{c}$$

$$\cos A = \frac{\text{adjacent side}}{\text{hypotenuse}} = \frac{b}{c}$$

$$\tan A = \frac{\text{opposite side}}{\text{adjacent side}} = \frac{a}{b}$$

$$\csc A = \frac{\text{hypotenuse}}{\text{opposite side}} = \frac{c}{a}$$

$$\sec A = \frac{\text{hypotenuse}}{\text{adjacent side}} = \frac{c}{b}$$

$$\cot A = \frac{\text{adjacent side}}{\text{opposite side}} = \frac{b}{a}$$

In the diagram below, angle $C$ is the right angle, and side $c$ is the hypotenuse. Side $a$ is the side adjacent to angle $B$ and side $b$ is the side adjacent to angle $A$. These formulas will work for any acute angle in a right triangle. They will NOT work for any triangle that is not a right triangle. Also, they will not work for the right angle in a right triangle, since there is not a distinct adjacent side to differentiate from the hypotenuse.

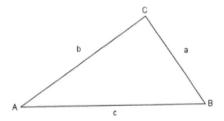

## PYTHAGOREAN THEOREM

The side of a triangle opposite the right angle is called the hypotenuse. The other two sides are called the legs. The Pythagorean Theorem states a relationship among the legs and hypotenuse of a right triangle: $a^2 + b^2 = c^2$, where $a$ and $b$ are the lengths of the legs of a right triangle, and $c$ is the length of the hypotenuse. Note that this formula will only work with right triangles.

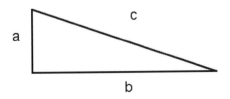

> **Review Video: Pythagorean Theorem**
> Visit mometrix.com/academy and enter code: 906576

**43**

Copyright © Mometrix Media. You have been licensed one copy of this document for personal use only. Any other reproduction or redistribution is strictly prohibited. All rights reserved.
This content is provided for test preparation purposes only and does not imply an endorsement by Mometrix of any particular political, scientific, or religious point of view.

## SIMILARITY AND CONGRUENCE RULES

**Similar triangles** are triangles whose corresponding angles are equal and whose corresponding sides are proportional. Represented by AAA. Similar triangles whose corresponding sides are congruent are also congruent triangles.

Triangles can be shown to be **congruent** in 5 ways:

- **SSS**: Three sides of one triangle are congruent to the three corresponding sides of the second triangle.
- **SAS**: Two sides and the included angle (the angle formed by those two sides) of one triangle are congruent to the corresponding two sides and included angle of the second triangle.
- **ASA**: Two angles and the included side (the side that joins the two angles) of one triangle are congruent to the corresponding two angles and included side of the second triangle.
- **AAS**: Two angles and a non-included side of one triangle are congruent to the corresponding two angles and non-included side of the second triangle.
- **HL**: The hypotenuse and leg of one right triangle are congruent to the corresponding hypotenuse and leg of the second right triangle.

> **Review Video: Similar Triangles**
> Visit mometrix.com/academy and enter code: 398538

## POLYGONS

Each straight line segment of a polygon is called a side.

The point at which two sides of a polygon intersect is called the vertex. In a polygon, the number of sides is always equal to the number of vertices.

A polygon with all sides congruent and all angles equal is called a regular polygon.

A line segment from the center of a polygon perpendicular to a side of the polygon is called the apothem. In a regular polygon, the apothem can be used to find the area of the polygon using the formula $A = \frac{1}{2}ap$, where $a$ is the apothem and $p$ is the perimeter.

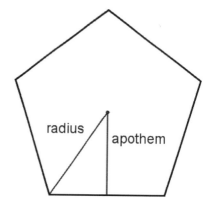

A line segment from the center of a polygon to a vertex of the polygon is called a radius. The radius of a regular polygon is also the radius of a circle that can be circumscribed about the polygon.

44

Copyright © Mometrix Media. You have been licensed one copy of this document for personal use only. Any other reproduction or redistribution is strictly prohibited. All rights reserved.
This content is provided for test preparation purposes only and does not imply an endorsement by Mometrix of any particular political, scientific, or religious point of view.

Triangle – 3 sides

Quadrilateral – 4 sides

Pentagon – 5 sides

Hexagon – 6 sides

Heptagon – 7 sides

Octagon – 8 sides

Nonagon – 9 sides

Decagon – 10 sides

Dodecagon – 12 sides

More generally, an $n$-gon is a polygon that has $n$ angles and $n$ sides.

The sum of the interior angles of an $n$-sided polygon is $(n-2) \times 180°$. For example, in a triangle $n = 3$. So the sum of the interior angles is $(3-2) \times 180° = 180°$. In a quadrilateral, $n = 4$, and the sum of the angles is $(4-2) \times 180° = 360°$.

A diagonal is a line segment that joins two non-adjacent vertices of a polygon.

A convex polygon is a polygon whose diagonals all lie within the interior of the polygon.

A concave polygon is a polygon with a least one diagonal that lies outside the polygon. In the diagram below, quadrilateral $ABCD$ is concave because diagonal $\overline{AC}$ lies outside the polygon.

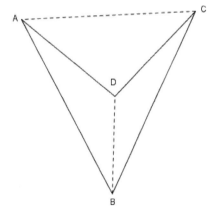

The number of diagonals a polygon has can be found by using the formula: number of diagonals = $\frac{n(n-3)}{2}$, where $n$ is the number of sides in the polygon. This formula works for all polygons, not just regular polygons.

Copyright © Mometrix Media. You have been licensed one copy of this document for personal use only. Any other reproduction or redistribution is strictly prohibited. All rights reserved.
This content is provided for test preparation purposes only and does not imply an endorsement by Mometrix of any particular political, scientific, or religious point of view.

Congruent figures are geometric figures that have the same size and shape. All corresponding angles are equal, and all corresponding sides are equal. It is indicated by the symbol ≅.

Congruent polygons

Similar figures are geometric figures that have the same shape, but do not necessarily have the same size. All corresponding angles are equal, and all corresponding sides are proportional, but they do not have to be equal. It is indicated by the symbol ~.

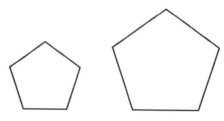

Similar polygons

Note that all congruent figures are also similar, but not all similar figures are congruent.

Line of Symmetry: The line that divides a figure or object into two symmetric parts. Each symmetric half is congruent to the other. An object may have no lines of symmetry, one line of symmetry, or more than one line of symmetry.

Lines of symmetry:

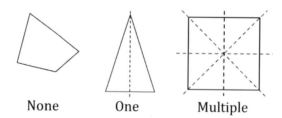

None          One          Multiple

Quadrilateral: A closed two-dimensional geometric figure composed of exactly four straight sides. The sum of the interior angles of any quadrilateral is 360°.

Parallelogram: A quadrilateral that has exactly two pairs of opposite parallel sides. The sides that are parallel are also congruent. The opposite interior angles are always congruent, and the

Copyright © Mometrix Media. You have been licensed one copy of this document for personal use only. Any other reproduction or redistribution is strictly prohibited. All rights reserved.
This content is provided for test preparation purposes only and does not imply an endorsement by Mometrix of any particular political, scientific, or religious point of view.

consecutive interior angles are supplementary. The diagonals of a parallelogram bisect each other. Each diagonal divides the parallelogram into two congruent triangles.

Trapezoid: Traditionally, a quadrilateral that has exactly one pair of parallel sides. Some math texts define trapezoid as a quadrilateral that has at least one pair of parallel sides. Because there are no rules governing the second pair of sides, there are no rules that apply to the properties of the diagonals of a trapezoid.

Rectangles, rhombuses, and squares are all special forms of parallelograms.

Rectangle: A parallelogram with four right angles. All rectangles are parallelograms, but not all parallelograms are rectangles. The diagonals of a rectangle are congruent.

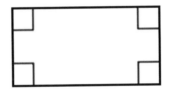

Copyright © Mometrix Media. You have been licensed one copy of this document for personal use only. Any other reproduction or redistribution is strictly prohibited. All rights reserved.
This content is provided for test preparation purposes only and does not imply an endorsement by Mometrix of any particular political, scientific, or religious point of view.

Rhombus: A parallelogram with four congruent sides. All rhombuses are parallelograms, but not all parallelograms are rhombuses. The diagonals of a rhombus are perpendicular to each other.

Square: A parallelogram with four right angles and four congruent sides. All squares are also parallelograms, rhombuses, and rectangles. The diagonals of a square are congruent and perpendicular to each other.

A quadrilateral whose diagonals bisect each other is a parallelogram. A quadrilateral whose opposite sides are parallel (2 pairs of parallel sides) is a parallelogram.

A quadrilateral whose diagonals are perpendicular bisectors of each other is a rhombus. A quadrilateral whose opposite sides (both pairs) are parallel and congruent is a rhombus.

A parallelogram that has a right angle is a rectangle. (Consecutive angles of a parallelogram are supplementary. Therefore, if there is one right angle in a parallelogram, there are four right angles in that parallelogram.)

A rhombus with one right angle is a square. Because the rhombus is a special form of a parallelogram, the rules about the angles of a parallelogram also apply to the rhombus.

## CIRCLES

The center is the single point inside the circle that is equidistant from every point on the circle. (Point $O$ in the diagram below.)

The radius is a line segment that joins the center of the circle and any one point on the circle. All radii of a circle are equal. (Segments $OX$, $OY$, and $OZ$ in the diagram below.)

The diameter is a line segment that passes through the center of the circle and has both endpoints on the circle. The length of the diameter is exactly twice the length of the radius. (Segment $XZ$ in the diagram below.)

Copyright © Mometrix Media. You have been licensed one copy of this document for personal use only. Any other reproduction or redistribution is strictly prohibited. All rights reserved. This content is provided for test preparation purposes only and does not imply an endorsement by Mometrix of any particular political, scientific, or religious point of view.

Concentric circles are circles that have the same center, but not the same length of radii. A bulls-eye target is an example of concentric circles.

An arc is a portion of a circle. Specifically, an arc is the set of points between and including two points on a circle. An arc does not contain any points inside the circle. When a segment is drawn from the endpoints of an arc to the center of the circle, a sector is formed.

A central angle is an angle whose vertex is the center of a circle and whose legs intercept an arc of the circle. Angle *XOY* in the diagram above is a central angle. A minor arc is an arc that has a measure less than 180°. The measure of a central angle is equal to the measure of the minor arc it intercepts. A major arc is an arc having a measure of at least 180°. The measure of the major arc can be found by subtracting the measure of the central angle from 360°.

A semicircle is an arc whose endpoints are the endpoints of the diameter of a circle. A semicircle is exactly half of a circle.

An inscribed angle is an angle whose vertex lies on a circle and whose legs contain chords of that circle. The portion of the circle intercepted by the legs of the angle is called the intercepted arc. The measure of the intercepted arc is exactly twice the measure of the inscribed angle. In the diagram below, angle *ABC* is an inscribed angle. $\widehat{AC} = 2(m\angle ABC)$

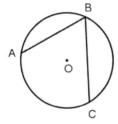

Any angle inscribed in a semicircle is a right angle. The intercepted arc is 180°, making the inscribed angle half that, or 90°. In the diagram below, angle *ABC* is inscribed in semicircle *ABC*, making angle *ABC* equal to 90°.

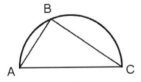

A sector is the portion of a circle formed by two radii and their intercepted arc. While the arc length is exclusively the points that are also on the circumference of the circle, the sector is the entire area bounded by the arc and the two radii.

Copyright © Mometrix Media. You have been licensed one copy of this document for personal use only. Any other reproduction or redistribution is strictly prohibited. All rights reserved.
This content is provided for test preparation purposes only and does not imply an endorsement by Mometrix of any particular political, scientific, or religious point of view.

# Measurement

## AREA AND PERIMETER FORMULAS

### TRIANGLE

The perimeter of any triangle is found by summing the three side lengths; $P = a + b + c$. For an equilateral triangle, this is the same as $P = 3s$, where $s$ is any side length, since all three sides are the same length.

### FIND THE SIDE OF A TRIANGLE

You may have problems that give you the perimeter of a triangle. So, you are asked to find one of the sides.

Example: The perimeter of a triangle is 35 cm. One side length is 10 cm. Another side length is 20cm. Find the length of the missing side.

First:   Set up the equation to set apart a side length.

Now, the equation is $35 = 10 + 20 + c$. So, you are left with $35 = 30 + c$.

Second: Subtract 30 from both sides: $35 - 30 = 30 - 30 + c$

Then, you are left with $5 = c$

The area of any triangle can be found by taking half the product of one side length (base or $b$) and the perpendicular distance from that side to the opposite vertex (height or $h$). In equation form, $A = \frac{1}{2}bh$. For many triangles, it may be difficult to calculate $h$, so using one of the other formulas given here may be easier.

### FIND THE HEIGHT OR THE AREA OF THE BASE

You may have problems that give you the area of a triangle. So, you are asked to find the height or the base.

Example: The area of a triangle is 70 cm², and the height is 10. Find the base.

First: Set up the equation to set apart the base.

The equation is $70 = \frac{1}{2}10b$.

Now, multiply both sides by 2: $70 \times 2 = \frac{1}{2}10b \times 2$.

So, you are left with: $140 = 10b$.

Second: Divide both sides by 10 to get the base: $\frac{140}{10} = \frac{10b}{10}$

50

Copyright © Mometrix Media. You have been licensed one copy of this document for personal use only. Any other reproduction or redistribution is strictly prohibited. All rights reserved. This content is provided for test preparation purposes only and does not imply an endorsement by Mometrix of any particular political, scientific, or religious point of view.

Then, you have $14 = b$.

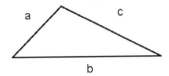

**Review Video: Area and Perimeter of a Triangle**
Visit mometrix.com/academy and enter code: 853779

Another formula that works for any triangle is $A = \sqrt{s(s-a)(s-b)(s-c)}$, where $A$ is the area, $s$ is the semiperimeter $s = \frac{a+b+c}{2}$, and $a$, $b$, and $c$ are the lengths of the three sides.

The area of an equilateral triangle can be found by the formula $A = \frac{\sqrt{3}}{4}s^2$, where $A$ is the area and $s$ is the length of a side. You could use the $30° - 60° - 90°$ ratios to find the height of the triangle and then use the standard triangle area formula, but this is faster.

The area of an isosceles triangle can be found by the formula, $A = \frac{1}{2}b\sqrt{a^2 - \frac{b^2}{4}}$, where $A$ is the area, $b$ is the base (the unique side), and $a$ is the length of one of the two congruent sides. If you do not remember this formula, you can use the Pythagorean Theorem to find the height so you can use the standard formula for the area of a triangle.

## SQUARE

The area of a square is found by using the formula $A = s^2$, where and $s$ is the length of one side.

### FIND THE SIDE OF A SQUARE

You may have problems that give you the area of a square. So, you are asked to find the side.

Example: The area of a square is 9 cm². Find the side.

First: Set up the equation to set apart $s$.

The equation is $9 = s^2$.

Second: Now, you can take the square root of both sides: $\sqrt{9} = \sqrt{s^2}$.

So, you are left with: $3 = s$

The perimeter of a square is found by using the formula $P = 4s$, where $s$ is the length of one side. Because all four sides are equal in a square, it is faster to multiply the length of one side by 4 than to

Copyright © Mometrix Media. You have been licensed one copy of this document for personal use only. Any other reproduction or redistribution is strictly prohibited. All rights reserved.
This content is provided for test preparation purposes only and does not imply an endorsement by Mometrix of any particular political, scientific, or religious point of view.

add the same number four times. You could use the formulas for rectangles and get the same answer.

### FIND THE SIDE OF A SQUARE

You may have problems that give you the perimeter of a square. So, you are asked to find the side.

Example: The perimeter of a square is 60 cm. Find the side.

First: Set up the equation to set apart $s$.

The equation is $60 = 4s$.

Second: Now, you can divide both sides by 4: $\frac{60}{4} = \frac{4s}{4}$. You are left with $15 = s$

## RECTANGLE

The area of a rectangle is found by the formula $A = lw$, where $A$ is the area of the rectangle, $l$ is the length (usually considered to be the longer side) and $w$ is the width (usually considered to be the shorter side). The numbers for $l$ and $w$ are interchangeable.

### FIND THE WIDTH OR LENGTH OF A RECTANGLE

You may have problems that give you the area of a rectangle. So, you are asked to find the width.

Example: The area of a rectangle is 150cm², and the length is 10cm. Find the width.

First: Set up the equation to set apart width. The equation is $150 = 10w$.

Second: Divide both sides by 10: $\frac{150}{10} = \frac{10w}{10}$. You are left with $15 = w$

Note: When you need to find the length, you can follow the steps above to find it.

The perimeter of a rectangle is found by the formula $P = 2l + 2w$ or $P = 2(l + w)$, where $l$ is the length, and $w$ is the width. It may be easier to add the length and width first and then double the result, as in the second formula.

### FIND THE WIDTH OR LENGTH OF A RECTANGLE

You may have problems that give you the perimeter of a rectangle. So, you are asked to find the width.

Example: The perimeter of a rectangle is 100cm, and the length is 20cm. Find the width.

First: Set up the equation to set apart the width. The equation is $100 = 2(20 + w)$

Second: Distribute the 2 across $(20 + w)$: $100 = 40 + 2w$

Then, subtract 40 from both sides: $100 - 40 = 40 + 2w - 40$

So, you are left with: $60 = 2w$. Then, divide both sides by 2: $\frac{60}{2} = \frac{2w}{2}$.

Now, you have $30 = w$.

Note: When you need to find the length, you can follow the steps above to find it.

Copyright © Mometrix Media. You have been licensed one copy of this document for personal use only. Any other reproduction or redistribution is strictly prohibited. All rights reserved.
This content is provided for test preparation purposes only and does not imply an endorsement by Mometrix of any particular political, scientific, or religious point of view.

## PARALLELOGRAM

The area of a parallelogram is found by the formula $A = bh$, where $b$ is the length of the base, and $h$ is the height. Note that the base and height correspond to the length and width in a rectangle, so this formula would apply to rectangles as well. Do not confuse the height of a parallelogram with the length of the second side. The two are only the same measure in the case of a rectangle.

### FIND THE LENGTH OF THE BASE OR THE HEIGHT OF A PARALLELOGRAM

You may have problems that give you the area of a parallelogram. So, you are asked to find the area of the base or the height.

Example: The area of the parallelogram is 84 cm². The base is 7cm. Find the height.

Set up the equation to set apart the height.
So, you have $84 = 7h$. Now, divide both sides by 7: $\frac{84}{7} = \frac{7h}{7}$.
Then, you are left with $12 = h$

The perimeter of a parallelogram is found by the formula $P = 2a + 2b$ or $P = 2(a + b)$, where $a$ and $b$ are the lengths of the two sides.

### FIND THE MISSING SIDE OF A PARALLELOGRAM

You may have problems that give you the perimeter of a parallelogram. So, you are asked to find one of the sides. Example: The perimeter of a parallelogram is 100cm, and one side is 20cm. Find the other side.

First: Set up the equation to set apart one of the side lengths.

The equation is $100 = 2(20 + b)$

Second: Distribute the 2 across $(20 + b)$: $100 = 40 + 2b$

Then, subtract 40 from both sides: $100 - 40 = 40 + 2b - 40$

So, you are left with: $60 = 2b$. Then, divide both sides by 2: $\frac{60}{2} = \frac{2b}{2}$

Now, you have $30 = b$.

> **Review Video: Area and Perimeter of a Parallelogram**
> Visit mometrix.com/academy and enter code: 718313

## TRAPEZOID

The area of a trapezoid is found by the formula $A = \frac{1}{2}h(b_1 + b_2)$, where $h$ is the height (segment joining and perpendicular to the parallel bases), and $b_1$ and $b_2$ are the two parallel sides (bases). Do not use one of the other two sides as the height unless that side is also perpendicular to the parallel bases.

### FIND THE HEIGHT OF A TRAPEZOID

You may have problems that give you the area of a trapezoid. So, you are asked to find the height.

Example: The area of a trapezoid is 30cm². B₁ is 3cm, and B₂ is 9cm. Find the height.

First: Set up the equation to set apart the height. The equation is $30 = \frac{1}{2}h(3 + 9)$.

Copyright © Mometrix Media. You have been licensed one copy of this document for personal use only. Any other reproduction or redistribution is strictly prohibited. All rights reserved. This content is provided for test preparation purposes only and does not imply an endorsement by Mometrix of any particular political, scientific, or religious point of view.

Second: Now, multiply both sides by 2: $30 \times 2 = \frac{1}{2}(12)h \times 2$.

So, you are left with: $60 = (12)h$.

Third: Divide both sides by 12: $\frac{60}{12} = \frac{(12)h}{12}$. Now, you have $5 = h$

### FIND A BASE OF A TRAPEZOID

You may have problems that give you the area of a trapezoid and the height. So, you are asked to find one of the bases.

Example: The area of a trapezoid is 90cm². $b_1$ is 5cm, and the height is 12cm. Find $b_2$.

First: Set up the equation to set apart $b_2$.

The equation is $90 = \frac{1}{2}12(5 + b_2)$.

Second: Now, multiply the height by $\frac{1}{2}$: $90 = 6(5 + b_2)$.

So, you can distribute the 6 across $(5 + b_2)$: $90 = 30 + 6b_2$

Third: Subtract 30 from both sides $90 - 30 = 30 + 6b_2 - 30$.

Now, you have $60 = 6b_2$.

Then, divide both sides by 6: $\frac{60}{6} = \frac{6b_2}{6}$. So, $b_2 = 10$.

The perimeter of a trapezoid is found by the formula $P = a + b_1 + c + b_2$, where $a$, $b_1$, $c$, and $b_2$ are the four sides of the trapezoid.

### FIND THE MISSING SIDE OF A TRAPEZOID

Example: The perimeter of a trapezoid is 50cm. $B_1$ is 20cm, $B_2$ is 10cm, and a is 5cm. Find the length of side c.

First: Set up the equation to set apart the missing side.

The equation is $50 = 5 + 20 + c + 10$. So, you have $50 = 35 + c$

Second: Subtract 35 from both sides: $50 - 35 = 35 + c - 35$.

So, you are left with $15 = c$

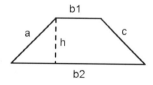

┌─────────────────────────────────────────────────────────┐
│  **Review Video: <u>Area and Perimeter of a Trapezoid</u>**  │
│  Visit mometrix.com/academy and enter code: 587523       │
└─────────────────────────────────────────────────────────┘

Copyright © Mometrix Media. You have been licensed one copy of this document for personal use only. Any other reproduction or redistribution is strictly prohibited. All rights reserved. This content is provided for test preparation purposes only and does not imply an endorsement by Mometrix of any particular political, scientific, or religious point of view.

## CIRCLES

The area of a circle is found by the formula $A = \pi r^2$, where $r$ is the length of the radius. If the diameter of the circle is given, remember to divide it in half to get the length of the radius before proceeding.

### FIND THE RADIUS OF A CIRCLE

You may have problems that give you the area of a circle. So, you are asked to find the radius.

Example: The area of a circle is 30cm². Find the radius.

First: Set up the equation to set apart the radius.

The equation is $30 = \pi r^2$. Now, divide both sides by $\pi$: $\dfrac{30}{\pi} = \dfrac{\pi r^2}{\pi}$

Second: Take the square root of both sides: $\sqrt{9.55} = \sqrt{r^2}$.

So, you are left with: $3.09 = r$.

Note: You may have the area, and you are asked to find the diameter of the circle. So, follow the steps above to find the radius. Then, multiply the radius by 2 for the diameter.

The circumference of a circle is found by the formula $C = 2\pi r$, where $r$ is the radius. Again, remember to convert the diameter if you are given that measure rather than the radius.

### FIND THE RADIUS OF A CIRCLE

You may have problems that give you the circumference of a circle. So, you are asked to find the radius. Example: The circumference is 20cm. Find the radius.

First: Set up the equation to set apart the radius.

The equation is $20 = 2\pi r$. Now divide both sides by 2: $\dfrac{20}{2} = \dfrac{2\pi r}{2}$.

Second: Divide both sides by $\pi$: $\dfrac{10}{\pi} = \dfrac{\pi r}{\pi}$. So, you are left with $3.18 = r$

Note: You may have the circumference, and you are asked to find the diameter of the circle. So, follow the steps above to find the radius. Then, multiply the radius by 2 for the diameter.

The area of a sector of a circle is found by the formula, $A = \dfrac{\theta r^2}{2}$, where $A$ is the area, $\theta$ is the measure of the central angle in radians, and $r$ is the radius. To find the area when the central angle is in degrees, use the formula, $A = \dfrac{\theta \pi r^2}{360}$, where $\theta$ is the measure of the central angle in degrees and $r$ is the radius.

A circle is inscribed in a polygon if each of the sides of the polygon is tangent to the circle. A polygon is inscribed in a circle if each of the vertices of the polygon lies on the circle.

A circle is circumscribed about a polygon if each of the vertices of the polygon lies on the circle. A polygon is circumscribed about the circle if each of the sides of the polygon is tangent to the circle.

Copyright © Mometrix Media. You have been licensed one copy of this document for personal use only. Any other reproduction or redistribution is strictly prohibited. All rights reserved.
This content is provided for test preparation purposes only and does not imply an endorsement by Mometrix of any particular political, scientific, or religious point of view.

If one figure is inscribed in another, then the other figure is circumscribed about the first figure.

Circle circumscribed about a pentagon
Pentagon inscribed in a circle

## VOLUME AND SURFACE AREA

The surface area of a solid object is the area of all sides or exterior surfaces. For objects such as prisms and pyramids, a further distinction is made between base surface area (B) and lateral surface area (LA). For a prism, the total surface area (SA) is $SA = LA + 2B$. For a pyramid or cone, the total surface area is $SA = LA + B$.

### SPHERE

The surface area of a sphere can be found by the formula $A = 4\pi r^2$, where $r$ is the radius.

#### FIND THE RADIUS OF A SPHERE

You may have problems that give you the surface area of a sphere. So, you are asked to find the radius.

Example: The surface area of a sphere is 100 cm². Find the radius.

First: Set up the equation to set apart the radius.

You begin with: $SA = 4\pi r^2$. Then, you move $4\pi$ to the other side of the equal sign and cancel out the $4\pi$ on the right side of the formula: $\frac{SA}{4\pi} = r^2$.

Next, you square both sides to set apart the radius:

$\sqrt{\frac{SA}{4\pi}} = \sqrt{r^2}$. So, you are left with $r = \sqrt{\frac{SA}{4\pi}}$

Second: Solve the equation.

$\sqrt{\frac{100}{4\pi}} = \sqrt{\frac{100}{12.57}} = 2.82$. So, the radius equals 2.82 cm.

Copyright © Mometrix Media. You have been licensed one copy of this document for personal use only. Any other reproduction or redistribution is strictly prohibited. All rights reserved.
This content is provided for test preparation purposes only and does not imply an endorsement by Mometrix of any particular political, scientific, or religious point of view.

The volume is given by the formula $V = \frac{4}{3}\pi r^3$, where $r$ is the radius. Both quantities are generally given in terms of $\pi$.

## FIND THE RADIUS OF A SPHERE

You may have problems that give you the volume of a sphere. So, you are asked to find the radius.

Example: The volume of a sphere is 100 cm³. Find the radius.

First: Set up the equation and cancel out the fraction.

$$\frac{3}{4} \times \frac{4}{3}\pi r^3 = 100 \times \frac{3}{4}.$$ So, you are left with: $\pi r^3 = 75$

Second: Cancel out $\pi$.

$$\frac{\pi r^3}{\pi} = \frac{75}{\pi}.$$ So, you are left with: $r^3 = \frac{75}{\pi} = 23.87$

Third: Take the cubed root of r³ and 23.87 to solve for the radius.

$$\sqrt[3]{r^3} = \sqrt[3]{23.87}.$$ So, you have the result of r= 2.88

## PRISMS

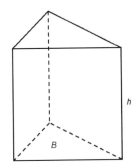

The volume of any prism is found by the formula $V = Bh$, where $B$ is the area of the base, and $h$ is the height (perpendicular distance between the bases).

> **Review Video: Volume and Surface Area of a Prism**
> Visit mometrix.com/academy and enter code: 420158

## FIND THE AREA OF THE BASE OR THE HEIGHT OF A PRISM

You may have problems that give you the volume of a prism. So, you are asked to find the area of the base or the height.

Example: The volume of the prism is 200 cm³. The area of the base is 10cm. Find the height.

First: Set up the equation to set apart the height. So, you have $200 = 10h$.

Second: Now, divide both sides by 10: $\frac{200}{10} = \frac{10h}{10}$. Then, you are left with $20 = h$

Note: When you need to find the area of the base, you can follow the steps above to solve for it.

The surface area of any prism is the sum of the areas of both bases and all sides. It can be calculated as $SA = 2B + Ph$, where $P$ is the perimeter of the base.

Copyright © Mometrix Media. You have been licensed one copy of this document for personal use only. Any other reproduction or redistribution is strictly prohibited. All rights reserved.
This content is provided for test preparation purposes only and does not imply an endorsement by Mometrix of any particular political, scientific, or religious point of view.

FIND THE AREA OF THE BASE

You may have problems that give you the surface area of a prism. So, you are asked to find the area of the base.

Example: The surface area of the prism is 100 cm². The perimeter of the base is 10cm, and the height is 2cm. Find the area of the base.

First: Set up the equation to set apart the area of the base.

So, you have $100 = 2B + 20$.

Second: Subtract 20 from both sides: $100 - 20 = 2B + 20 - 20$.

Now, you are left with $80 = 2B$. So, divide both sides by 2.

Then, you have $40 = B$.

FIND THE PERIMETER OF THE BASE OR THE HEIGHT OF A PRISM

You may have problems that give you the surface area of a prism and the area of the base. So, you are asked to find the perimeter of the base or the height.

Example: The surface area of the prism is 280 cm². The area of the base is 15cm², and the perimeter of the base is 10cm. Find the height.

First: Set up the equation to set apart the height.

The equation is $280 = 2(15) + (10)h$. So, you have $250 = 30 + (10)h$

Second: Subtract 30 from both sides: $280 - 30 = 30 + (10)h - 30$.

Now, you are left with: $250 = (10)h$. Then, divide both sides by 10.

$\frac{250}{10} = \frac{(10)h}{10} = 25$. So, the height of the prism is 25cm.

Note: When you need to find the perimeter of the base, you can follow the steps above to find it.

RECTANGULAR PRISM

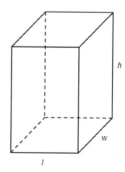

For a rectangular prism, the volume can be found by the formula $V = lwh$, where $V$ is the volume, $l$ is the length, $w$ is the width, and $h$ is the height.

┌─────────────────────────────────────────────────────────────┐
│ **Review Video: <u>Volume and Surface Area of a Rectangular Prism</u>** │
│ Visit mometrix.com/academy and enter code: 282814 │
└─────────────────────────────────────────────────────────────┘

Copyright © Mometrix Media. You have been licensed one copy of this document for personal use only. Any other reproduction or redistribution is strictly prohibited. All rights reserved.
This content is provided for test preparation purposes only and does not imply an endorsement by Mometrix of any particular political, scientific, or religious point of view.

## FIND THE LENGTH, WIDTH, OR HEIGHT OF A RECTANGULAR PRISM

You may have problems that give you the volume of a rectangular prism. So, you are asked to find the length, width, or height.

Example: The volume of the rectangular prism is 200 cm³. The width is 10cm, and the height is 10cm. Find the length.

First: Set up the equation to set apart the length.

So, you have $200 = l(10)(10)$ that becomes $200 = (100)l$.

Second: Divide both sides by 100.

Now, you have $\frac{200}{100} = \frac{(100)l}{100}$. So, you are left with $2 = l$.

Note: When you need to find the width or height, you can follow the steps above to solve for either.

The surface area can be calculated as $SA = 2lw + 2hl + 2wh$ or $SA = 2(lw + hl + wh)$.

## FIND THE LENGTH, WIDTH, OR HEIGHT OF A RECTANGULAR PRISM

You may have problems that give you the surface area of a rectangular prism. So, you are asked to find the length, width, or height.

Example: The surface area of the rectangular prism is 200 cm². The width is 15cm, and the height is 5cm. Find the length.

First: Set up the equation to set apart the length.

So, you have $200 = 2(15)l + 2(5)l + 2(15)(5)$ that becomes:

$200 = (40)l + 150$.

Second: Subtract 150 from both sides.

So, $200 - 150 = (40)l + 150 - 150$ becomes $50 = (40)l$.

Then, divide both sides by 40 to set apart $l$: $\frac{50}{40} = \frac{(40)l}{40}$.

You are left with $1.25 = l$.

Note: When you need to find the width or height, you can follow the steps above to solve for either.

## CUBE

The volume of a cube can be found by the formula $V = s^3$, where $s$ is the length of a side.

## FIND THE SIDE OF A CUBE

You may have problems that give you the volume of a cube. So, you are asked to find the side.

Example: The volume of a cube is 20 cm³. Find the side.

First: Set up the equation to set apart the side length. Then, take the cube root of both sides. So, $20 = s^3$ becomes $\sqrt[3]{20} = \sqrt[3]{s^3}$ Then, you are left with $\sqrt[3]{20} = s$

Copyright © Mometrix Media. You have been licensed one copy of this document for personal use only. Any other reproduction or redistribution is strictly prohibited. All rights reserved.
This content is provided for test preparation purposes only and does not imply an endorsement by Mometrix of any particular political, scientific, or religious point of view.

Second: Solve for the side length.

$$\sqrt[3]{20} = 2.71. \text{ So, } s \text{ equals } 2.71.$$

The surface area of a cube is calculated as $SA = 6s^2$, where $SA$ is the total surface area and $s$ is the length of a side. These formulas are the same as the ones used for the volume and surface area of a rectangular prism, but simplified since all three quantities (length, width, and height) are the same.

## FIND THE SIDE OF A CUBE

You may have problems that give you the surface area of a cube. So, you are asked to find the side.

Example: The surface area of a cube is 60 cm². Find the side.

First: Set up the equation to set apart the side length.

So, $60 = 6s^2$ becomes $\frac{60}{6} = \frac{6s^2}{6}$. Then, you are left with $10 = s^2$

Second: Take the square root of both sides to set apart the $s$.

So, $10 = s^2$ becomes $\sqrt{10} = \sqrt{s^2}$.

Then, you are left with $3.16 = s$

## CYLINDER

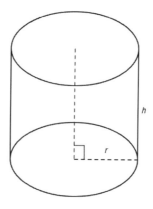

The volume of a cylinder can be calculated by the formula $V = \pi r^2 h$, where $r$ is the radius, and $h$ is the height.

> **Review Video: <u>Finding the Volume and Surface Area of a Right Circular Cylinder</u>**
> Visit mometrix.com/academy and enter code: 226463

## FIND THE HEIGHT OF A CYLINDER

You may have problems that give you the volume of a cylinder. So, you are asked to find the height.

Example: The volume of a cylinder is 300 cm³ and the radius is 5 cm. Find the height.

First: Set up the equation and put in the known numbers.

You begin with $300 = \pi 5^2 h$. Now, $\pi 5^2 h = 78.5h$.

Copyright © Mometrix Media. You have been licensed one copy of this document for personal use only. Any other reproduction or redistribution is strictly prohibited. All rights reserved. This content is provided for test preparation purposes only and does not imply an endorsement by Mometrix of any particular political, scientific, or religious point of view.

So, you have $300 = 78.5h$

Second: Set apart h to solve for the height.

$\frac{300}{78.5} = \frac{78.5h}{78.5}$. So, you are left with: $\frac{300}{78.5} = h$

Solve: $\frac{300}{78.5} = 3.82$cm is the height.

## FIND THE RADIUS OF A CYLINDER

You may have problems that give you the volume of a cylinder. So, you are asked to find the radius.

Example: The volume of a cylinder is 200 cm³ and the radius is 15cm. Find the radius.

First: Set up the equation to set apart the radius.

You begin with $200 = \pi(15)r^2$. Now, you move $\pi$ and (15) to both sides of the equation: $\frac{200}{\pi(15)} = \frac{\pi(15)r^2}{\pi(15)}$. Then, you are left with: $\frac{200}{\pi(15)} = r^2$.

Second: Take the square root of both sides to solve for the radius: $\sqrt{\frac{200}{\pi(15)}} = \sqrt{r^2}$.

Then, you have $\sqrt{4.25} = r$. So, the radius is equal to 2.06.

The surface area of a cylinder can be found by the formula $SA = 2\pi r^2 + 2\pi rh$. The first term is the base area multiplied by two, and the second term is the perimeter of the base multiplied by the height.

## FIND THE HEIGHT OF A CYLINDER

You may have problems that give you the surface area of a cylinder. So, you are asked to find the height. Example: The surface area of a cylinder is 150 cm² and the radius is 2 cm. Find the height.

First: Set up the equation and put in the known numbers.

You begin with $150 = 2\pi 2^2 + 2\pi(2)h$.

So, you have $150 = 25.12 + 12.56h$.

Second: Subtract 25.12 from both sides of the equation.

So, $150 - 25.12 = 25.12 + 12.56h - 25.12$ becomes $124.85 = 12.56h$.

Then, divide both sides by 12.56.

Now, you are left with $9.94 = h$.

## FIND THE RADIUS OF A CYLINDER

You may have problems that give you the surface area of a cylinder. So, you are asked to find the radius. Example: The surface area of a cylinder is 327 cm², and the height is 12cm. Find the radius.

First: Set up the equation and put in the known numbers.

You begin with $327 = 2\pi r^2 + 2\pi 12(r)$. So, you have $327 = 2\pi r^2 + 75.36r$.

**61**

Copyright © Mometrix Media. You have been licensed one copy of this document for personal use only. Any other reproduction or redistribution is strictly prohibited. All rights reserved.
This content is provided for test preparation purposes only and does not imply an endorsement by Mometrix of any particular political, scientific, or religious point of view.

Second: Set up the quadratic formula.

So, you now have $6.28r^2 + 75.36r - 327 = 0$

Third: Solve the equation using the quadratic formula steps.

Now, radius $= \frac{-75.36 \pm \sqrt{(75.36)^2 - 4(6.28)(-327)}}{2(6.28)}$

So, the radius equals a positive 3.39.

## PYRAMID

The volume of a pyramid is found by the formula $V = \frac{1}{3}Bh$, where $B$ is the area of the base, and $h$ is the height (perpendicular distance from the vertex to the base). Notice this formula is the same as $\frac{1}{3}$ times the volume of a prism. Like a prism, the base of a pyramid can be any shape.

### FIND THE AREA OF THE BASE OR THE HEIGHT OF A PYRAMID

You may have problems that give you the volume of a pyramid. So, you are asked to find the area of the base or the height.

Example: The volume of the pyramid is 100 cm³. The area of the base is 5cm². Find the height.

First: Set up the equation to set apart the height.

The equation is $100 = \frac{1}{3}5h$.

Now, you start by multiplying both sides by 3: $100 \times 3 = \frac{1}{3}5h \times 3$.

Second: You have $300 = 5h$. Now, divide both sides by 5: $\frac{300}{5} = \frac{5h}{5}$.

So, you have found that the height is 60.

Note: When you need to find the area of the base, you can follow the steps above to find it.

If the pyramid is a right pyramid, meaning the base is a regular polygon and the vertex is directly over the center of that polygon, the surface area can be calculated as $SA = B + \frac{1}{2}Ph_s$, where $P$ is the perimeter of the base, and $h_s$ is the slant height (distance from the vertex to the midpoint of one side of the base).

If the pyramid is irregular, the area of each triangle side must be calculated individually and then summed, along with the base.

> **Review Video: Finding the Volume and Surface Area of a Pyramid**
> Visit mometrix.com/academy and enter code: 621932

### FIND THE AREA OF THE BASE, THE PERIMETER OF THE BASE, OR THE HEIGHT

You may have problems that give you the surface area of a pyramid. So, you are asked to find the area of the base, the perimeter of the base, or the height.

Copyright © Mometrix Media. You have been licensed one copy of this document for personal use only. Any other reproduction or redistribution is strictly prohibited. All rights reserved. This content is provided for test preparation purposes only and does not imply an endorsement by Mometrix of any particular political, scientific, or religious point of view.

Example: The surface area of the pyramid is 100 cm². The area of the base is 40cm², and the height is 12cm.

First: Set up the equation to set apart the perimeter of the base.

The equation is $100 = 40 + \frac{1}{2}12P$

Now, you can multiply the height by $\frac{1}{2}$.

So, you have: $100 = 40 + 6P$

Second: Subtract both sides of the equation by 40: $100 - 40 = 40 + 6P - 40$.

So, you have: $60 = 6P$

Now, divide both sides by 6: $\frac{60}{6} = \frac{6P}{6}$. So, you are left with: P=10cm.

Note: When you need to find the area of the base or the height, you can follow the steps above.

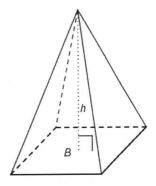

| Review Video: **Finding the Volume and Surface Area of a Pyramid** |
| :---: |
| Visit mometrix.com/academy and enter code: 621932 |

## CONE

The volume of a cone is found by the formula $V = \frac{1}{3}\pi r^2 h$, where $r$ is the radius, and $h$ is the height. Notice this is the same as $\frac{1}{3}$ times the volume of a cylinder.

### FIND THE RADIUS OR HEIGHT OF A CONE

You may have problems that give you the volume of a cone. So, you are asked to find the radius or the height.

Example: The volume of the cone is 47.12 cm³. The height is 5cm. Find the radius.

First: Set up the equation to set apart the radius.

The equation is $47.12 = \frac{1}{3}\pi 5r^2$

Now, you can multiply both sides by 3: $47.12 \times 3 = \frac{1}{3}\pi 5r^2 \times 3$

Copyright © Mometrix Media. You have been licensed one copy of this document for personal use only. Any other reproduction or redistribution is strictly prohibited. All rights reserved. This content is provided for test preparation purposes only and does not imply an endorsement by Mometrix of any particular political, scientific, or religious point of view.

So, you have $141.36 = \pi 5 r^2$.

Second: Divide both sides by 5: $\frac{141.36}{5} = \frac{\pi 5 r^2}{5}$.

Now, you have: $28.27 = \pi r^2$

You can divide both sides by $\pi$: $\frac{28.27}{\pi} = \frac{\pi r^2}{\pi}$.

So, you have $9 = \pi r^2$.

Third: Take the square root of both sides: $\sqrt{9} = \sqrt{r^2}$.

Now, you have $3 = r$

Note: When you need to find the height, you can follow the steps above to find it.

The surface area can be calculated as $SA = \pi r^2 + \pi r s$, where s is the slant height. The slant height can be calculated using the Pythagorean Thereom to be $\sqrt{r^2 + h^2}$, so the surface area formula can also be written as $SA = \pi r^2 + \pi r \sqrt{r^2 + h^2}$.

### FIND THE RADIUS OF A CONE

You may have problems that give you the surface area of a cone. So, you are asked to find the radius.

Example: The surface area of the cone is 43.96 cm². The slant height is 5cm. Find the radius.

First: Set up the equation to set apart the radius.

The equation is $43.96 = \pi r^2 + 5\pi r$

Then, you can factor out the $\pi$: $43.96 = \pi(r^2 + 5r)$

Second: Now, you can divide both sides by $\pi$: $\frac{43.96}{\pi} = \frac{\pi(r^2 + 5r)}{\pi}$

So, you have: $14 = r^2 + 5r$. Then, subtract 14 from both sides, and you have:

$x = r^2 + 5r - 14$

Third: Use the quadratic formula

$$x = \frac{-5 \pm \sqrt{5^2 - 4(1)(-14)}}{2(1)}$$

So, the radius equals a positive 2.

### FIND THE SLANT HEIGHT OF A CONE

You may have problems that give you the surface area of a cone. So, you are asked to find the slant height.

Example: The surface area of the cone is 37.68 cm². The radius is 2cm. Find the slant height.

First: Set up the equation to set apart the slant height.

Copyright © Mometrix Media. You have been licensed one copy of this document for personal use only. Any other reproduction or redistribution is strictly prohibited. All rights reserved. This content is provided for test preparation purposes only and does not imply an endorsement by Mometrix of any particular political, scientific, or religious point of view.

The equation is $37.68 = \pi 2^2 + \pi 2s$

Now, calculate both sides: $37.68 = 12.56 + 6.28s$

Second: Divide 6.28 across all three terms: $\frac{37.68}{6.28} = \frac{12.56}{6.28} + \frac{6.28s}{6.28}$

Then, you have $6 = 2 + s$. Now, subtract 2 from both sides: $6 - 2 = 2 + s - 2$

So, you are left with $4 = s$

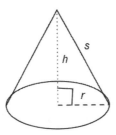

**Review Video: Volume and Surface Area of a Right Circular Cone**
Visit mometrix.com/academy and enter code: 573574

# Data Analysis, Probability, and Statistics

## STATISTICS

Statistics is the branch of mathematics that deals with collecting, recording, interpreting, illustrating, and analyzing large amounts of data. The following terms are often used in the discussion of data and statistics:

Data – the collective name for pieces of information (singular is datum).

Quantitative data – measurements (such as length, mass, and speed) that provide information about quantities in numbers

Qualitative data – information (such as colors, scents, tastes, and shapes) that cannot be measured using numbers

Discrete data – information that can be expressed only by a specific value, such as whole or half numbers; For example, since people can be counted only in whole numbers, a population count would be discrete data.

Continuous data – information (such as time and temperature) that can be expressed by any value within a given range

Primary data – information that has been collected directly from a survey, investigation, or experiment, such as a questionnaire or the recording of daily temperatures; Primary data that has not yet been organized or analyzed is called raw data.

Secondary data – information that has been collected, sorted, and processed by the researcher

Ordinal data – information that can be placed in numerical order, such as age or weight

Copyright © Mometrix Media. You have been licensed one copy of this document for personal use only. Any other reproduction or redistribution is strictly prohibited. All rights reserved.
This content is provided for test preparation purposes only and does not imply an endorsement by Mometrix of any particular political, scientific, or religious point of view.

Nominal data – information that cannot be placed in numerical order, such as names or places

## MEASURES OF CENTRAL TENDENCY

The quantities of mean, median, and mode are all referred to as measures of central tendency. They can each give a picture of what the whole set of data looks like with just a single number. Knowing what each of these values represents is vital to making use of the information they provide.

The mean, also known as the arithmetic mean or average, of a data set is calculated by summing all of the values in the set and dividing that sum by the number of values. For example, if a data set has 6 numbers and the sum of those 6 numbers is 30, the mean is calculated as 30/6 = 5.

The median is the middle value of a data set. The median can be found by putting the data set in numerical order, and locating the middle value. In the data set (1, 2, 3, 4, 5), the median is 3. If there is an even number of values in the set, the median is calculated by taking the average of the two middle values. In the data set, (1, 2, 3, 4, 5, 6), the median would be (3 + 4)/2 = 3.5.

The mode is the value that appears most frequently in the data set. In the data set (1, 2, 3, 4, 5, 5, 5), the mode would be 5 since the value 5 appears three times. If multiple values appear the same number of times, there are multiple values for the mode. If the data set were (1, 2, 2, 3, 4, 4, 5, 5), the modes would be 2, 4, and 5. If no value appears more than any other value in the data set, then there is no mode.

## MEASURES OF DISPERSION

The standard deviation expresses how spread out the values of a distribution are from the mean. Standard deviation is given in the same units as the original data and is represented by a lower-case sigma ($\sigma$). A high standard deviation means that the values are very spread out. A low standard deviation means that the values are close together.

If every value in a distribution is increased or decreased by the same amount, the mean, median, and mode are increased or decreased by that amount, but the standard deviation stays the same. If every value in a distribution is multiplied or divided by the same number, the mean, median, mode, and standard deviation will all be multiplied or divided by that number.

The range of a distribution is the difference between the highest and lowest values in the distribution. For example, in the data set (1, 3, 5, 7, 9, 11), the highest and lowest values are 11 and 1, respectively. The range then would be calculated as 11 – 1 = 10.

The three quartiles are the three values that divide a data set into four equal parts. Quartiles are generally only calculated for data sets with a large number of values. As a simple example, for the data set consisting of the numbers 1 through 99, the first quartile (Q1) would be 25, the second quartile (Q2), always equal to the median, would be 50, and the third quartile (Q3) would be 75. The difference between Q1 and Q3 is known as the interquartile range.

## PROBABILITY

Probability is a branch of statistics that deals with the likelihood of something taking place. One classic example is a coin toss. There are only two possible results: heads or tails. The likelihood, or probability, that the coin will land as heads is 1 out of 2 (1/2, 0.5, 50%). Tails has the same probability. Another common example is a 6-sided die roll. There are six possible results from

Copyright © Mometrix Media. You have been licensed one copy of this document for personal use only. Any other reproduction or redistribution is strictly prohibited. All rights reserved.
This content is provided for test preparation purposes only and does not imply an endorsement by Mometrix of any particular political, scientific, or religious point of view.

rolling a single die, each with an equal chance of happening, so the probability of any given number coming up is 1 out of 6.

**Review Video: Intro to Probability**
Visit mometrix.com/academy and enter code: 212374

Terms frequently used in probability:

Event – a situation that produces results of some sort (a coin toss)

Compound event – event that involves two or more items (rolling a pair of dice; taking the sum)

Outcome – a possible result in an experiment or event (heads, tails)

**Desired outcome** (or success)—an outcome that meets a particular set of criteria (a roll of 1 or 2 if we are looking for numbers less than 3)

**Independent events**—two or more events whose outcomes do not affect one another (two coins tossed at the same time)

**Dependent events**—two or more events whose outcomes affect one another (two cards drawn consecutively from the same deck)

**Certain outcome**—probability of outcome is 100% or 1

**Impossible outcome**—probability of outcome is 0% or 0

Mutually exclusive outcomes – two or more outcomes whose criteria cannot all be satisfied in a single outcome (a coin coming up heads and tails on the same toss)

Theoretical probability is the likelihood of a certain outcome occurring for a given event. It can be determined without actually performing the event. It is calculated as P (probability of success) = (desired outcomes)/(total outcomes).

Example:

There are 20 marbles in a bag and 5 are red. The theoretical probability of randomly selecting a red marble is 5 out of 20, (5/20 = 1/4, 0.25, or 25%).

Most of the time, when we talk about probability, we mean theoretical probability. Experimental probability, or relative frequency, is the number of times an outcome occurs in a particular experiment or a certain number of observed events.

While theoretical probability is based on what *should* happen, experimental probability is based on what *has* happened. Experimental probability is calculated in the same way as theoretical probability, except that actual outcomes are used instead of possible outcomes.

Theoretical and experimental probability do not always line up with one another. Theoretical probability says that out of 20 coin tosses, 10 should be heads. However, if we were actually to toss 20 coins, we might record just 5 heads. This doesn't mean that our theoretical probability is incorrect; it just means that this particular experiment had results that were different from what was predicted.

Copyright © Mometrix Media. You have been licensed one copy of this document for personal use only. Any other reproduction or redistribution is strictly prohibited. All rights reserved.
This content is provided for test preparation purposes only and does not imply an endorsement by Mometrix of any particular political, scientific, or religious point of view.

## EXPECTED VALUE

**Expected value** is a method of determining the expected outcome in a random situation. It is a sum of the weighted probabilities of the possible outcomes. Multiply the probability of an event occurring by the weight assigned to that probability (such as the amount of money won or lost). A practical application of the expected value is to determine whether a game of chance is really fair. If the sum of the weighted probabilities is equal to zero, the game is generally considered fair because the player has a fair chance to at least break even. If the expected value is less than zero, then players are expected to lose more than they win. For example, a lottery drawing allows the player to choose any three-digit number, 000–999. The probability of choosing the winning number is 1:1000. If it costs $1 to play, and a winning number receives $500, the expected value is $\left(-\$1 \cdot \frac{999}{1,000}\right) + \left(\$500 \cdot \frac{1}{1,000}\right) = -0.499$ or $-\$0.50$. You can expect to lose on average 50 cents for every dollar you spend.

## COMMON CHARTS AND GRAPHS

*Charts* and *Tables* are ways of organizing information into separate rows and columns. These rows and columns are labeled to find and to explain the information in them. Some charts and tables are organized horizontally with rows giving the details about the labeled information. Other charts and tables are organized vertically with columns giving the details about the labeled information.

*Frequency Tables* show how many times each value comes up within the set. A *Relative Frequency Table* shows the proportions of each value compared to the entire set. Relative frequencies are given as percents. However, the total percent for a relative frequency table may not equal 100 percent because of rounding.

This is an example of a frequency table with relative frequencies:

| Favorite Color | Frequency | Relative Frequency |
| --- | --- | --- |
| Blue | 4 | 13% |
| Red | 7 | 22% |
| Purple | 3 | 9% |
| Green | 6 | 19% |
| Cyan | 12 | 38% |

A *Bar Graph* is one of the few graphs that can be drawn correctly in two ways: horizontally and vertically. A bar graph is similar to a line plot because of how the data is organized on the graph. Both axes must have their categories defined for the graph to be useful. A thick line is drawn from zero to the exact value of the data. This line can be used for a number, a percentage, or other numerical value. Longer bar lengths point to greater data values. To understand a bar graph, read the labels for the axes to know the units being reported. Then look where the bars end and match

Copyright © Mometrix Media. You have been licensed one copy of this document for personal use only. Any other reproduction or redistribution is strictly prohibited. All rights reserved.
This content is provided for test preparation purposes only and does not imply an endorsement by Mometrix of any particular political, scientific, or religious point of view.

this to the scale on the other axis. This will show you the connection between the axes. This bar graph shows the responses from a survey about the favorite colors of a group.

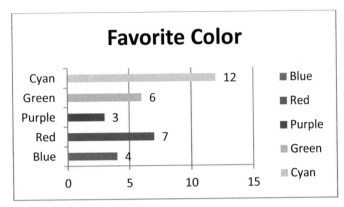

*Line Graphs* have one or more lines of different styles (e.g., solid or broken). These lines show the different values for a data set. Each point on the graph is shown as an ordered pair. This is similar to a Cartesian plane. In this case, the *x-* and *y-* axes are given certain units (e.g., dollars or time). Each point that is for one measurement is joined by line segments. Then, these lines show what the values are doing.

The lines may be increasing (i.e., line sloping upward), decreasing (i.e., line sloping downward), or staying the same (i.e., horizontal line). More than one set of data can be put on the same line graph. This is done to compare more than one piece of data. An example of this would be graphing test scores for different groups of students over the same stretch of time. This allows you to see which group had the greatest increase or decrease in performance over a certain amount of years. This example is shown in the graph below.

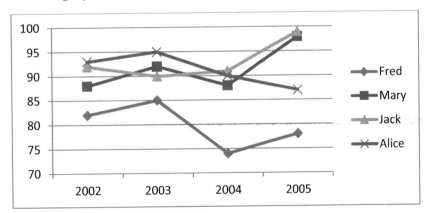

A *Line Plot*, or a *Dot Plot*, has plotted points that are NOT connected by line segments. In this graph, the horizontal axis lists the different possible values for the data. The vertical axis lists how many times one value happens. A single dot is graphed for each value. The dots in a line plot are connected. If the dots are connected, then this will not correctly represent the data.

The *5-Number Summary* of a set of data gives a very informative picture of the set. The five numbers in the summary are the minimum value, maximum value, and the three quartiles. This information gives you the range and the median of the set. Also, this information hints at how the data is spread across the median.

Copyright © Mometrix Media. You have been licensed one copy of this document for personal use only. Any other reproduction or redistribution is strictly prohibited. All rights reserved.
This content is provided for test preparation purposes only and does not imply an endorsement by Mometrix of any particular political, scientific, or religious point of view.

A *Box-and-Whiskers Plot* shows the 5-number summary on a graph. To draw a box-and-whiskers plot, place the points of the 5-number summary on a number line. Draw a box whose ends come through the points for the first and third quartiles. This is called the interquartile range. Draw a vertical line in the box that comes through the median and divides the box in half. Then, draw a line segment from the first quartile point to the minimum value. Also, draw a point from the third quartile point to the maximum value.

A *Pictograph* is a graph that is given in the horizontal format. This graph uses pictures or symbols to show the data. Each pictograph must have a key that defines the picture or symbol. Also, this key should give the number that stands for each picture or symbol. The pictures or symbols on a pictograph are not always shown as whole elements.

In this case, the fraction of the picture or symbol stands for the same fraction of the quantity that a whole picture or symbol represents. For example, there is a row in the pictograph with $3\frac{1}{2}$ ears of corn. Each ear of corn represents 100 stalks of corn in a field. So, this would equal $3\frac{1}{2} \times 100 = 350$ stalks of corn in the field.

*Circle Graphs*, or *Pie Charts*, show the relationship of each type of data compared to the whole set of data. The circle graph is divided into sections by drawing radii (i.e., plural for radius) to make central angles. These angles stand for a percentage of the circle. Each 1% of data is equal to 3.6° in the graph. So, data that stands for a 90° section of the circle graph makes up 25% of the whole. The pie chart below shows the data from the frequency table where people were asked about their favorite color.

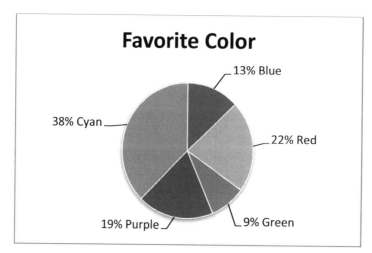

At first glance, a *Histogram* looks like a vertical bar graph. The difference is that a bar graph has a separate bar for each piece of data. A histogram has one bar for each stretch of data. For example, a histogram may have one bar for the stretch of 0–9 and one bar for the stretch of 10–19. A bar graph has numerical values on one axis.

A histogram has numbers on both axes. Each range is of equal size, and they are ordered left to right from lowest to highest. The height of each column on a histogram stands for the number of

Copyright © Mometrix Media. You have been licensed one copy of this document for personal use only. Any other reproduction or redistribution is strictly prohibited. All rights reserved.
This content is provided for test preparation purposes only and does not imply an endorsement by Mometrix of any particular political, scientific, or religious point of view.

data values within that range. Like a stem and leaf plot, a histogram makes it easy to look at the graph and find which range has the greatest number of values. Below is an example of a histogram.

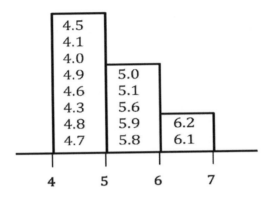

A *Stem and Leaf Plot* can outline groups of data that fall into a range of values. Each piece of data is split into two parts: the first, or left, part is called the stem. The second, or right, part is called the leaf. Each stem is listed in a column from smallest to largest. Each leaf that has the common stem is listed in that stem's row from smallest to largest.

For example, in a set of two-digit numbers, the digit in the tens place is the stem. So, the digit in the ones place is the leaf. With a stem and leaf plot, you can see which subset of numbers (10s, 20s, 30s, etc.) is the largest. This information can be found by looking at a histogram. However, a stem and leaf plot also lets you look closer and see which values fall in that range. Using all of the test scores from the line graph, we can put together a stem and leaf plot:

| Test Scores | | | | | | | | |
|---|---|---|---|---|---|---|---|---|
| **7** | 4 | 8 | | | | | | |
| **8** | 2 | 5 | 7 | 8 | 8 | | | |
| **9** | 0 | 0 | 1 | 2 | 2 | 3 | 5 | 8 | 9 |

Again, a stem-and-leaf plot is similar to histograms and frequency plots. However, a stem-and-leaf plot keeps all of the original data. In this example, you can see that almost half of the students scored in the 80s. Also, all of the data has been maintained. These plots can be used for larger numbers as well. However, they work better for small sets of data.

*Bivariate Data* is data from two different variables. The prefix *bi-* means *two*. In a *Scatter Plot*, each value in the set of data is put on a grid. This is similar to the Cartesian plane where each axis represents one of the two variables. When you look at the pattern made by the points on the grid, you may know if there is a relationship between the two variables. Also, you may know what that relationship is and if it exists.

The variables may be directly proportionate, inversely proportionate, or show no proportion. Also, you may be able to see if the data is linear. If the data is linear, you can find an equation to show the

Copyright © Mometrix Media. You have been licensed one copy of this document for personal use only. Any other reproduction or redistribution is strictly prohibited. All rights reserved.
This content is provided for test preparation purposes only and does not imply an endorsement by Mometrix of any particular political, scientific, or religious point of view.

two variables. The following scatter plot shows the relationship between preference for brand "A" and the age of the consumers surveyed.

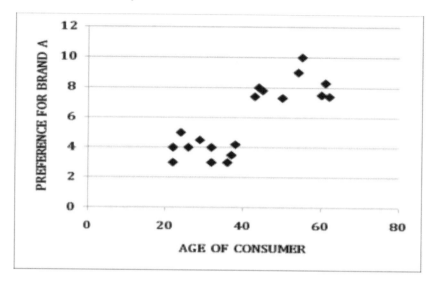

Scatter Plots are useful for knowing the types of functions that are given with the data. Also, they are helpful for finding the simple regression. A simple regression is a regression that uses an independent variable.

A regression is a chart that is used to predict future events. Linear scatter plots may be positive or negative. Many nonlinear scatter plots are exponential or quadratic. Below are some common types of scatter plots:

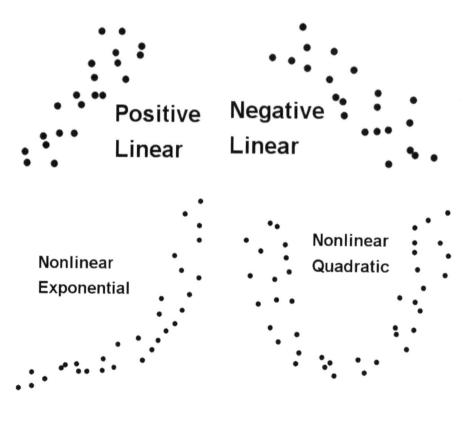

Copyright © Mometrix Media. You have been licensed one copy of this document for personal use only. Any other reproduction or redistribution is strictly prohibited. All rights reserved. This content is provided for test preparation purposes only and does not imply an endorsement by Mometrix of any particular political, scientific, or religious point of view.

# Reading Comprehension

## Reading and Reasoning

### TYPES OF PASSAGES

A **narrative** passage is a story that can be fiction or nonfiction. However, there are a few elements that a text must have in order to be classified as a narrative. First, the text must have a plot (i.e., a series of events). Narratives often proceed in a clear sequence, but this is not a requirement. If the narrative is good, then these events will be interesting to readers. Second, a narrative has characters. These characters could be people, animals, or even inanimate objects--so long as they participate in the plot. Third, a narrative passage often contains figurative language which is meant to stimulate the imagination of readers by making comparisons and observations. For instance, a metaphor, a common piece of figurative language, is a description of one thing in terms of another. *The moon was a frosty snowball* is an example of a metaphor. In the literal sense this is obviously untrue, but the comparison suggests a certain mood for the reader.

> **Review Video: Narratives**
> Visit mometrix.com/academy and enter code: 280100

An **expository** passage aims to inform and enlighten readers. The passage is nonfiction and usually centers around a simple, easily defined topic. Since the goal of exposition is to teach, such a passage should be as clear as possible. Often, an expository passage contains helpful organizing words, like *first*, *next*, *for example*, and *therefore*. These words keep the reader oriented in the text.

Although expository passages do not need to feature colorful language and artful writing, they are often more effective with these features. For a reader, the challenge of expository passages is to maintain steady attention. Expository passages are not always about subjects that will naturally interest a reader, and the writer is often more concerned with clarity and comprehensibility than with engaging the reader. By reading actively, you will ensure a good habit of focus when reading an expository passage.

> **Review Video: Expository Passages**
> Visit mometrix.com/academy and enter code: 256515

A **technical** passage is written to describe a complex object or process. Technical writing is common in medical and technological fields, in which complex ideas of mathematics, science, and engineering need to be explained simply and clearly. To ease comprehension, a technical passage usually proceeds in a very logical order. Technical passages often have clear headings and subheadings, which are used to keep the reader oriented in the text. Additionally, you will find that these passages divide sections up with numbers or letters. Many technical passages look more like an outline than a piece of prose.

The amount of jargon or difficult vocabulary will vary in a technical passage depending on the intended audience. As much as possible, technical passages try to avoid language that the reader will have to research in order to understand the message, yet readers will find that jargon cannot always be avoided.

> **Review Video: Technical Passages**
> Visit mometrix.com/academy and enter code: 478923

73

Copyright © Mometrix Media. You have been licensed one copy of this document for personal use only. Any other reproduction or redistribution is strictly prohibited. All rights reserved. This content is provided for test preparation purposes only and does not imply an endorsement by Mometrix of any particular political, scientific, or religious point of view.

## ORGANIZATION OF THE PASSAGE

The way a text is organized can help readers to understand the author's intent and his or her conclusions. There are various ways to organize a text, and each one has a purpose and use.

Occasionally, authors will organize information logically in a passage so the reader can follow and locate the information within the text. Since this is not always the case with passages in an exam, you need to be familiar with other examples of provided information. Two common organizational structures are cause and effect and chronological order. When using **chronological order**, the author presents information in the order that it happened. For example, biographies are written in chronological order. The subject's birth and childhood are presented first, followed by their adult life, and lastly by the events leading up to the person's death.

In **cause and effect**, an author presents one thing that makes something else happen. For example, if one were to go to bed very late and awake very early, then they would be tired in the morning. The cause is lack of sleep, with the effect of being tired the next day.

Identifying the cause-and-effect relationships in a text can be tricky, but there are a few ways to approach this task. Often, these relationships are signaled with certain terms. When an author uses words like *because*, *since*, *in order*, and *so*, he or she is likely describing a cause-and-effect relationship. Consider the sentence: *He called her because he needed the homework.* This is a simple causal relationship in which the cause was his need for the homework, and the effect was his phone call. Yet, not all cause-and-effect relationships are marked in this way. Consider the sentences: *He called her. He needed the homework.* When the cause-and-effect relationship is not indicated with a keyword, the relationship can be discovered by asking why something happened. He called her: why? The answer is in the next sentence: He needed the homework.

## PURPOSES FOR WRITING

In order to be an effective reader, one must pay attention to the author's **position** and purpose. Even those texts that seem objective and impartial, like textbooks, have a position and bias. Readers need to take these positions into account when considering the author's message. When an author uses emotional language or clearly favors one side of an argument, his or her position is clear. However, the author's position may be evident not only in what he or she writes, but also in what he or she doesn't write.

In a normal setting, a reader would want to review some other texts on the same topic in order to develop a view of the author's position. If this was not possible, then you would want to acquire some background about the author. However, since you are in the middle of an exam and the only source of information is the text, you should look for language and argumentation that seems to indicate a particular stance on the subject.

> **Review Video: Author's Position**
> Visit mometrix.com/academy and enter code: 827954

Usually, identifying the **purpose** of an author is easier than identifying his or her position. In most cases, the author has no interest in hiding his or her purpose. A text that is meant to entertain, for instance, should be written to please the reader. Most narratives, or stories, are written to entertain, though they may also inform or persuade. Informative texts are easy to identify, while the most difficult purpose of a text to identify is persuasion because the author has an interest in making this purpose hard to detect. When a reader discovers that the author is trying to persuade, he or she should be skeptical of the argument. For this reason, persuasive texts often try to

Copyright © Mometrix Media. You have been licensed one copy of this document for personal use only. Any other reproduction or redistribution is strictly prohibited. All rights reserved.
This content is provided for test preparation purposes only and does not imply an endorsement by Mometrix of any particular political, scientific, or religious point of view.

establish an entertaining tone and hope to amuse the reader into agreement. On the other hand, an informative tone may be implemented to create an appearance of authority and objectivity.

> **Review Video: Understanding the Author's Intent**
> Visit mometrix.com/academy and enter code: 511819

An **informative text** is written to educate and enlighten readers. Informative texts are almost always nonfiction and are rarely structured as a story. The intention of an informative text is to deliver information in the most comprehensible way. So, look for the structure of the text to be very clear. In an informative text, the thesis statement is one or two sentences that normally appears at the end of the first paragraph. The author may use some colorful language, but he or she is likely to put more emphasis on clarity and precision. Informative essays do not typically appeal to the emotions. They often contain facts and figures and rarely include the opinion of the author; however, readers should remain aware of the possibility for a bias as those facts are presented. Sometimes a persuasive essay can resemble an informative essay, especially if the author maintains an even tone and presents his or her views as if they were established fact.

When an author intends to **express feelings,** he or she may use expressive and bold language. An author may write with emotion for any number of reasons. Sometimes, authors will express feelings because they are describing a personal situation of great pain or happiness. In other situations, authors will attempt to persuade the reader and will use emotion to stir up the passions. This kind of expression is easy to identify when the writer uses phrases like *I felt* and *I sense*. However, readers may find that the author will simply describe feelings without introducing them. As a reader, you must know the importance of recognizing when an author is expressing emotion and not to become overwhelmed by sympathy or passion. Readers should maintain some detachment so that they can still evaluate the strength of the author's argument or the quality of the writing.

In a sense, almost all writing is descriptive, insofar as an author seeks to describe events, ideas, or people to the reader. Some texts, however, are primarily concerned with **description**. A descriptive text focuses on a particular subject and attempts to depict the subject in a way that will be clear to readers. Descriptive texts contain many adjectives and adverbs (i.e., words that give shades of meaning and create a more detailed mental picture for the reader). A descriptive text fails when it is unclear to the reader. A descriptive text will certainly be informative and may be persuasive and entertaining as well.

## WRITING DEVICES

Authors will use different stylistic and writing devices to make their meaning clear for readers. One of those devices is comparison and contrast. As mentioned previously, when an author describes the ways in which two things are alike, he or she is **comparing** them. When the author describes the ways in which two things are different, he or she is **contrasting** them. The "compare and contrast" essay is one of the most common forms in nonfiction. These passages are often signaled with certain words: a comparison may have indicating terms such as *both, same, like, too,* and *as well*; while a contrast may have terms like *but, however, on the other hand, instead,* and *yet*. Of course, comparisons and contrasts may be implicit without using any such signaling language. A single sentence may both compare and contrast. Consider the sentence *Brian and Sheila love ice*

Copyright © Mometrix Media. You have been licensed one copy of this document for personal use only. Any other reproduction or redistribution is strictly prohibited. All rights reserved.
This content is provided for test preparation purposes only and does not imply an endorsement by Mometrix of any particular political, scientific, or religious point of view.

*cream, but Brian prefers vanilla and Sheila prefers strawberry.* In one sentence, the author has described both a similarity (love of ice cream) and a difference (favorite flavor).

**Review Video: <u>Compare and Contrast</u>**
Visit mometrix.com/academy and enter code: 171799

One of the most common text structures is **cause and effect**. A cause is an act or event that makes something happen, and an effect is the thing that happens as a result of the cause. A cause-and-effect relationship is not always explicit, but there are some terms in English that signal causes, such as *since, because,* and *due to.* Furthermore, terms that signal effects include *consequently, therefore, this lead(s) to.* As an example, consider the sentence *Because the sky was clear, Ron did not bring an umbrella.* The cause is the clear sky, and the effect is that Ron did not bring an umbrella. However, readers may find that sometimes the cause-and-effect relationship will not be clearly noted. For instance, the sentence *He was late and missed the meeting* does not contain any signaling words, but the sentence still contains a cause (he was late) and an effect (he missed the meeting).

Authors often use analogies to add meaning to their passages. An **analogy** is a comparison of two things. The words in the analogy are connected by a certain, often undetermined relationship. Look at this analogy: *moo is to cow as quack is to duck.* This analogy compares the sound that a cow makes with the sound that a duck makes. Even if the word *quack* was not given, one could figure out the correct word to complete the analogy based on the relationship between the words *moo* and *cow.* Some common relationships for analogies include synonyms, antonyms, part to whole, definition, and actor to action.

Another element that impacts a text is the author's point-of-view. The **point of view** of a text is the perspective from which a passage is told. An author will always have a point of view about a story before he or she draws up a plot line. The author will know what events they want to take place, how they want the characters to interact, and how they want the story to resolve. An author will also have an opinion on the topic or series of events which is presented in the story that is based on their prior experience and beliefs.

The two main points of view that authors use--especially in a work of fiction--are first person and third person. If the narrator of the story is also the main character, or *protagonist,* the text is written in first-person point of view. In first person, the author writes from the perspective of *I.* Third-person point of view is probably the most common that authors use in their passages. Using third person, authors refer to each character by using *he* or *she.* In third-person omniscient, the narrator is not a character in the story and tells the story of all of the characters at the same time.

**Review Video: <u>Point of View</u>**
Visit mometrix.com/academy and enter code: 383336

**Transitional words** and phrases are devices that guide readers through a text. You are no doubt familiar with the common transitions, though you may never have considered how they operate. Some transitional phrases (*after, before, during, in the middle of*) give information about time. Some indicate that an example is about to be given (*for example, in fact, for instance*). Writers use them to compare (*also, likewise*) and contrast (*however, but, yet*). Transitional words and phrases can suggest addition (*and, also, furthermore, moreover*) and logical relationships (*if, then, therefore, as a*

Copyright © Mometrix Media. You have been licensed one copy of this document for personal use only. Any other reproduction or redistribution is strictly prohibited. All rights reserved. This content is provided for test preparation purposes only and does not imply an endorsement by Mometrix of any particular political, scientific, or religious point of view.

*result, since*). Finally, transitional words and phrases can separate the steps in a process (*first, second, last*).

> **Review Video: Transitional Words and Phrases**
> Visit mometrix.com/academy and enter code: 197796

## UNDERSTANDING A PASSAGE

One of the most important skills in reading comprehension is the identification of **topics** and **main ideas.** There is a subtle difference between these two features. The topic is the **subject** of a text (i.e., what the text is all about). The main idea, on the other hand, is the **most important point** being made by the author. The topic is usually expressed in a few words at the most while the main idea often needs a full sentence to be completely defined. As an example, a short passage might have the topic of penguins and the main idea could be written as *Penguins are different from other birds in many ways.* In most nonfiction writing, the topic and the main idea will be stated directly and often appear in a sentence at the very beginning or end of the text. When being tested on an understanding of the author's topic, you may be able to skim the passage for the general idea, by reading only the first sentence of each paragraph. A body paragraph's first sentence is often—but not always—the main topic sentence which gives you a summary of the content in the paragraph.

However, there are cases in which the reader must figure out an unstated topic or main idea. In these instances, you must read every sentence of the text and try to come up with an overarching idea that is supported by each of those sentences.

Note: A thesis statement should not be confused with the main idea of the passage. While the main idea gives a brief, general summary of a text, the thesis statement provides a specific perspective on an issue that the author supports with evidence.

> **Review Video: Topics and Main Ideas**
> Visit mometrix.com/academy and enter code: 407801

**Supporting details** provide evidence and backing for the main point. In order to show that a main idea is correct, or valid, authors add details that prove their point. All texts contain details, but they are only classified as supporting details when they serve to reinforce some larger point. Supporting details are most commonly found in informative and persuasive texts. In some cases, they will be clearly indicated with terms like *for example* or *for instance*, or they will be enumerated with terms like *first*, *second*, and *last*. However, you need to be prepared for texts that do not contain those indicators.

As a reader, you should consider whether the author's supporting details really back up his or her main point. Supporting details can be factual and correct, yet they may not be relevant to the author's point. Conversely, supporting details can seem pertinent, but they can be ineffective because they are based on opinion or assertions that cannot be proven.

> **Review Video: Supporting Details**
> Visit mometrix.com/academy and enter code: 396297

An example of a **main idea** is: *Giraffes live in the Serengeti of Africa.* A **supporting detail** about giraffes could be: *A giraffe in this region benefits from a long neck by reaching twigs and leaves on tall trees.* The main idea expresses that the text is about giraffes in general. The supporting detail gives a specific fact about how the giraffes eat.

Copyright © Mometrix Media. You have been licensed one copy of this document for personal use only. Any other reproduction or redistribution is strictly prohibited. All rights reserved. This content is provided for test preparation purposes only and does not imply an endorsement by Mometrix of any particular political, scientific, or religious point of view.

As opposed to a main idea, themes are seldom expressed directly in a text and can be difficult to identify. A **theme** is an issue, an idea, or a question raised by the text. For instance, a theme of *Cinderella* (the Charles Perrault version) is perseverance as the title character serves her step-sisters and step-mother, and the prince seeks to find the girl with the missing slipper. A passage may have many themes, and a dedicated reader must take care to identify only themes that you are asked to find. One common characteristic of themes is that they raise more questions than they answer. In a good piece of fiction, authors are trying to elevate the reader's perspective and encourage him or her to consider the themes in a deeper way. In the process of reading, one can identify themes by constantly asking about the general issues that the text is addressing. A good way to evaluate an author's approach to a theme is to begin reading with a question in mind (e.g., How does this text approach the theme of love?) and to look for evidence in the text that addresses that question.

> **Review Video: Themes in Literature**
> Visit mometrix.com/academy and enter code: 732074

## EVALUATING A PASSAGE

When reading informational texts, there is importance in understanding the logical conclusion of the author's ideas. **Identifying a logical conclusion** can help you determine whether you agree with the writer or not. Coming to this conclusion is much like making an inference: the approach requires you to combine the information given by the text with what you already know in order to make a logical conclusion. If the author intended the reader to draw a certain conclusion, then you can expect the author's argumentation and detail to be leading in that direction. One way to approach the task of drawing conclusions is to make brief notes of all the points made by the author. When the notes are arranged on paper, they may clarify the logical conclusion. Another way to approach conclusions is to consider whether the reasoning of the author raises any pertinent questions. Sometimes you will be able to draw several conclusions from a passage. On occasion these will be conclusions that were never imagined by the author. Therefore, be aware that these conclusions must be supported directly by the text.

> **Review Video: How to Support a Conclusion**
> Visit mometrix.com/academy and enter code: 281653

The term **text evidence** refers to information that supports a main point or minor points and can help lead the reader to a conclusion. Information used as text evidence is precise, descriptive, and factual. A main point is often followed by supporting details that provide evidence to back-up a claim. For example, a passage may include the claim that winter occurs during opposite months in the Northern and Southern hemispheres. Text evidence based on this claim may include countries where winter occurs in opposite months along with reasons that winter occurs at different times of the year in separate hemispheres (due to the tilt of the Earth as it rotates around the sun).

> **Review Video: Textual Evidence**
> Visit mometrix.com/academy and enter code: 486236

A reader should always be drawing conclusions from the text. Sometimes conclusions are implied from written information, and other times the information is **stated directly** within the passage. One should always aim to draw conclusions from information stated within a passage, rather than to draw them from mere implications. At times an author may provide some information and then describe a counterargument. Readers should be alert for direct statements that are subsequently rejected or weakened by the author. Furthermore, you should always read through the entire

Copyright © Mometrix Media. You have been licensed one copy of this document for personal use only. Any other reproduction or redistribution is strictly prohibited. All rights reserved.
This content is provided for test preparation purposes only and does not imply an endorsement by Mometrix of any particular political, scientific, or religious point of view.

passage before drawing conclusions. Many readers are trained to expect the author's conclusions at either the beginning or the end of the passage, but many texts do not adhere to this format.

Drawing conclusions from information implied within a passage requires confidence on the part of the reader. **Implications** are things that the author does not state directly, but readers can assume based on what the author does say. Consider the following passage: *I stepped outside and opened my umbrella. By the time I got to work, the cuffs of my pants were soaked.* The author never states that it is raining, but this fact is clearly implied. Conclusions based on implication must be well supported by the text. In order to draw a solid conclusion, readers should have multiple pieces of evidence. If readers have only one piece, they must be assured that there is no other possible explanation than their conclusion. A good reader will be able to draw many conclusions from information implied by the text which will be a great help in the exam.

As an aid to drawing conclusions, **outlining** the information contained in the passage should be a familiar skill to readers. An effective outline will reveal the structure of the passage and will lead to solid conclusions. An effective outline will have a title that refers to the basic subject of the text though the title needs not recapitulate the main idea. In most outlines, the main idea will be the first major section. Each major idea of the passage will be established as the head of a category. For instance, the most common outline format calls for the main ideas of the passage to be indicated with Roman numerals. In an effective outline of this kind, each of the main ideas will be represented by a Roman numeral and none of the Roman numerals will designate minor details or secondary ideas. Moreover, all supporting ideas and details should be placed in the appropriate place on the outline. An outline does not need to include every detail listed in the text, but the outline should feature all of those that are central to the argument or message. Each of these details should be listed under the appropriate main idea.

> **Review Video: Outlining as an Aid to Drawing Conclusions**
> Visit mometrix.com/academy and enter code: 584445

Ideas from a text can also be organized using **graphic organizers**. A graphic organizer is a way to simplify information and take key points from the text. A graphic organizer such as a timeline may have an event listed for a corresponding date on the timeline while an outline may have an event listed under a key point that occurs in the text. Each reader needs to create the type of graphic organizer that works the best for him or her in terms of being able to recall information from a story. Examples include a *spider-map,* which takes a main idea from the story and places it in a bubble with supporting points branching off the main idea. An *outline* is useful for diagramming the main and supporting points of the entire story, and a *Venn diagram* classifies information as separate or overlapping.

> **Review Video: Graphic Organizers**
> Visit mometrix.com/academy and enter code: 665513

A helpful tool is the ability to **summarize** the information that you have read in a paragraph or passage format. This process is similar to creating an effective outline. First, a summary should accurately define the main idea of the passage though the summary does not need to explain this main idea in exhaustive detail. The summary should continue by laying out the most important supporting details or arguments from the passage. All of the significant supporting details should be included, and none of the details included should be irrelevant or insignificant. Also, the summary should accurately report all of these details. Too often, the desire for brevity in a summary leads to the sacrifice of clarity or accuracy. Summaries are often difficult to read because they omit all of the

Copyright © Mometrix Media. You have been licensed one copy of this document for personal use only. Any other reproduction or redistribution is strictly prohibited. All rights reserved.
This content is provided for test preparation purposes only and does not imply an endorsement by Mometrix of any particular political, scientific, or religious point of view.

graceful language, digressions, and asides that distinguish great writing. However, an effective summary should contain much the same message as the original text.

> **Review Video: Summarizing Text**
> Visit mometrix.com/academy and enter code: 172903

**Paraphrasing** is another method that the reader can use to aid in comprehension. When paraphrasing, one puts what they have read into their words by rephrasing what the author has written, or one "translates" all of what the author shared into their words by including as many details as they can.

## RESPONDING TO A PASSAGE

When reading a good passage, readers are moved to engage actively in the text. One part of being an active reader involves making predictions. A **prediction** is a guess about what will happen next. Readers constantly make predictions based on what they have read and what they already know.

> **Review Video: Predictive Reading**
> Visit mometrix.com/academy and enter code: 437248

Consider the following sentence: *Staring at the computer screen in shock, Kim blindly reached over for the brimming glass of water on the shelf to her side.* The sentence suggests that Kim is agitated, and that she is not looking at the glass that she is going to pick up. So, a reader might predict that Kim is going to knock over the glass. Of course, not every prediction will be accurate: perhaps Kim will pick the glass up cleanly. Nevertheless, the author has certainly created the expectation that the water might be spilled. Predictions are always subject to revision as the reader acquires more information.

*Test-taking tip*: To respond to questions requiring future predictions, your answers should be based on evidence of past or present behavior.

Readers are often required to understand a text that claims and suggests ideas without stating them directly. An **inference** is a piece of information that is implied but not written outright by the author. For instance, consider the following sentence: *After the final out of the inning, the fans were filled with joy and rushed the field.* From this sentence, a reader can infer that the fans were watching a baseball game and their team won the game. Readers should take great care to avoid using information beyond the provided passage before making inferences. As you practice drawing inferences, you will find that they require concentration and attention.

> **Review Video: Inference**
> Visit mometrix.com/academy and enter code: 379203

*Test-taking tip*: While being tested on your ability to make correct inferences, you must look for contextual clues. An answer can be *true* but not *correct*. The contextual clues will help you find the answer that is the best answer out of the given choices. Be careful in your reading to understand the context in which a phrase is stated. When asked for the implied meaning of a statement made in the passage, you should immediately locate the statement and read the context in which the statement was made. Also, look for an answer choice that has a similar phrase to the statement in question.

Copyright © Mometrix Media. You have been licensed one copy of this document for personal use only. Any other reproduction or redistribution is strictly prohibited. All rights reserved. This content is provided for test preparation purposes only and does not imply an endorsement by Mometrix of any particular political, scientific, or religious point of view.

Readers must be able to identify a text's **sequence**, or the order in which things happen. Often, when the sequence is very important to the author, the text is indicated with signal words like *first*, *then*, *next*, and *last*. However, a sequence can be merely implied and must be noted by the reader.

Consider the sentence *He walked through the garden and gave water and fertilizer to the plants.* Clearly, the man did not walk through the garden before he collected water and fertilizer for the plants. So, the implied sequence is that he first collected water, then he collected fertilizer, next he walked through the garden, and last he gave water or fertilizer as necessary to the plants. Texts do not always proceed in an orderly sequence from first to last. Sometimes they begin at the end and start over at the beginning. As a reader, you can enhance your understanding of the passage by taking brief notes to clarify the sequence.

In addition to inference and prediction, readers must often **draw conclusions** about the information they have read. When asked for a *conclusion* that may be drawn, look for critical "hedge" phrases, such as *likely, may, can, will often*, among many others. When you are being tested on this knowledge, remember the question that writers insert into these hedge phrases to cover every possibility. Often an answer will be wrong simply because there is no room for exception. Extreme positive or negative answers (such as always or never) are usually not correct. The reader should not use any outside knowledge that is not gathered from the passage to answer the related questions. Correct answers can be derived straight from the passage.

## Building a Vocabulary

The **denotative** meaning of a word is the literal meaning. The **connotative** meaning goes beyond the denotative meaning to include the emotional reaction that a word may invoke. The connotative meaning often takes the denotative meaning a step further due to associations which the reader makes with the denotative meaning. Readers can differentiate between the denotative and connotative meanings by first recognizing how authors use each meaning. Most nonfiction, for example, is fact-based, and nonfiction authors rarely use flowery, figurative language. The reader can assume that the writer is using the denotative meaning of words. In fiction, the author may use the connotative meaning. Readers can determine whether the author is using the denotative or connotative meaning of a word by implementing context clues.

> **Review Video: Connotation and Denotation**
> Visit mometrix.com/academy and enter code: 310092

Readers of all levels will encounter words that they either have never seen or have only encountered on a limited basis. The best way to define a word in **context** is to look for nearby words that can assist in learning the meaning of the word. For instance, unfamiliar nouns are often accompanied by examples that provide a definition. Consider the following sentence: *Dave arrived at the party in hilarious garb: a leopard-print shirt, buckskin trousers, and high heels.* If a reader was unfamiliar with the meaning of garb, he or she could read the examples (i.e., a leopard-print shirt, buckskin trousers, and high heels) and quickly determine that the word means *clothing*. Examples will not always be this obvious. Consider this sentence: *Parsley, lemon, and flowers were just a few of items he used as garnishes.* Here, the word *garnishes* is exemplified by parsley, lemon, and flowers. Readers who have eaten in a few restaurants will probably be able to identify a garnish as something used to decorate a plate.

> **Review Video: Context Clues**
> Visit mometrix.com/academy and enter code: 613660

Copyright © Mometrix Media. You have been licensed one copy of this document for personal use only. Any other reproduction or redistribution is strictly prohibited. All rights reserved.
This content is provided for test preparation purposes only and does not imply an endorsement by Mometrix of any particular political, scientific, or religious point of view.

In addition to looking at the context of a passage, readers can use contrasts to define an unfamiliar word in context. In many sentences, the author will not describe the unfamiliar word directly; instead, he or she will describe the opposite of the unfamiliar word. Thus, you are provided with some information that will bring you closer to defining the word. Consider the following example: *Despite his intelligence, Hector's low brow and bad posture made him look obtuse.* The author writes that Hector's appearance does not convey intelligence. Therefore, *obtuse* must mean unintelligent. Here is another example: *Despite the horrible weather, we were beatific about our trip to Alaska.* The word *despite* indicates that the speaker's feelings were at odds with the weather. Since the weather is described as *horrible*, then *beatific* must mean something positive.

In some cases, there will be very few contextual clues to help a reader define the meaning of an unfamiliar word. When this happens, one strategy that readers may employ is **substitution**. A good reader will brainstorm some possible synonyms for the given word, and he or she will substitute these words into the sentence. If the sentence and the surrounding passage continue to make sense, then the substitution has revealed at least some information about the unfamiliar word. Consider the sentence: *Frank's admonition rang in her ears as she climbed the mountain.* A reader unfamiliar with *admonition* might come up with some substitutions like *vow, promise, advice, complaint,* or *compliment.* All of these words make general sense of the sentence though their meanings are diverse. The process has suggested; however, that an admonition is some sort of message. The substitution strategy is rarely able to pinpoint a precise definition, but this process can be effective as a last resort.

Occasionally, you will be able to define an unfamiliar word by looking at the descriptive words in the context. Consider the following sentence: *Fred dragged the recalcitrant boy kicking and screaming up the stairs.* The words *dragged, kicking,* and *screaming* all suggest that the boy does not want to go up the stairs. The reader may assume that *recalcitrant* means something like unwilling or protesting. In this example, an unfamiliar adjective was identified.

Additionally, using description to define an unfamiliar noun is a common practice compared to unfamiliar adjectives, as in this sentence: *Don's wrinkled frown and constantly shaking fist identified him as a curmudgeon of the first order.* Don is described as having a *wrinkled frown and constantly shaking fist* suggesting that a *curmudgeon* must be a grumpy person. Contrasts do not always provide detailed information about the unfamiliar word, but they at least give the reader some clues.

When a word has more than one meaning, readers can have difficulty with determining how the word is being used in a given sentence. For instance, the verb *cleave,* can mean either *join* or *separate.* When readers come upon this word, they will have to select the definition that makes the most sense. Consider the following sentence: *Hermione's knife cleaved the bread cleanly.* Since, a knife cannot join bread together, the word must indicate separation. A slightly more difficult example would be the sentence: *The birds cleaved together as they flew from the oak tree.* Immediately, the presence of the word *together* should suggest that in this sentence *cleave* is being used to mean *join.* Discovering the intent of a word with multiple meanings requires the same tricks as defining an unknown word: look for contextual clues and evaluate the substituted words.

As a person is exposed to more words, the extent of their vocabulary will expand. By reading on a regular basis, a person can increase the number of ways that they have seen a word in context. Based on experience, a person can recall how a word was used in the past and apply that knowledge to a new context. For example, a person may have seen the word *gull* used to mean a bird that is found near the seashore. However, a *gull* can be a person who is tricked easily. If the word in context is used in reference to a character, the reader can recognize the insult since gulls

Copyright © Mometrix Media. You have been licensed one copy of this document for personal use only. Any other reproduction or redistribution is strictly prohibited. All rights reserved. This content is provided for test preparation purposes only and does not imply an endorsement by Mometrix of any particular political, scientific, or religious point of view.

are not seen as extremely intelligent. When you use your knowledge about a word, you can find comparisons or figure out the meaning for a new use of a word.

# Figurative Language

There are many types of language devices that authors use to convey their meaning in a descriptive way. Understanding these concepts will help you understand what you read. These types of devices are called *figurative language* – language that goes beyond the literal meaning of a word or phrase. **Descriptive language** that evokes imagery in the reader's mind is one type of figurative language. **Exaggeration** is another type of figurative language. Also, when you compare two things, you are using figurative language. **Similes** and **metaphors** are ways of comparing things, and both are types of figurative language commonly found in poetry. An example of figurative language (a simile in this case): *The child howled like a coyote when her mother told her to pick up the toys*. In this example, the child's howling is compared to that of a coyote and helps the reader understand the sound being made by the child.

A **figure-of-speech**, sometimes termed a rhetorical figure or device is a word or phrase that departs from straightforward, literal language. Figures-of-speech are often used and crafted for emphasis, freshness of expression, or clarity. However, clarity of a passage may suffer from use of these devices. As an example of the figurative use of a word, consider the sentence: *I am going to crown you.* The author may mean:

- I am going to place a literal crown on your head.
- I am going to symbolically exalt you to the place of kingship.
- I am going to punch you in the head with my clenched fist.
- I am going to put a second checker's piece on top of your checker piece to signify that it has become a king.

> **Review Video: Figures of Speech**
> Visit mometrix.com/academy and enter code: 111295

An **allusion** is a comparison of someone or something to a person or event in history or literature. Allusions that refer to people or events that are more or less contemporary are called topical allusions. Those referring to specific persons are called personal allusions. For example, *His desire for power was his Achilles' heel.* This example refers to Achilles, a notable hero in Greek mythology who was known to be invincible with the exception of his heels. Today, the term *Achilles' heel* refers to an individual's weakness.

> **Review Video: Allusions**
> Visit mometrix.com/academy and enter code: 294065

A **metaphor** is a type of figurative language in which the writer equates one thing with a different thing. For instance: *The bird was an arrow arcing through the sky*. In this sentence, the arrow is serving as a metaphor for the bird. The point of a metaphor is to encourage the reader to consider the item being described in a different way. Let's continue with this metaphor for a bird: you are asked to envision the bird's flight as being similar to the arc of an arrow. So, you imagine the flight to be swift and bending. Metaphors are a way for the author to describe an item without being direct and obvious. This literary device is a lyrical and suggestive way of providing information. Note that the reference for a metaphor will not always be mentioned explicitly by the author. Consider the following description of a forest in winter: *Swaying skeletons reached for the sky and*

Copyright © Mometrix Media. You have been licensed one copy of this document for personal use only. Any other reproduction or redistribution is strictly prohibited. All rights reserved. This content is provided for test preparation purposes only and does not imply an endorsement by Mometrix of any particular political, scientific, or religious point of view.

*groaned as the wind blew through them.* In this example, the author is using *skeletons* as a metaphor for leafless trees. This metaphor creates a spooky tone while inspiring the reader's imagination.

**Review Video: Metaphors in Writing**
Visit mometrix.com/academy and enter code: 133295

**Hyperbole** is overstatement for effect. For example: *He jumped ten feet in the air when he heard the good news.* Obviously, no person has the natural ability to jump ten feet in the air. The author exaggerates because the hyperbole conveys the extremity of emotion. If the author simply said: *He jumped when he heard the good news,* then readers would be led to think that the character is not experiencing an extreme emotion. Hyperbole can be dangerous if the author does not exaggerate enough. For instance, if the author wrote, *He jumped two feet in the air when he heard the good news,* then readers may assume that the author is writing a factual statement, not an exaggeration. Readers should be cautious with confusing or vague hyperboles as some test questions may have a hyperbole and a factual statement listed in the answer options.

**Understatement** is the opposite of hyperbole. This device discounts or downplays something. Think about someone who climbs Mount Everest. Then, they say that the journey was *a little stroll.* As with other types of figurative language, understatement has a range of uses. The device may show self-defeat or modesty as in the Mount Everest example. However, some may think of understatement as false modesty (i.e., an attempt to bring attention to you or a situation). For example, a woman is praised on her diamond engagement ring. The woman says, *Oh, this little thing?* Her understatement might be heard as stuck-up or unfeeling.

**Review Video: Hyperbole and Understatement**
Visit mometrix.com/academy and enter code: 308470

A **simile** is a figurative expression that is similar to a metaphor, yet the expression requires the use of the distancing words *like* or *as.* Some examples: *The sun was like an orange, eager as a beaver,* and *nimble as a mountain goat.* Because a simile includes *like* or a*s,* the device creates a space between the description and the thing being described. If an author says that *a house was like a shoebox,* then the tone is different than the author saying that the house *was* a shoebox. In a simile, authors indicate an awareness that the description is not the same thing as the thing being described. In a metaphor, there is no such distinction. Authors will use metaphors and similes depending on their intended tone.

**Review Video: Similes**
Visit mometrix.com/academy and enter code: 642949

Another type of figurative language is **personification.** This is the description of a nonhuman thing as if the item were human. Literally, the word means the process of making something into a person. The general intent of personification is to describe things in a manner that will be comprehensible to readers. When an author states that a tree *groans* in the wind, he or she does not mean that the tree is emitting a low, pained sound from a mouth. Instead, the author means that the tree is making a noise similar to a human groan. Of course, this personification establishes a tone of sadness or suffering. A different tone would be established if the author said that the tree was *swaying* or *dancing.*

**Review Video: Personification**
Visit mometrix.com/academy and enter code: 260066

Copyright © Mometrix Media. You have been licensed one copy of this document for personal use only. Any other reproduction or redistribution is strictly prohibited. All rights reserved.
This content is provided for test preparation purposes only and does not imply an endorsement by Mometrix of any particular political, scientific, or religious point of view.

**Irony** is a statement that suggests the opposite of what one expects to occur. In other words, the device is used when an author or character says one thing but means another. For example, imagine a man who is covered in mud and dressed in tattered clothes and walks in his front door to meet his wife. Then, his wife asks him, "How was your day?", and he says, "Great!" The man's response to his wife is an example of irony. As in this example, irony often depends on information that the reader obtains elsewhere. There is a fine distinction between irony and sarcasm. Irony is any statement in which the literal meaning is opposite from the intended meaning. Sarcasm is similar, yet the statement is insulting to the person at whom the words are directed. A sarcastic statement suggests that the other person is foolish to believe that an obviously false statement is true.

> **Review Video: What is the Definition of Irony?**
> Visit mometrix.com/academy and enter code: 374204

Copyright © Mometrix Media. You have been licensed one copy of this document for personal use only. Any other reproduction or redistribution is strictly prohibited. All rights reserved.
This content is provided for test preparation purposes only and does not imply an endorsement by Mometrix of any particular political, scientific, or religious point of view.

# Essay

## PRACTICE MAKES PREPARED WRITERS

Writing is a skill that continues to need development throughout a person's life. For some people, writing seems to be a natural gift. They rarely struggle with writer's block. When you read their papers, they have persuasive ideas. For others, writing is an intimidating task that they endure. As you practice, you can improve your skills and be better prepared for writing a time-sensitive essay.

A traditional way to prepare for the writing section is to read. When you read newspapers, magazines, and books, you learn about new ideas. You can read newspapers and magazines to become informed about issues that affect many people. As you think about those issues and ideas, you can take a position and form opinions. Try to develop these ideas and your opinions by sharing them with friends. After you develop your opinions, try writing them down as if you were going to spread your ideas beyond your friends.

Remember that you are practicing for more than an exam. Two of the most valuable skills in life are the abilities to **read critically** and to **write clearly**. When you work on evaluating the arguments of a passage and explain your thoughts well, you are developing skills that you will use for a lifetime. In this overview of essay writing, you will find strategies and tools that will prepare you to write better essays.

## ESSAY OVERVIEW

For your exam you need to write an essay that shows your ability to understand and respond to an assignment. When you talk with others, you give beliefs, opinions, and ideas about the world around you. As you talk, you have the opportunity to share information with spoken words, facial expressions, or hand motions. If your audience seems confused about your ideas, you can stop and explain. However, when you write, you have a different assignment. As you write, you need to share information in a clear, precise way. Your readers will not have the chance to ask questions about your ideas. So, before you write your essay, you need to understand the assignment. As you write, you should be clear and precise about your ideas.

## BRAINSTORM

Spend the first three to five minutes brainstorming for ideas. Write down any ideas that you might have on the topic. The purpose is to pull any helpful information from the depths of your memory. In this stage, anything goes down on note paper regardless of how good or bad the idea may seem at first glance. You may not bring your own paper for these notes. Instead, you will be provided with paper at the time of your test.

## STRENGTH THROUGH DIFFERENT VIEWPOINTS

The best papers will contain several examples and mature reasoning. As you brainstorm, you should consider different perspectives. There are more than two sides to every topic. In an argument, there are countless perspectives that can be considered. On any topic, different groups are impacted and many reach the same conclusion or position. Yet, they reach the same conclusion through different paths. Before writing your essay, try to *see* the topic through as many different *eyes* as you can.

In addition, you don't have to use information on how the topic impacts others. You can draw from your own experience as you wish. If you prefer to use a personal narrative, then explain the

86

Copyright © Mometrix Media. You have been licensed one copy of this document for personal use only. Any other reproduction or redistribution is strictly prohibited. All rights reserved. This content is provided for test preparation purposes only and does not imply an endorsement by Mometrix of any particular political, scientific, or religious point of view.

experience and your emotions from that moment. Anything that you've seen in your community can be expanded upon to round out your position on the topic.

Once you have finished with your creative flow, you need to stop and review what you brainstormed. *Which idea allowed you to come up with the most supporting information?* Be sure to pick an angle that will allow you to have a thorough coverage of the prompt.

Every garden of ideas has weeds. The ideas that you brainstormed are going to be random pieces of information of different values. Go through the pieces carefully and pick out the ones that are the best. The best ideas are strong points that will be easy to write a paragraph in response.

Now, you have your main ideas that you will focus on. So, align them in a sequence that will flow in a smooth, sensible path from point to point. With this approach, readers will go smoothly from one idea to the next in a reasonable order. Readers want an essay that has a sense of continuity (i.e., Point 1 to Point 2 to Point 3 and so on).

## START YOUR ENGINES

Now, you have a logical flow of the main ideas for the start of your essay. Begin by expanding on the first point, then move to your second point. Pace yourself. Don't spend too much time on any one of the ideas that you are expanding on. You want to have time for all of them. <u>Make sure that you watch your time</u>. If you have twenty minutes left to write out your ideas and you have four ideas, then you can only use five minutes per idea. Writing so much information in so little time can be an intimidating task. Yet, when you pace yourself, you can get through all of your points. If you find that you are falling behind, then you can remove one of your weaker arguments. This will allow you to give enough support to your remaining paragraphs.

Once you finish expanding on an idea, go back to your brainstorming session where you wrote out your ideas. You can scratch through the ideas as you write about them. This will let you see what you need to write about next and what you have left to cover.

Your introductory paragraph should have several easily identifiable features.

- First, the paragraph should have a quick description or paraphrasing of the topic. Use your own words to briefly explain what the topic is about.
- Second, you should list your writing points. What are the main ideas that you came up with earlier? If someone was to read only your introduction, they should be able to get a good summary of the entire paper.
- Third, you should explain your opinion of the topic and give an explanation for why you feel that way. What is your decision or conclusion on the topic?

Each of your following paragraphs should develop one of the points listed in the main paragraph. Use your personal experience and knowledge to support each of your points. Examples should back up everything.

Once you have finished expanding on each of your main points, you need to conclude your essay. Summarize what you written in a conclusion paragraph. Explain once more your argument on the prompt and review why you feel that way in a few sentences. At this stage, you have already backed up your statements. So, there is no need to do that again. You just need to refresh your readers on the main points that you made in your essay.

Copyright © Mometrix Media. You have been licensed one copy of this document for personal use only. Any other reproduction or redistribution is strictly prohibited. All rights reserved.
This content is provided for test preparation purposes only and does not imply an endorsement by Mometrix of any particular political, scientific, or religious point of view.

## DON'T PANIC

Whatever you do during essay, do not panic. When you panic, you will put fewer words on the page and your ideas will be weak. Therefore, panicking is not helpful. If your mind goes blank when you see the prompt, then you need to take a deep breath. Force yourself to go through the steps listed above: brainstorm and put anything on scratch paper that comes to mind.

Also, don't get clock fever. You may be overwhelmed when you're looking at a page that is mostly blank. Your mind is full of random thoughts and feeling confused, and the clock is ticking down faster. You have already brainstormed for ideas. Therefore, you don't have to keep coming up with ideas. If you're running out of time and you have a lot of ideas that you haven't written down, then don't be afraid to make some cuts. Start picking the best ideas that you have left and expand on them. Don't feel like you have to write on all of your ideas.

A short paper that is well written and well organized is better than a long paper that is poorly written and poorly organized. Don't keep writing about a subject just to add sentences and avoid repeating a statement or idea that you have explained already. The goal is 1 to 2 pages of quality writing. That is your target, but you should not mess up your paper by trying to get there. You want to have a natural end to your work without having to cut something short. If your essay is a little long, then that isn't a problem as long as your ideas are clear and flow well from paragraph to paragraph. Remember to expand on the ideas that you identified in the brainstorming session.

Leave time at the end (at least three minutes) to go back and check over your work. Reread and make sure that everything you've written makes sense and flows well. Clean up any spelling or grammar mistakes. Also, go ahead and erase any brainstorming ideas that you weren't able to include. Then, clean up any extra information that you might have written that doesn't fit into your paper.

As you proofread, make sure that there aren't any fragments or run-ons. Check for sentences that are too short or too long. If the sentence is too short, then look to see if you have a specific subject and an active verb. If it is too long, then break up the long sentence into two sentences. Watch out for any "big words" that you may have used. Be sure that you are using difficult words correctly. Don't misunderstand; you should try to increase your vocabulary and use difficult words in your essay. However, your focus should be on developing and expressing ideas in a clear and precise way.

## THE SHORT OVERVIEW

Depending on your preferences and personality, the essay may be your hardest or your easiest section. You are required to go through the entire process of writing a paper in a limited amount of time which is very challenging.

Stay focused on each of the steps for brainstorming. Go through the process of creative flow first. You can start by generating ideas about the prompt. Next, organize those ideas into a smooth flow. Then, pick out the ideas that are the best from your list.

Create a recognizable essay structure in your paper. Start with an introduction that explains what you have decided to argue. Then, choose your main points. Use the body paragraphs to touch on those main points and have a conclusion that wraps up the topic.

Save a few moments to go back and review what you have written. Clean up any minor mistakes that you might have made and make those last few critical touches that can make a huge difference. Finally, be proud and confident of what you have written!

88

Copyright © Mometrix Media. You have been licensed one copy of this document for personal use only. Any other reproduction or redistribution is strictly prohibited. All rights reserved. This content is provided for test preparation purposes only and does not imply an endorsement by Mometrix of any particular political, scientific, or religious point of view.

# Practice Test #1

Want to take this practice test in an online interactive format?
Check out the bonus page, which includes interactive practice questions and
much more: **mometrix.com/bonus948/iseeupper**

## Section 1 – Verbal Reasoning

*DIRECTIONS: Each of the following questions consists of one word followed by four words. Select the one word whose meaning is closest to the word in capital letters. You are not allowed to use scrap paper, a dictionary, or a thesaurus.*

### PART ONE – SYNONYMS

**1. ENTHRALL**
- a. bizarre
- b. devote
- c. extreme
- d. fascinate

**2. COWARD**
- a. boor
- b. brave
- c. gutless
- d. judge

**3. NOVICE**
- a. beginner
- b. expert
- c. naught
- d. nurse

**4. TEMPERATE**
- a. extreme
- b. lenient
- c. moderate
- d. taut

**5. AUTHENTIC**
- a. colorful
- b. flimsy
- c. genuine
- d. laughable

Copyright © Mometrix Media. You have been licensed one copy of this document for personal use only. Any other reproduction or redistribution is strictly prohibited. All rights reserved.
This content is provided for test preparation purposes only and does not imply an endorsement by Mometrix of any particular political, scientific, or religious point of view.

## 6. SALVAGE

- a. bless
- b. recover
- c. slobber
- d. swagger

## 7. VERNACULAR

- a. ballad
- b. language
- c. poison
- d. veracity

## 8. ATTEST

- a. accommodate
- b. bewitch
- c. heed
- d. vouch

## 9. DERELICT

- a. abandoned
- b. corrupted
- c. depressed
- d. dispirited

## 10. ORDAIN

- a. adorn
- b. arrange
- c. command
- d. create

## 11. HAUGHTY

- a. arrogant
- b. bitter
- c. obscure
- d. perilous

## 12. LAPSE

- a. award
- b. error
- c. margin
- d. prank

## 13. NAUSEATE

- a. annoy
- b. crave
- c. repulse
- d. rival

Copyright © Mometrix Media. You have been licensed one copy of this document for personal use only. Any other reproduction or redistribution is strictly prohibited. All rights reserved. This content is provided for test preparation purposes only and does not imply an endorsement by Mometrix of any particular political, scientific, or religious point of view.

## 14. PALTRY

    a. cheap
    b. lurid
    c. peaceful
    d. severely

## 15. REFINED

    a. aromatic
    b. blatant
    c. cultured
    d. frightened

## 16. VIRTUAL

    a. potent
    b. real
    c. simulated
    d. visible

## 17. LOATHE

    a. charge
    b. exist
    c. fear
    d. hate

## 18. MIMIC

    a. curtail
    b. delve
    c. imitate
    d. recall

## 19. BRITTLE

    a. broad
    b. fragile
    c. radical
    d. smooth

## 20. WRETCHED

    a. absorbed
    b. awry
    c. miserable
    d. wicked

Copyright © Mometrix Media. You have been licensed one copy of this document for personal use only. Any other reproduction or redistribution is strictly prohibited. All rights reserved.
This content is provided for test preparation purposes only and does not imply an endorsement by Mometrix of any particular political, scientific, or religious point of view.

## PART TWO – SENTENCE COMPLETION

*DIRECTIONS: Select the answer choice that best completes the sentence. You are not allowed to use scrap paper, a dictionary, or a thesaurus.*

21. The teacher _____ her students when they gave the wrong answer.
    a. applauded
    b. belittled
    c. commended
    d. praised

22. Many rainforest species have _____ due to deforestation.
    a. immigrated
    b. perished
    c. persisted
    d. survived

23. She had many reasons for choosing to _____ a year of her life by putting her _____ variety of skills to work for others.
    a. aspire . . . immense
    b. benchmark . . . incognizant
    c. earmark . . . renown
    d. economize. . . . acrimonious

24. Overcome with _____, the students built a monument to _____ their teacher after his death.
    a. blissfulness . . . commemorate
    b. gratitude . . . politicize
    c. melancholy . . . memorialize
    d. sadness . . . criticize

25. Her son's misbehavior _____ her, but she managed to calm down before she spoke to him.
    a. blighted
    b. embroiled
    c. interlaced
    d. revived

26. The obstacles he faced seemed _____, but through hard work and _____ he was successful in his efforts.
    a. insuppressible . . . retention
    b. insurmountable . . . diligence
    c. licentious . . . persistence
    d. mountainous . . . indolence

27. Her _____ is to _____ the globe in a hot air balloon.
    a. affliction . . . circumambulate
    b. aspiration . . . circumnavigate
    c. dream . . . circulate
    d. enmity . . . circumscribe

Copyright © Mometrix Media. You have been licensed one copy of this document for personal use only. Any other reproduction or redistribution is strictly prohibited. All rights reserved. This content is provided for test preparation purposes only and does not imply an endorsement by Mometrix of any particular political, scientific, or religious point of view.

28. Paul made a bad decision to hike in _____ weather conditions.

    a.  adverse
    b.  affable
    c.  malleable
    d.  onerous

29. The teacher's predictable lecture was so _____ that the students fell asleep soon after it started.

    a.  banal
    b.  flippant
    c.  inconceivable
    d.  morbid

30. The mysterious, _____ music floated through the trees and charmed the listeners.

    a.  ethereal
    b.  frantic
    c.  poignant
    d.  timorous

31. Rhonda's behavior only _____ an already bad situation.

    a.  exacerbated
    b.  manifested
    c.  pursued
    d.  safeguarded

32. Brian had a reputation for _____ trouble in high school, but he _____ after he started college.

    a.  alleviating . . . decreased
    b.  inciting . . . deteriorated
    c.  inferring . . . oscillated
    d.  instigating . . . mellowed

33. These birds are not _____ to North America; they were brought here by European immigrants.

    a.  exigent
    b.  fluent
    c.  indigenous
    d.  ingenuous

34. The varsity basketball team's perfect season _____ in a championship win over their biggest rival.

    a.  alleviated
    b.  culminated
    c.  dispersed
    d.  lamented

Copyright © Mometrix Media. You have been licensed one copy of this document for personal use only. Any other reproduction or redistribution is strictly prohibited. All rights reserved. This content is provided for test preparation purposes only and does not imply an endorsement by Mometrix of any particular political, scientific, or religious point of view.

35. In a(n) _____ decision, the jury _____ the mayor of all wrongdoing.
    a. acclaimed . . . expatriated
    b. gridlocked . . . subjugated
    c. frantic . . . augmented
    d. unprecedented . . . exonerated

36. His friends never knew what to expect from Chris; his behavior was so _____.
    a. apathetic
    b. dubious
    c. erratic
    d. palliative

37. Since Glenda was short of money, she decided that her current appliances were _____ for the present.
    a. ephemeral
    b. imperious
    c. pestilent
    d. sufficient

38. The forecaster said that the high winds would _____ about midnight and that the next day would have light breezes.
    a. capitulate
    b. dispatch
    c. intensify
    d. subside

39. Since Gloria did not feel hungry, she looked at her dinner plate rather _____.
    a. gluttonously
    b. indifferently
    c. ravenously
    d. voraciously

40. He believed that in order to _____ the problem fully, he would need to understand all of its _____.
    a. constrict . . . aspirations
    b. deplore . . . vertigo
    c. elude . . . kindred
    d. grapple . . . intricacies

Copyright © Mometrix Media. You have been licensed one copy of this document for personal use only. Any other reproduction or redistribution is strictly prohibited. All rights reserved.
This content is provided for test preparation purposes only and does not imply an endorsement by Mometrix of any particular political, scientific, or religious point of view.

# Section 2 - Quantitative Reasoning

## Part One: Word Problems

*In this section there are four possible answers after each question. Choose which one is best. You are not allowed a calculator, a calculator watch, a ruler, a protractor, or a compass.*

**1. Determine the number of diagonals of a dodecagon.**

    a.  12
    b.  24
    c.  54
    d.  108

**2. Jonas jogs three times faster than he walks. Which graph BEST represents the situation?**

a.

c.

b.

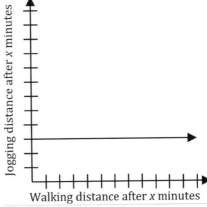

d.

**3. Jerry needs to load four pieces of equipment onto a factory elevator that has weight limit of 800 pounds. Jerry weighs 200 pounds. What would the average weight of each item have to be so that the elevator's weight limit is not exceeded?**

    a.  128 pounds
    b.  150 pounds
    c.  175 pounds
    d.  180 pounds

Copyright © Mometrix Media. You have been licensed one copy of this document for personal use only. Any other reproduction or redistribution is strictly prohibited. All rights reserved. This content is provided for test preparation purposes only and does not imply an endorsement by Mometrix of any particular political, scientific, or religious point of view.

**4. Chan receives a bonus from his job. He pays 30% in taxes, gives 20% to charity, uses another 20% to pay off an old debt, and sets aside 10% in a savings account. He has $600 remaining from his bonus. What was the total amount of Chan's bonus?**

    a.  $2400
    b.  $2800
    c.  $3000
    d.$3600

**5. A jar contains pennies and nickels. The ratio of nickels to pennies is 6:2. What percent of the coins are pennies?**

    a.  25%
    b.  33.3%
    c.  40%
    d.  50%

**6. Given the equation, $ax + b = c$, what is the value of x?**

    a.  $\frac{c+b}{a}$
    b.  $\frac{ca}{b}$
    c.  $c - ba$
    d.  $\frac{c-b}{a}$

**7. For the number set {7, 12, 5, 16, 23, 44, 18, 9, Z}, which of the following values could be equal to Z if Z is the median of the set?**

    a.  10
    b.  11
    c.  14
    d.  17

**8. If *c* is to be chosen at random from the set {1, 2, 3, 4} and *d* is to be chosen at random from the set {1, 2, 3, 4}, what is the probability *cd* will be odd?**

    a.  $\frac{1}{4}$
    b.  $\frac{1}{3}$
    c.  $\frac{3}{4}$
    d.  4

**9. If $x = 2y - 3$ and $2x + \frac{1}{2}y = 3$, then $y = ?$**

    a.  $-\frac{2}{3}$
    b.  1
    c.  2
    d.  $\frac{18}{7}$

Copyright © Mometrix Media. You have been licensed one copy of this document for personal use only. Any other reproduction or redistribution is strictly prohibited. All rights reserved. This content is provided for test preparation purposes only and does not imply an endorsement by Mometrix of any particular political, scientific, or religious point of view.

10. A bag contains 14 blue, 6 red, 12 green and 8 purple buttons. 25 buttons are removed from the bag randomly. How many of the removed buttons were red if the chance of drawing a red button from the bag is now $1/3$?

    a.  0
    b.  1
    c.  3
    d.  5

11. The sides of a triangle are equal to integral numbers of units. Two sides are 4 and 6 units long, respectively; what is the minimum value for the triangle's perimeter?

    a.  10 units
    b.  11 units
    c.  12 units
    d.  13 units

12. The average of six numbers is 4. If the average of two of those numbers is 2, what is the average of the other four numbers?

    a.  5
    b.  6
    c.  7
    d.  8

13. There are 64 squares on a checkerboard. Bobby puts one penny on the first square, two on the second square, four on the third, eight on the fourth. He continues to double the number of coins at each square until he has covered all 64 squares. How many coins must he place on the last square?

    a.  $2^{63}$
    b.  $2^{63} + 1$
    c.  $2^{64} - 1$
    d.  $2^{64}$

14. A commuter survey counts the people riding in cars on a highway in the morning. Each car contains only one man, only one woman, or both one man and one woman. Out of 25 cars, 13 contain a woman and 20 contain a man. How many contain both a man and a woman?

    a.  4
    b.  7
    c.  8
    d.  13

15. The length of Square A is 3 feet longer than the length of Square B. If the difference between their areas is 75 ft$^2$, what is the length of Square B?

    a.  11 feet
    b.  12 feet
    c.  13 feet
    d.  14 feet

Copyright © Mometrix Media. You have been licensed one copy of this document for personal use only. Any other reproduction or redistribution is strictly prohibited. All rights reserved.
This content is provided for test preparation purposes only and does not imply an endorsement by Mometrix of any particular political, scientific, or religious point of view.

16. One method for calculating the area of a circle is to dissect it into a number of wedges. The circle below has a radius $r$ and has been evenly dissected into 16 wedges.

If the wedges are rearranged alternately to create a shape resembling a rectangle, as shown below, what is the approximate length of the rectangle?

    a.   $\pi$
    b.   $\pi r$
    c.   $r$
    d.   $\pi r^2$

17. The cost, in dollars, of shipping x computers to California for sale is 3000 + 100x. The amount received when selling these computers is 400x dollars. What is the least number of computers that must be shipped and sold so that the amount received is at least equal to the shipping cost?

    a.   10
    b.   15
    c.   20
    d.   25

18. Given points $A$ and $B$ on a number line, where $A = -3$ and $B = 7$, find point $C$, located between $A$ and $B$, such that $C$ is four times farther from $A$ than it is from $B$.

    a.   −1
    b.   1
    c.   3
    d.   5

19. If $\frac{x}{8} = \frac{y}{4} = 4$, what is the value of $x - y$?

    a.   8
    b.   16
    c.   32
    d.   48

Copyright © Mometrix Media. You have been licensed one copy of this document for personal use only. Any other reproduction or redistribution is strictly prohibited. All rights reserved. This content is provided for test preparation purposes only and does not imply an endorsement by Mometrix of any particular political, scientific, or religious point of view.

**20. If *p* and *n* are positive consecutive integers such that *p* > *n*, and *p* + *n* = 15, what is the value of *n*?**

    a.  5
    b.  6
    c.  7
    d.  8

*In questions 21–37, note the given information, if any, and then compare the quantity in Column A to the quantity in Column B. Answer as follows:*

    a.  if the quantity in Column A is greater
    b.  if the quantity in Column B is greater
    c.  if the two quantities are equal
    d.  if the relationship cannot be determined from the information given

*In this section, you are not allowed a calculator, a calculator watch, a ruler, a protractor, or a compass.*

$$3x = y \text{ and } y = 4z$$

|  | **Column A** | **Column B** |
|---|---|---|
| **21.** | $y$ | $z$ |

|  | **Column A** | **Column B** |
|---|---|---|
| **22.** | $6x + 7 = 25$ | $x = 3$ |

On a floor plan drawn at a scale of 1:100, the area of a rectangular room is 30 cm$^2$.

|  | **Column A** | **Column B** |
|---|---|---|
| **23.** | The actual area of the room | 3,000 cm² |

|  | **Column A** | **Column B** |
|---|---|---|
| **24.** | $24 \div (6 - 2)$ | 12 |

Copyright © Mometrix Media. You have been licensed one copy of this document for personal use only. Any other reproduction or redistribution is strictly prohibited. All rights reserved.
This content is provided for test preparation purposes only and does not imply an endorsement by Mometrix of any particular political, scientific, or religious point of view.

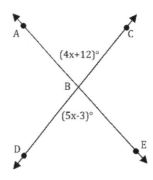

|  | Column A | Column B |
|---|---|---|
| **25.** | ∠ABC | ∠CBE |

A box of nails costs $15.75. Screws by the piece are $0.03 each.

|  | Column A | Column B |
|---|---|---|
| **26.** | The price of 10 screws | The price of 10 nails |

**Forty students in a class take a test that is graded on a scale of 1 to 10. The histogram in the figure shows the grade distribution, with the x-axis representing the grades and the y-axis representing the number of students obtaining each grade. The median value is represented by P, and the modal value is represented by Q.**

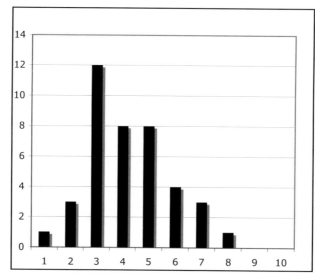

|  | Column A | Column. B |
|---|---|---|
| **27.** | P | Q |

|  | Column A | Column B |
|---|---|---|
| **28.** | $3 \times \sqrt[2]{81}$ | $81 \times 3$ |

Copyright © Mometrix Media. You have been licensed one copy of this document for personal use only. Any other reproduction or redistribution is strictly prohibited. All rights reserved.
This content is provided for test preparation purposes only and does not imply an endorsement by Mometrix of any particular political, scientific, or religious point of view.

Square A has side lengths of $x$. Square B has side lengths of $2x$.

| **Column A** | **Column B** |
|---|---|
| Area of Square A | Half the area of Square B |

**29.**

| **Column A** | **Column B** |
|---|---|
| $1 + x$ | $1 - x$ |

**30.**

A spinner has eight equally-spaced sections labeled 1 - 8. In addition, a die with six sides numbered 1-6 is rolled.

| **Column A** | **Column B** |
|---|---|
| Probability that the spinner lands on the number 1 or on a number that is greater than 5. | Probability that the die lands on the number 3 or on a number that is greater than 2. |

**31.**

David bought 200 shares of Oracle stock yesterday and sold it today at closing. The chart below shows the closing prices of stocks on the market today. His profit was $20.00.

| Stock | Price per Share | Shares Traded |
|---|---|---|
| Microsoft | $45.14 | 89,440,000 |
| Oracle | $19.10 | 12,415,000 |
| Apple Computer | $16.90 | 17,953,000 |
| Cisco Systems | $3.50 | 73,019,000 |
| Garmin | $29.30 | 53,225,000 |

| **Column A** | **Column B** |
|---|---|
| The price at which he bought the stock yesterday | The profit that he obtained |

**32.**

| **Column A** | **Column B** |
|---|---|
| The number of faces that share an edge with any one face on a cube. | The number of sides on any square. |

**33.**

| **Column A** | **Column B** |
|---|---|
| $6(7 + 17)$ | $(6 \times 7) + (6 \times 17)$ |

**34.**

Copyright © Mometrix Media. You have been licensed one copy of this document for personal use only. Any other reproduction or redistribution is strictly prohibited. All rights reserved.
This content is provided for test preparation purposes only and does not imply an endorsement by Mometrix of any particular political, scientific, or religious point of view.

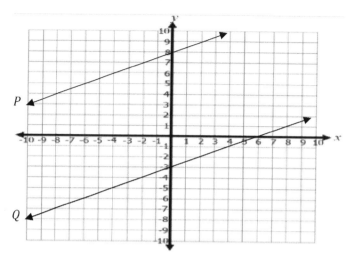

| **Column A** | **Column B** |
|---|---|
| 35. Slope of Line $P$ | Slope of Line $Q$ |

A bag contains 2 red marbles, 3 blue marbles, and 5 green marbles. In addition, a die with six sides numbered 1-6 is rolled.

| **Column A** | **Column B** |
|---|---|
| Probability that a red or a green marble is drawn. | Probability that a prime number or the number 6 is rolled. |
| 36. | |

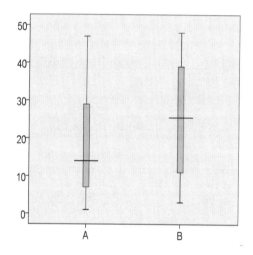

| **Column A** | **Column B** |
|---|---|
| The boxplot for data set B has a larger interquartile range | The boxplot for data set A has a larger median |
| 37. | |

Copyright © Mometrix Media. You have been licensed one copy of this document for personal use only. Any other reproduction or redistribution is strictly prohibited. All rights reserved.
This content is provided for test preparation purposes only and does not imply an endorsement by Mometrix of any particular political, scientific, or religious point of view.

## Section 3 – Reading Comprehension

*You are not allowed to use scrap paper, a dictionary, or a thesaurus.*

### Close Relationships in the 21st Century

We all know the drill: the consequences of urban sprawl, American's long work hours, and devotion to television and the internet are doing nothing good for American
5 communities.

A new study by sociologists at Duke University and the University of Arizona adds more grist to this mill, noting that Americans in 2004 had smaller networks of people with
10 whom they talk about matters important to them than they did in 1985. (*Social Isolation in America: Changes in Core Discussion Networks Over Two Decades*, American Sociological Review, June 2006.) In 1985,
15 Americans had three confidants, in 2004, we averaged two. The number of Americans who had no one with whom to talk about important matters almost doubled in 2004 to over 25%. Increasingly, most confidants are
20 family: in 2004, 80% of people talked only to family about important matters and about 9% of people depended totally on their spouse.

This decrease in confidants is part (a result) of the same trend that's leaving fewer
25 people knowing their neighbors or participating in social clubs or public affairs than in the past (phenomena noted in the book Better Together: Restoring the American Community by Robert Putnam and
30 Lewis Feldstein). We know a lot of people, but not necessarily very well.

Left to our own devices and cultural trends then, we seem to be moving in an unpleasant direction. Communities are
35 formed ad hoc, around specific shared individual interests. This wouldn't be bad, of course, except that those communities seem to exist only within the constraints of those shared interests, and don't develop into close
40 and meaningful relationships. The transient and specific nature of many of our relationships today can keep us socially busy without building the lasting relationships and communities that we want.

45 So, what do we do about it if we want to change things? Harvard University's School of Government put together 150 ways to increase what they call "social capital" (i.e., the value of our social networks). Among
50 their suggestions are: support local merchants; audition for community theater or volunteer to usher; participate in political campaigns; start or join a carpool; eat breakfast at a local gathering spot on
55 Saturdays; and stop and make sure the person on the side of the highway is OK.

Copyright © Mometrix Media. You have been licensed one copy of this document for personal use only. Any other reproduction or redistribution is strictly prohibited. All rights reserved.
This content is provided for test preparation purposes only and does not imply an endorsement by Mometrix of any particular political, scientific, or religious point of view.

**1. According to the author, which of the following was true in 2004:**

    a. The average American had three confidants and 9% of people depended totally on their spouse for discussion of important matters.

    b. The average American had two confidants, and 80% of people discussed important matters only with their spouses.

    c. The average American had two confidants, and 9% of people discussed important matters only with family members.

    d. The average American had two confidants, and 80% of people discussed important matters only with family members.

**2. The author argues that the transient nature of many of today's relationships is problematic for what reason?**

    a. we don't share specific interests

    b. we don't know many people

    c. it prevents us building lasting relationships and communities

    d. we have too much social capital

**3. Which of the following are some of the causes to which the author attributes problems in American communities:**

    a. too much homework and devotion to television

    b. urban sprawl and long work hours

    c. long work hours and too much homework

    d. urban sprawl and decline of sports team membership

**4. Which of the following is not something the author states was suggested by Harvard University as a way to increase social capital:**

    a. eat breakfast at a local gathering spot

    b. join a bowling team

    c. support local merchants

    d. join a carpool

**5. How many ways did Harvard University's School of Government suggest to increase social capital?**

    a. 25

    b. 80

    c. 100

    d. 150

**6. According to the author, "social capital" means which of the following:**

    a. the value of our social networks

    b. the number of confidants with whom we share information

    c. the value we place on friendships outside family members

    d. the number of activities in which we engage

Copyright © Mometrix Media. You have been licensed one copy of this document for personal use only. Any other reproduction or redistribution is strictly prohibited. All rights reserved. This content is provided for test preparation purposes only and does not imply an endorsement by Mometrix of any particular political, scientific, or religious point of view.

An Excerpt from *Pride and Prejudice* by Jane Austen:

It is a truth universally acknowledged, that a single man in possession of a good fortune, must be in want of a wife.

However little known the feelings or
5  views of such a man may be on his first entering a neighbourhood, this truth is so well fixed in the minds of the surrounding families, that he is considered the rightful property of some one or other of their
10  daughters.

"My dear Mr. Bennet," said his lady to him one day, "have you heard that Netherfield Park is let at last?"

Mr. Bennet replied that he had not.

15  "But it is," returned she; "for Mrs. Long has just been here, and she told me all about it."

Mr. Bennet made no answer.

"Do you not want to know who has taken
20  it?" cried his wife impatiently.

"You want to tell me, and I have no objection to hearing it."

This was invitation enough.

"Why, my dear, you must know, Mrs. Long
25  says that Netherfield is taken by a young man of large fortune from the north of England; that he came down on Monday in a chaise and four to see the place, and was so much

delighted with it, that he agreed with Mr.
30  Morris immediately; that he is to take possession before Michaelmas, and some of his servants are to be in the house by the end of next week."

"What is his name?"

35  "Bingley."

"Is he married or single?"

"Oh! Single, my dear, to be sure! A single man of large fortune; four or five thousand a year. What a fine thing for our girls!"

40  "How so? How can it affect them?"

"My dear Mr. Bennet," replied his wife, "how can you be so tiresome! You must know that I am thinking of his marrying one of them."

45  "Is that his design in settling here?"

"Design! Nonsense, how can you talk so! But it is very likely that he may fall in love with one of them, and therefore you must visit him as soon as he comes."

50  "I see no occasion for that. You and the girls may go, or you may send them by themselves, which perhaps will be still better, for as you are as handsome as any of them, Mr. Bingley may like you the best of the
55  party."

## 7. What is the central idea of this selection?

a. A new neighbor is due to arrive who may become good friends with Mr. and Mrs. Bennet.
b. A new neighbor is due to arrive who may be a prospective husband for one of the Bennet daughters.
c. A new neighbor is due to arrive who may be a good business connection for Mr. Bennet.
d. A new neighbor is due to arrive who has already expressed an interest in marrying one of the Bennet daughters.

Copyright © Mometrix Media. You have been licensed one copy of this document for personal use only. Any other reproduction or redistribution is strictly prohibited. All rights reserved. This content is provided for test preparation purposes only and does not imply an endorsement by Mometrix of any particular political, scientific, or religious point of view.

**8. How does Mrs. Bennet feel about the arrival of Mr. Bingley?**

    a.  Mrs. Bennet is excited about the arrival of Mr. Bingley.

    b.  Mrs. Bennet is nervous about the arrival of Mr. Bingley.

    c.  Mrs. Bennet is afraid the arrival of Mr. Bingley will upset Mr. Bennet.

    d.  Mrs. Bennet is indifferent to the arrival of Mr. Bingley.

**9. What does Mrs. Bennet expect from Mr. Bennet?**

    a.  Mrs. Bennet expects Mr. Bennet to invite Mr. Bingley to a dinner party.

    b.  Mrs. Bennet expects Mr. Bennet to offer one of his daughters in marriage to Mr. Bingley.

    c.  Mrs. Bennet expects Mr. Bennet to pay a visit to Mr. Bingley.

    d.  Mrs. Bennet expects Mr. Bennet to invite Mr. Bingley to a ball in his honor.

**10. What does Mrs. Bennet expect from Mr. Bingley?**

    a.  Mrs. Bennet expects Mr. Bingley to be interested in marrying one of her daughters.

    b.  Mrs. Bennet expects Mr. Bingley to be interested in receiving a visit from Mr. Bennet.

    c.  Mrs. Bennet expects Mr. Bingley to love living at Netherfield Park.

    d.  Mrs. Bennet expects Mr. Bingley to ask for her help in choosing a wife for himself.

**11. Which of the following statements best describes Mrs. Bennet's feelings about her husband as indicated by this selection?**

    a.  Mrs. Bennet is tired of her husband.

    b.  Mrs. Bennet is exasperated by her husband.

    c.  Mrs. Bennet is afraid of her husband.

    d.  Mrs. Bennet is indifferent toward her husband.

**12. Which of the following statements best describes Mr. Bennet's feelings about his wife as indicated by this selection?**

    a.  Mr. Bennet thinks his wife is a great beauty.

    b.  Mr. Bennet thinks his wife is a wonderful mother.

    c.  Mr. Bennet thinks his wife is intolerable.

    d.  Mr. Bennet thinks his wife is silly.

Copyright © Mometrix Media. You have been licensed one copy of this document for personal use only. Any other reproduction or redistribution is strictly prohibited. All rights reserved.
This content is provided for test preparation purposes only and does not imply an endorsement by Mometrix of any particular political, scientific, or religious point of view.

## Helen Keller

Helen Keller was born on June 27, 1880. She was a happy and healthy child until the age of 19 months when she fell ill with a terrible fever. Although Helen recovered from
5 the fever, it left her both deaf and blind.

Helen was loved and cared for by her doting parents, but her behavior became erratic after she lost her hearing and sight, with unpredictable outbursts of temper. Her
10 parents were at a loss how to reach her and teach her how to behave. Helen herself was frustrated and lonely in her dark, silent world. All of that began to change in March 1887 when Anne Sullivan came to live with
15 the Kellers and be Helen's teacher.

Anne taught Helen to communicate by forming letters with her fingers held in another person's hand. In this way, Teacher, as Helen called her, taught her pupil to spell
20 cake, doll, and milk. However, it was not until Anne spelled w-a-t-e-r in Helen's hands as cold water gushed over both of them that Helen made the exciting connection between the words and the world around her. This
25 connection engendered an insatiable curiosity within Helen. After that day, Helen learned at an incredible rate with Teacher by her side.

Helen went on to graduate from Radcliffe
30 College. She became a famous writer, speaker, and advocate. The story of Helen's remarkable life is known worldwide. Anne Sullivan and Helen Keller were inseparable until Anne's death in 1936. Teacher shined a
35 light in Helen's dark world and showed her the way.

**13. Which organizational pattern does the author use?**
   a. Comparison and contrast
   b. Chronological order
   c. Cause and effect
   d. Problem/solution

**14. What is the author's primary purpose in writing this passage?**
   a. To inform people about Helen Keller's college career
   b. To inform people about Anne Sullivan's life
   c. To inform people about services available for the deaf and blind
   d. To inform people about Helen Keller's life

**15. How does the author make a connection between the second and third paragraphs?**
   a. The author begins the third paragraph by continuing to talk about Helen's parents who were introduced in the second paragraph.
   b. The author organizes the second and third paragraphs the same way.
   c. The author ends the second paragraph with the advent of Anne Sullivan in Helen's life, and begins the third paragraph with the most important contribution Anne made to Helen's education.
   d. The author uses the third paragraph to elaborate on Helen's frustration and resulting temper tantrums introduced in the second paragraph.

**16. What is the author's tone in this passage?**
   a. Indifferent
   b. Censorious
   c. Admiring
   d. Impartial

Copyright © Mometrix Media. You have been licensed one copy of this document for personal use only. Any other reproduction or redistribution is strictly prohibited. All rights reserved.
This content is provided for test preparation purposes only and does not imply an endorsement by Mometrix of any particular political, scientific, or religious point of view.

**17. What was the turning point in Helen's life?**

a. When Helen learned to connect feeling water on her hands with the word "water."
b. When Helen graduated from Radcliffe College.
c. When Helen contracted the fever that took away her hearing and sight.
d. When Anne Sullivan came to live with the Kellers and be Helen's teacher.

**18. Which of the following can you infer was true about Helen's parents?**

a. Helen's parents were frustrated that they were unable to help Helen communicate.
b. Helen's parents were jealous that Anne Sullivan was closer to Helen than they were.
c. Helen's parents were glad to give Anne Sullivan full responsibility for Helen.
d. Helen's parents wanted their daughter to graduate from Radcliffe College.

Black History Month

Black History Month is still a meaningful observance. Despite the election of our first African American president being a huge achievement, education about African
5 American history is still unmet to a substantial degree. Black History Month is a powerful tool in working towards meeting that need. There is no reason to give up that tool now, and it can easily coexist with an
10 effort to develop a more comprehensive and inclusive yearly curriculum.

Having a month set aside for the study of African American history doesn't limit its study and celebration to that month; it
15 merely focuses complete attention on it for that month. There is absolutely no contradiction between having a set-aside month and having it be present in the curriculum the rest of the year.

20 Equally important is that the debate *itself* about the usefulness of Black History Month can, and should, remind parents that they can't necessarily count on schools to teach African American history as thoroughly as

25 many parents would want. Although Black History Month has, to an extent, become a shallow ritual, it doesn't have to be. Good teachers and good materials could make the February curriculum deeply informative,
30 thought-provoking, and inspiring. The range of material that can be covered is rich, varied, and full of limitless possibilities.

Finally, it is worthwhile to remind ourselves and our children of the key events
35 that happened during the month of February. In 1926, Woodson organized the first Black History Week to honor the birthdays of essential civil rights activists Abraham Lincoln and Frederick Douglass. W. E. B.
40 DuBois was born on February 23, 1868. The 15th Amendment, which granted African Americans the right to vote, was passed on February 3, 1870. The first black U.S. senator, Hiram R. Revels, took his oath of office on
45 February 25, 1870. The National Association for the Advancement of Colored People (NAACP) was founded on February 12, 1909. Malcolm X was shot on February 21, 1965.

**19. Based on this passage, what would be the author's argument against the study and celebration of Black History Month being limited to one month of the year?**

a. Black History Month is still a meaningful observance.
b. Black History Month is a powerful tool in meeting the need for education about African American history.
c. Having a month set aside for the study of African American history does not limit its study and celebration to that month.
d. Black History Month does not have to be a shallow ritual.

Copyright © Mometrix Media. You have been licensed one copy of this document for personal use only. Any other reproduction or redistribution is strictly prohibited. All rights reserved. This content is provided for test preparation purposes only and does not imply an endorsement by Mometrix of any particular political, scientific, or religious point of view.

**20. Why does the author of believe that the debate itself about Black History Month can be useful?**

    a. The people on opposing sides can come to an intelligent resolution about whether to keep it.

    b. African American history is discussed in the media when the debate is ongoing.

    c. The debate is a reminder to parents that they can't count on schools to teach their children about African American history.

    d. Black History Month doesn't have to be a shallow ritual.

**21. What does the author say about the range of material that can be taught during Black History Month?**

    a. It is rich and varied.

    b. It is important.

    c. It is an unmet need.

    d. It is comprehensive.

**22. In line 7, the word "substantial" most nearly means:**

    a. base

    b. considerable

    c. minor

    d. trivial

**23. The author's tone in this passage can be described as:**

    a. doubtful

    b. emboldening

    c. jovial

    d. menacing

**24. Which of the following can be inferred from the last paragraph (lines 34-49)?**

    a. The most important events in black history happened in the 19th century.

    b. Black history has been influenced by more men than women.

    c. There are several avenues from which to draw on larger lessons of black history.

    d. The most influential black figures served in politics.

Copyright © Mometrix Media. You have been licensed one copy of this document for personal use only. Any other reproduction or redistribution is strictly prohibited. All rights reserved.
This content is provided for test preparation purposes only and does not imply an endorsement by Mometrix of any particular political, scientific, or religious point of view.

## An Excerpt from "To Build a Fire" by Jack London

But all this—the mysterious, far-reaching hair-line trail, the absence of sun from the sky, the tremendous cold, and the strangeness and weirdness of it all—made no
5 impression on the man. It was not because he was long used to it. He was a newcomer in the land, a chechaquo, and this was his first winter. The trouble with him was that he was without imagination. He was quick and alert
10 in the things of life, but only in the things, and not in the significances. Fifty degrees below zero meant eighty-odd degrees of frost. Such fact impressed him as being cold and uncomfortable, and that was all. It did not
15 lead him to meditate upon his frailty as a creature of temperature, and upon man's frailty in general, able only to live within certain narrow limits of heat and cold; and from there on it did not lead him to the
20 conjectural field of immortality and man's place in the universe. Fifty degrees below zero stood for a bite of frost that hurt and that must be guarded against by the use of mittens, ear-flaps, warm moccasins, and thick
25 socks. Fifty degrees below zero was to him just precisely fifty degrees below zero. That there should be anything more to it than that was a thought that never entered his head.

. . . .

30 At the man's heels trotted a dog, a big native husky, the proper wolf-dog, gray-coated and without any visible or temperamental difference from its brother, the wild wolf. The animal was depressed by
35 the tremendous cold. It knew that it was no time for travelling. Its instinct told it a truer tale than was told to the man by the man's judgment. In reality, it was not merely colder than fifty below zero; it was colder than sixty
40 below, than seventy below. It was seventy-five below zero. Since the freezing-point is thirty-two above zero, it meant that one hundred and seven degrees of frost obtained. The dog did not know anything about
45 thermometers. Possibly in its brain there was no sharp consciousness of a condition of very cold such as was in the man's brain. But the brute had its instinct. It experienced a vague but menacing apprehension that subdued it
50 and made it slink along at the man's heels, and that made it question eagerly every unwonted movement of the man as if expecting him to go into camp or to seek shelter somewhere and build a fire. The dog
55 had learned fire, and it wanted fire, or else to burrow under the snow and cuddle its warmth away from the air.

**25. In this short story, the main character struggles against the cold and eventually freezes to death. Given this information, which of the following devices is the author using in the first paragraph of this passage?**

    a. First person point of view
    b. Hyperbole
    c. Onomatopoeia
    d. Foreshadowing

**26. What is the point of view used in this passage?**

    a. First person
    b. First person plural
    c. Unreliable narrator
    d. Third person omniscient

Copyright © Mometrix Media. You have been licensed one copy of this document for personal use only. Any other reproduction or redistribution is strictly prohibited. All rights reserved. This content is provided for test preparation purposes only and does not imply an endorsement by Mometrix of any particular political, scientific, or religious point of view.

**27. Which statement best captures the author's meaning in the statement, "The trouble with him was that he was without imagination"?**

    I. The man was not smart
    II. The man did not need imagination because he was rational
    III. The man did not have the foresight to realize that he was putting himself in danger

  a. I only
  b. II only
  c. III only
  d. I and II

**28. In what sense should the passage be taken when it mentions immortality and man's place in the universe?**

  a. Humans are frail
  b. Humans are stronger than nature
  c. Humans will one day attain immortality
  d. Humans are smarter than animals

**29. In what way does the narrator say the dog is better off than the man?**

  a. The dog is better equipped for the cold because of its fur.
  b. The dog has a better conscious idea of what the cold means
  c. The dog's instinct guides it, while the man's intellect fails him
  d. The dog understands mankind's place in the universe

**30. In line 15, the word "frailty" most nearly means:**

  a. advantage
  b. brawn
  c. vigor
  d. weakness

Copyright © Mometrix Media. You have been licensed one copy of this document for personal use only. Any other reproduction or redistribution is strictly prohibited. All rights reserved.
This content is provided for test preparation purposes only and does not imply an endorsement by Mometrix of any particular political, scientific, or religious point of view.

## "The Gettysburg Address" by Abraham Lincoln

Four score and seven years ago our fathers brought forth, upon this continent, a new nation, conceived in Liberty, and dedicated to the proposition that all men are
5 created equal.

Now we are engaged in a great civil war, testing whether that nation, or any nation so conceived, and so dedicated, can long endure. We are met here on a great battlefield of that
10 war. We have come to dedicate a portion of it as a final resting place for those who here gave their lives that that nation might live. It is altogether fitting and proper that we should do this.

15 But in a larger sense we cannot dedicate - we cannot consecrate - we cannot hallow this ground. The brave men, living and dead, who struggled here, have consecrated it far above our poor power to add or detract. The world
20 will little note, nor long remember, what we say here, but can never forget what they did here.

It is for us, the living, rather to be dedicated here to the unfinished work which
25 they have, thus far, so nobly carried on. It is rather for us to be here dedicated to the great task remaining before us - that from these honored dead we take increased devotion to that cause for which they here gave the last
30 full measure of devotion - that we here highly resolve that these dead shall not have died in vain; that this nation shall have a new birth of freedom; and that this government of the people, by the people, for the people, shall not
35 perish from the earth.

**31. What is the main message of this speech?**
   a. Those who died in this battle honor this land we are dedicating today better than anyone else.
   b. As we honor those who died in this battle, we should move forward with renewed dedication to ensuring the nation our founding fathers created continues to function the way they intended.
   c. We need to put the regrets of the past aside, without remembering the sacrifices of those who gave their lives for our country.
   d. The war we are fighting is far from over, as evidenced by the number of lives lost in this battle.

**32. The phrase "the world will little note" means what?**
   a. The world will not soon forget.
   b. The world will record what we say here.
   c. The world will not pay much attention.
   d. The world will recall what we do with perfect accuracy.

**33. There were nearly 100 years between the American Revolution and the Civil War. The speech connects ideas about these two conflicts by saying that the ideas of the Civil War**
   a. threaten those of the Revolution.
   b. are similar to those of the Revolution.
   c. are newer than those of the Revolution.
   d. are better than those of the Revolution.

Copyright © Mometrix Media. You have been licensed one copy of this document for personal use only. Any other reproduction or redistribution is strictly prohibited. All rights reserved. This content is provided for test preparation purposes only and does not imply an endorsement by Mometrix of any particular political, scientific, or religious point of view.

**34. Why does Lincoln most likely talk about the past before he talks about the present?**

    a.  to incite listeners of his message to protest
    b.  to remember what has been lost in the past
    c.  to establish context for his main message
    d.  to try to get listeners to side with his position

**35. What is the following sentence addressing?**

> *Now we are engaged in a great civil war, testing whether that nation, or any nation so conceived, and so dedicated, can long endure.*

    a.  whether or not a nation based on ideas of freedom and equality can survive for any significant length of time
    b.  whether or not the Union will be able to preserve the existing structure of the United States by preventing the Confederacy from seceding
    c.  whether or not the Confederacy will be successful in seceding from the United States and surviving on its own
    d.  whether or not Lincoln should continue dedicating troops to the war

**36. In line 32, the word "vain" most nearly means:**

    a.  decisive
    b.  frivolous
    c.  momentous
    d.  practical

Copyright © Mometrix Media. You have been licensed one copy of this document for personal use only. Any other reproduction or redistribution is strictly prohibited. All rights reserved.
This content is provided for test preparation purposes only and does not imply an endorsement by Mometrix of any particular political, scientific, or religious point of view.

## Section 4 – Mathematics Achievement

*In this section there are four possible answers after each question. In this section, you are not allowed a calculator, a calculator watch, a ruler, a protractor, or a compass.*

**1. The scientific notation for the diameter of a red blood cell is approximately $7.4 \times 10^{-4}$ centimeters. What is that amount in standard form?**

    a.  0.00074
    b.  0.0074
    c.  7.40000
    d.  296

**2. What is the area of the shaded region? (Each square represents one unit.)**

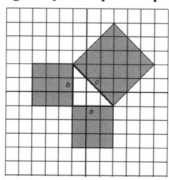

    a.  16
    b.  18
    c.  24
    d.  36

**3. 5 more than 6 times a number is 77. What is the number?**

    a.  12
    b.  17
    c.  72
    d.  82

**4. For vector $v = (4, 3)$ and vector $w = (-3, 4)$, find $2(v + w)$.**

    a.  $(2, 14)$
    b.  $(14, -2)$
    c.  $(1, 7)$
    d.  $(7, -1)$

**5. Simplify $(3 \times 10^4) \times (2 \times 10^5)$.**

    a.  $5 \times 10^9$
    b.  $5 \times 10^{20}$
    c.  $6 \times 10^9$
    d.  $6 \times 10^{20}$

Copyright © Mometrix Media. You have been licensed one copy of this document for personal use only. Any other reproduction or redistribution is strictly prohibited. All rights reserved. This content is provided for test preparation purposes only and does not imply an endorsement by Mometrix of any particular political, scientific, or religious point of view.

6. **Which of the following is the factored form of the expression, $x^2 + 3x - 28$?**

    a. $(x - 14)(x + 2)$
    b. $(x + 6)(x - 3)$
    c. $(x + 4)(x - 1)$
    d. $(x - 4)(x + 7)$

7. **Given $x^2 - 7x + 10 \geq 0$, what is the solution set for $x$?**

    a. $2 \leq x \leq 5$
    b. $x \leq 2$ or $x \geq 5$
    c. $7 \leq x \leq 10$
    d. $x \leq 7$ or $x \geq 10$

8. **Equation A is $5y - 100x = 25$. What are the slope and y-intercept of the line?**

    a. The slope is 100, and the y-intercept is 5.
    b. The slope is 5, and the y-intercept is 100.
    c. The slope is 20, and the y-intercept is 5.
    d. The slope is 25, and the $y$-intercept is 5.

9. **The Charleston Recycling Company collects 50,000 tons of recyclable material every month. The chart shows the kinds of materials that are collected by the company's five trucks.**

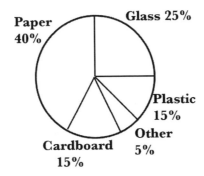

**About how much paper is recycled every month?**

    a. 15,000 tons
    b. 20,000 tons
    c. 40,000 tons
    d. 50,000 tons

10. **The volume of a rectangular box is found by multiplying its length, width, and height. If the dimensions of a box are $\sqrt{3}$, $2\sqrt{5}$, and 4, what is its volume?**

    a. $2\sqrt{60}$
    b. $4\sqrt{15}$
    c. $8\sqrt{15}$
    d. $24\sqrt{5}$

Copyright © Mometrix Media. You have been licensed one copy of this document for personal use only. Any other reproduction or redistribution is strictly prohibited. All rights reserved. This content is provided for test preparation purposes only and does not imply an endorsement by Mometrix of any particular political, scientific, or religious point of view.

**11. Simplify** $(8 \times 10^3) + (1 \times 10^3)$.

    a.  $8 \times 10^3$

    b.  $8 \times 10^6$

    c.  $9 \times 10^3$

    d.  $9 \times 10^6$

**12. Which function represents the graph?**

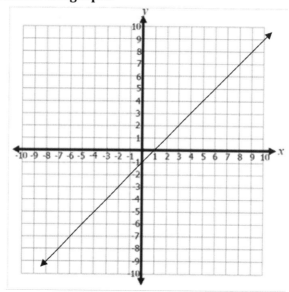

    a.  $y = x + 1$

    b.  $y = x - 1$

    c.  $y = -x + 1$

    d.  $y = -x - 1$

**13. If** $A = \begin{bmatrix} 1 & -3 \\ -4 & 2 \end{bmatrix}$ **and** $B = \begin{bmatrix} 1 & -3 \\ -4 & -2 \end{bmatrix}$, **then** $A - B = ?$

    a.  $\begin{bmatrix} 2 & -6 \\ -8 & 0 \end{bmatrix}$

    b.  $\begin{bmatrix} 0 & 0 \\ 0 & 0 \end{bmatrix}$

    c.  $\begin{bmatrix} 0 & 0 \\ 0 & 4 \end{bmatrix}$

    d.  $\begin{bmatrix} 0 & 3 \\ 4 & 2 \end{bmatrix}$

**14. A dress is marked down by 20% and placed on a clearance rack, on which is posted a sign reading, "Take an extra 25% off already reduced merchandise." What fraction of the original price is the final sale price of the dress?**

    a.  $\dfrac{2}{5}$

    b.  $\dfrac{9}{20}$

    c.  $\dfrac{11}{20}$

    d.  $\dfrac{3}{5}$

Copyright © Mometrix Media. You have been licensed one copy of this document for personal use only. Any other reproduction or redistribution is strictly prohibited. All rights reserved. This content is provided for test preparation purposes only and does not imply an endorsement by Mometrix of any particular political, scientific, or religious point of view.

**15. On his last math test, Sam got 2 questions correct for every 3 questions he missed. If the test had a total of 60 questions, how many questions did Sam answer correctly?**

    a.  12
    b.  24
    c.  36
    d.  60

**16. Which class has the greatest interquartile range of test scores?**

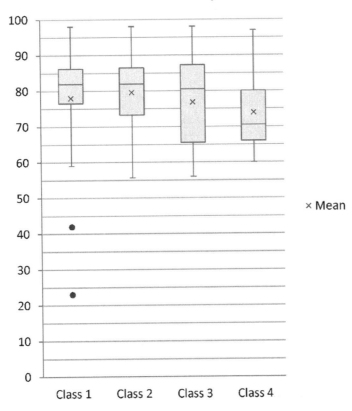

    a.  Class 1
    b.  Class 2
    c.  Class 3
    d.  Class 4

**17. Solve $(3x + 1)(7x + 10)$**

    a.  $12x^2 + 17x + 10$
    b.  $21x^2 + 37x + 10$
    c.  $21x^2 + 23x + 10$
    d.  $21x^2 + 37x + 9$

Copyright © Mometrix Media. You have been licensed one copy of this document for personal use only. Any other reproduction or redistribution is strictly prohibited. All rights reserved.
This content is provided for test preparation purposes only and does not imply an endorsement by Mometrix of any particular political, scientific, or religious point of view.

18. In the figure below, lines *a* and *b* are parallel.  Find the value of *x*.

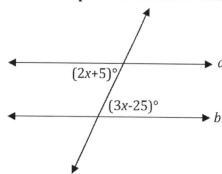

   a.  x = 22
   b.  x = 30
   c.  x = 40
   d.  *x* = 65

19. Joseph purchased 12 pounds of peaches at 80 cents per pound. He calculated the total amount as $12 \times \$0.80 = \$9.60$. Another method Joseph could have used to calculate the total cost of the peaches is:
   a.  (10 x $0.80) + (2 x $0.80)
   b.  (12 x $0.40) + (2 x $0.80)
   c.  (12 x $0.20) + (12 x $0.20)
   d.  (2 x $0.80) + (10 x $0.40)

20. How many solutions does the equation $6x + 1 = 4x + 9$ have?
   a.  None
   b.  One
   c.  Two
   d.  Infinitely many solutions

21. Joshua has to earn more than 92 points on the state test in order to qualify for an academic scholarship. Each question is worth 4 points, and the test has a total of 30 questions. Let x represent the number of test questions.

Which of the following inequalities can be solved to determine the number of questions Joshua must answer correctly?
   a.  $4x < 30$
   b.  $4x < 92$
   c.  $4x > 30$
   d.  $4x > 92$

22. If $\frac{4}{x-3} - \frac{2}{x} = 1$, then $x = ?$
   a.  $-6$
   b.  $-1$
   c.  $-6$ or $-1$
   d.  $-1$ or $6$

Copyright © Mometrix Media. You have been licensed one copy of this document for personal use only. Any other reproduction or redistribution is strictly prohibited. All rights reserved.
This content is provided for test preparation purposes only and does not imply an endorsement by Mometrix of any particular political, scientific, or religious point of view.

**23. A committee of 12 people is electing four of its members for president, vice president, secretary, and treasurer. In how many different ways can they elect these four positions?**

  a.  1680
  b.  9240
  c.  11,880
  d.  20,736

**24. Simplify $\frac{2+3i}{4-2i}$ .**

  a.  $\frac{1}{10}+\frac{4}{5}i$
  b.  $\frac{1}{10}$
  c.  $\frac{7}{6}+\frac{2}{3}i$
  d.  $\frac{1}{10}+\frac{3}{10}i$

**25. If $a \neq 0$, then $12a^2b \div 3a = ?$**

  a.  $4b$
  b.  $4ab$
  c.  $9b^2$
  d.  $9ab$

**26. If the square of twice the sum of $x$ and three is equal to the product of twenty-four and $x$, which of these is a possible value of $x$?**

  a.  $6 + 3\sqrt{2}$
  b.  $\frac{3}{2}$
  c.  $-3i$
  d.  $-3$

Copyright © Mometrix Media. You have been licensed one copy of this document for personal use only. Any other reproduction or redistribution is strictly prohibited. All rights reserved.
This content is provided for test preparation purposes only and does not imply an endorsement by Mometrix of any particular political, scientific, or religious point of view.

**27. Which of the following figures show parallelogram** $WXYZ$ **being carried onto its image** $W'X'Y'Z'$ **by a reflection across the** $x$**-axis?**

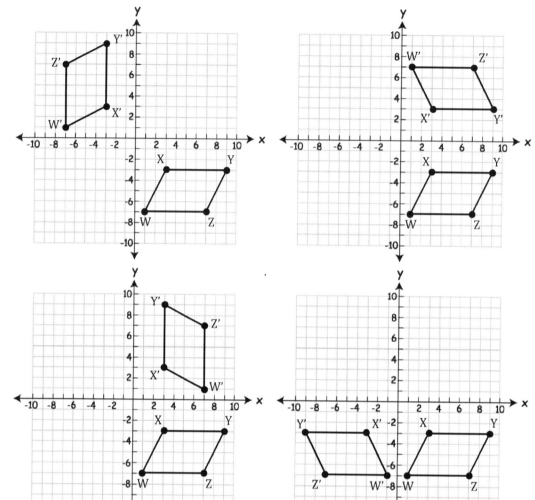

**28. A teacher wishes to divide her class of twenty students into four groups, each of which will have three boys and two girls. How many possible groups can she form?**

  a.  248
  b.  6,160
  c.  73,920
  d.  95,040

Copyright © Mometrix Media. You have been licensed one copy of this document for personal use only. Any other reproduction or redistribution is strictly prohibited. All rights reserved. This content is provided for test preparation purposes only and does not imply an endorsement by Mometrix of any particular political, scientific, or religious point of view.

29. In △$ABC$, cos $A$ =

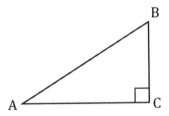

   a.   $\frac{AC}{AB}$

   b.   $\frac{AC}{BC}$

   c.   $\frac{BC}{AC}$

   d.   $\frac{BC}{AB}$

30. The expression $-2i \times 7i$ is equal to

   a.   -14

   b.   14

   c.   $14\sqrt{-1}$

   d.   $-14\sqrt{-1}$

31. **Which of the following represents the expected value of the number of tails Adam will get after tossing a coin 6 times?**

   a.   2

   b.   3

   c.   6

   d.   12

32. **Based on the figure below, if $BG$ = 6$x$ – 4 and $GD$ = 2$x$ + 8, what is the length of $\overline{GD}$?**

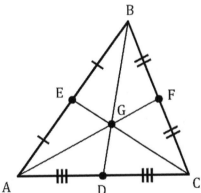

   a.   10

   b.   14

   c.   28

   d.   56

Copyright © Mometrix Media. You have been licensed one copy of this document for personal use only. Any other reproduction or redistribution is strictly prohibited. All rights reserved.
This content is provided for test preparation purposes only and does not imply an endorsement by Mometrix of any particular political, scientific, or religious point of view.

**33. Which of the following boxplots correctly represents the data set shown below?**

7, 8, 8, 11, 13, 14, 15, 15, 16, 17, 21, 23, 23, 24, 31, 35, 35, 35, 38, 38, 40, 45, 49, 50, 50

a.

c.

b.

d.
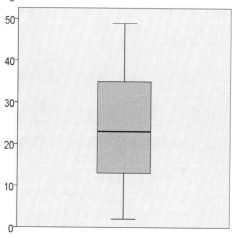

**34. Matthew has to earn more than 96 points on his high school entrance exam in order to be eligible for varsity sports. Each question is worth 3 points, and the test has a total of 40 questions. Let x represent the number of test questions.**

**How many questions can Matthew answer incorrectly and still qualify for varsity sports?**
  a.  $x > 32$
  b.  $x > 8$
  c.  $0 \leq x < 8$
  d.  $0 < x \leq 8$

**35. A box in the form of a rectangular solid has a square base of 5 feet in length, a width of 5 feet, and a height of $h$ feet. If the volume of the rectangular solid is 200 cubic feet, which of the following equations may be used to find $h$?**
  a.  5h = 200
  b.  5h² = 200
  c.  25h = 200
  d.  h = 200 ÷ 5

Copyright © Mometrix Media. You have been licensed one copy of this document for personal use only. Any other reproduction or redistribution is strictly prohibited. All rights reserved.
This content is provided for test preparation purposes only and does not imply an endorsement by Mometrix of any particular political, scientific, or religious point of view.

36. Solve: $\begin{bmatrix} 4 & 2 \\ 7 & 12 \end{bmatrix} + \begin{bmatrix} -1 & 15 \\ 3 & -5 \end{bmatrix}$.

   a. $\begin{bmatrix} 3 & 17 \\ 10 & 7 \end{bmatrix}$

   b. $\begin{bmatrix} 3 & 1 \\ 10 & 15 \end{bmatrix}$

   c. $\begin{bmatrix} 19 & 17 \\ 2 & 7 \end{bmatrix}$

   d. $\begin{bmatrix} 19 & 1 \\ 2 & 15 \end{bmatrix}$

37. Robert is planning to drive 1,800 miles on a cross-country trip. If his car gets 30 miles to the gallon, and his tank holds 12 gallons of gas, how many tanks of gas will he need to complete the trip?

   a. 3 tanks of gas
   b. 5 tanks of gas
   c. 30 tanks of gas
   d. 60 tanks of gas

38. Which line appears to have a slope of 2?

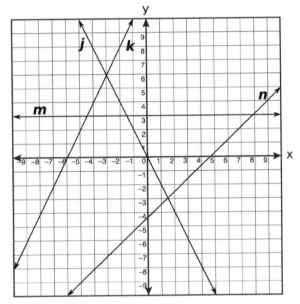

   a. Line j
   b. Line k
   c. Line m
   d. Line n

39. Three quarters of the students running a 100-yard race finished with an average time of 16 seconds. The remaining 25% of students finished with an average time of 12 seconds. What was the average time overall?

   a. 13 seconds
   b. 14 seconds
   c. 15 seconds
   d. 16 seconds

Copyright © Mometrix Media. You have been licensed one copy of this document for personal use only. Any other reproduction or redistribution is strictly prohibited. All rights reserved.
This content is provided for test preparation purposes only and does not imply an endorsement by Mometrix of any particular political, scientific, or religious point of view.

**40. A bag contains 8 red marbles, 3 blue marbles, and 4 green marbles. What is the probability Carlos draws a red marble, does not replace it, and then draws another red marble?**

a. $\frac{2}{15}$

b. $\frac{4}{15}$

c. $\frac{64}{225}$

d. $\frac{32}{105}$

**41. If $\sqrt{3x-2} = x-2$, then $x = ?$**

a. 1

b. 6

c. −1 or 6

d. 1 or 6

**42. If $7\sqrt{x} + 16 = 79$, what is the value of $x$?**

a. 6

b. 9

c. 27

d. 81

**43. Which of the following is equivalent to $27x^3 + y^3$ ?**

a. $(3x+y)(3x+y)(3x+y)$

b. $(3x+y)(9x^2 - 3xy + y^2)$

c. $(3x-y)(9x^2 + 3xy + y^2)$

d. $(3x-y)(9x^2 + 9xy + y^2)$

**44. What is the expected value of drawing a card from a deck when the cards are labeled 1 – 5?**

a. 1.5

b. 2

c. 2.5

d. 3

**45. On a road map, $\frac{1}{4}$ inch represents 8 miles of actual road distance. The towns of Dinuba and Clovis are measured to be $2\frac{1}{8}$ inches apart on the map. What is the actual distance, in miles, between the two towns?**

a. 32

b. 40

c. 60

d. 68

Copyright © Mometrix Media. You have been licensed one copy of this document for personal use only. Any other reproduction or redistribution is strictly prohibited. All rights reserved. This content is provided for test preparation purposes only and does not imply an endorsement by Mometrix of any particular political, scientific, or religious point of view.

**46. In the figure below, ΔJKL is dilated to the image ΔJ'K'L'.**

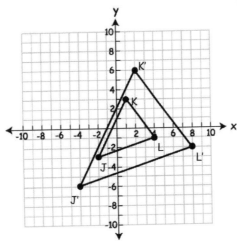

**What is the scale factor of the dilation?**

a. $\frac{1}{3}$

b. $\frac{1}{2}$

c. 2

d. 3

**47. In the Figure shown here, the arc $\widehat{AB}$ is 4 meters long, and the total perimeter of the circle is 48 meters. Which of the following best represents the measure of ∠AOB, which subtends arc $\widehat{AB}$?**

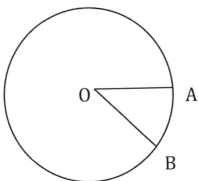

a. 15 degrees

b. 30 degrees

c. 45 degrees

d. 60 degrees

Copyright © Mometrix Media. You have been licensed one copy of this document for personal use only. Any other reproduction or redistribution is strictly prohibited. All rights reserved. This content is provided for test preparation purposes only and does not imply an endorsement by Mometrix of any particular political, scientific, or religious point of view.

## Section 5 – Essay

*Write an essay on the following prompt on the paper provided. Your essay should NOT exceed 2 pages and must be written in ink. Erasing is not allowed. You are not allowed to use scrap paper, a dictionary, or a thesaurus.*

**Prompt:** The city council has raised the issue of setting a curfew for children under the age of 17 to keep young drivers off the road after a certain time at night. They know it is legal, but still plan to discuss it at the next meeting, including whether the idea is worthwhile, whether the curfew would be all the time or only on school nights, and whether or not the age of 17 is too high. The subject will be open for ideas.

Copyright © Mometrix Media. You have been licensed one copy of this document for personal use only. Any other reproduction or redistribution is strictly prohibited. All rights reserved. This content is provided for test preparation purposes only and does not imply an endorsement by Mometrix of any particular political, scientific, or religious point of view.

# Answers and Explanations for Test #1

## Section 1: Verbal Reasoning

**1. D:** To enthrall is to fascinate or mesmerize.

**2. C:** A coward is someone who is gutless or lacks courage when facing danger.

**3. A:** A novice is someone who is new to the circumstances, or the person is a beginner.

**4. C:** Temperate means to be moderate or restrained.

**5. C:** Something authentic is genuine or true.

**6. B:** To salvage something is to save or recover it from wreckage, destruction, or loss.

**7. B:** Vernacular is the speech or language of a place.

**8. D:** To attest is to vouch for or to certify.

**9. A:** Derelict means to be neglected or abandoned, e.g., "a derelict old home."

**10. C:** To ordain is to order or command.

**11. A:** To be haughty is to be proud or arrogant.

**12. B:** A lapse is an error or mistake, e.g., "a lapse of memory."

**13. C:** To nauseate is to disgust or repulse.

**14. A:** Something paltry is cheap, base, or common.

**15. C:** To be refined is to be cultured and well-bred.

**16. C:** Virtual means to be simulated, especially as related to computer software.

**17. D:** To loathe is to hate or abhor.

**18. C:** When you mimic, you imitate or copy someone or something.

**19. B:** Something brittle is fragile and easily damaged or destroyed.

**20. C:** Wretched means miserable or woeful.

**21. B:** "Wrong answer" is a clue that indicates a negative word. *Belittled* means to *criticize*. All the other answer choices have a positive connotation and, therefore, do not fit the intended meaning of the sentence.

**22. B:** *Deforestation* would have a negative effect on the rainforest: therefore, *perished* is the only word that makes sense in the context of the sentence.

**23. C:** The woman has a variety of skills, and she wants to be put them to use for others. So, she has chosen to do something about it for one year of her life. If she had to choose, then she has to leave

Copyright © Mometrix Media. You have been licensed one copy of this document for personal use only. Any other reproduction or redistribution is strictly prohibited. All rights reserved.
This content is provided for test preparation purposes only and does not imply an endorsement by Mometrix of any particular political, scientific, or religious point of view.

something else behind and set it aside for another time. So, she could choose to earmark (i.e., reserve or set aside) a year of her life and put her skills of renown (i.e., fame) to use for others.

**24. C:** Death is usually associated with sadness and grief, resulting in melancholy. Both choices C and D have words that seem to fit the first blank. However, a monument is not built to criticize the deceased, but to memorialize or praise them. Therefore, choice C is the best answer.

**25. A:** Misbehavior does not usually exhilarate or embroil (excite or involve). It can depress or infuriate those who observe it. Use the clue "calm down" to narrow the remaining choices down to the word *blighted*.

**26. B:** An obstacle could be insuppressible, mountainous, or insurmountable, so any of these choices could fit the first blank. Choice C is incorrect because licentious doesn't fit the context of the first blank. However, retention and indolence do not fit in the context of the second blank, so they can be ruled out. Choice B is the best answer and makes the sentence meaningful.

**27. B:** The goal is to go around the world in a hot air balloon. Circumscribe means to limit or restrict and does not fit the sentence meaning. Circulate means to distribute and makes no sense in context. Circumambulate means to walk around but it is unlikely that anyone would "ambulate" around the world. Circumnavigate means to travel completely around, and reflects the sentence's intended meaning. Circumnavigate is the best answer.

**28. A:** "Bad decision" relates to the weather conditions. Adverse means unfavorable, and therefore makes choice A the best answer. Affable means very agreeable or personable and doesn't work here. Onerous or burdensome is closer in meaning, but it is not as relevant as the word adverse. Meanwhile, the weather is never malleable, that is, able to be shaped the way we want it.

**29. A:** "Predictable" is the clue. Banal means to be common place or predictable. It can also be boring which is capable of putting the students to sleep.

**30. A:** Ethereal means to be light or spiritual. Ethereal is often used to describe music that touches the soul, making that word the best choice.

**31. A:** We're looking for a word capable of making a bad situation worse. Exacerbate means to increase in severity.

**32. D:** Inciting and instigating both fit the first blank. However, deteriorated does not make sense in the second blank. Choice D is the best answer choice. The other answer choices make very little sense in the overall context of the sentence.

**33. C:** Indigenous means originating or occurring naturally in an area or environment. This answer choice makes the most sense in the sentence context. The reason is that the birds were not native and were brought from Europe.

**34. B:** *Culminate* means to come to completion. The words "perfect season" and "championship win" allude to the happy ending of the basketball season. *Culminate* is the only choice that fits.

**35. D:** You are looking for a word that indicates that the mayor was free from guilt. Exonerated (i.e., excused or cleared) is the only word that fits in terms of meaning and is the best answer choice.

**36. C:** The blank in this sentence needs to describe the behavior of someone who regularly does unexpected things. Erratic (i.e., unpredictable) is the best fit.

Copyright © Mometrix Media. You have been licensed one copy of this document for personal use only. Any other reproduction or redistribution is strictly prohibited. All rights reserved. This content is provided for test preparation purposes only and does not imply an endorsement by Mometrix of any particular political, scientific, or religious point of view.

**37. D:** "Short on money" is a clue that Glenda could not afford new appliances. Sufficient means adequate or tolerable. If Glenda is not able to buy new appliances, then her current appliances will have to be satisfactory until she can afford new appliances.

**38. D:** The only two word choices which make any sense at all are subside and intensify. The next day's light breezes indicate that the winds would decrease, or subside, making subside the best choice. While it is possible that the already high winds could intensify, it is far more likely that the "light breezes" indicate that they did the opposite.

**39. B:** The sentence clearly states that Gloria was not hungry. All of the answer choices except choice B are indicative of hunger or excessive eating. It is far more likely that Gloria would have looked at her plate *indifferently*.

**40. D:** The best combination is choice (D) because the gentleman wants to grapple (i.e., deal with an issue) with the problem in order to know and understand the difficulties or intricacies of the problem.

## Section 2: Quantitative Reasoning

**1. C:** Because drawing a dodecagon and counting its diagonals is an arduous task, it is useful to employ a different problem-solving strategy. One such strategy is to draw polygons with fewer sides and look for a pattern in the number of the polygons' diagonals.

| | | |
|---|---|---|
| △ | 3 | 0 |
| ▣ | 4 | 2 |
| ⬠ | 5 | 5 |
| ⬡ | 6 | 9 |
| Heptagon | 7 | 14 |
| Octagon | 8 | 20 |

A quadrilateral has two more diagonals than a triangle, a pentagon has three more diagonals than a quadrilateral, and a hexagon has four more diagonals than a pentagon. Continue this pattern to find that a dodecagon has 54 diagonals.

**2. A:** (0.0) is a point because if Jonas doesn't walk, then his running speed is also 0. Another point is (1,3) because if Jonas moves a distance of 1 unit after walking $x$ minutes, then he moves a distance of 3 units after $x$ minutes from jogging.

**3. B:** To solve, first subtract Jerry's weight from the total permitted: 800-200 = 600. Divide 600 by 4 (the four pieces of equipment) to get 150, the average weight.

Copyright © Mometrix Media. You have been licensed one copy of this document for personal use only. Any other reproduction or redistribution is strictly prohibited. All rights reserved. This content is provided for test preparation purposes only and does not imply an endorsement by Mometrix of any particular political, scientific, or religious point of view.

**4. C:** The correct answer is $3000. Besides the $600 he has remaining, Chan has paid out a total of 80% (30% + 20% +20%+10%) of his bonus for the expenses described in the question. Therefore, the $600 represents the remaining 20%. To determine his total bonus, solve $\frac{100}{20} \times 600 = 3000$.

**5. A:** If the ratio of pennies to nickels is 2:6, the ratio of the pennies to the combined coins is 2:2+6, or 2:8. This is $\frac{1}{4}$ or, expressed as a percentage, 25%.

**6. D:** The literal equation may be solved for $x$ by first subtracting $b$ from both sides of the equation. Doing so gives $ax = c - b$. Dividing both sides of the equation by $a$ gives $x = \frac{c-b}{a}$.

**7. C:** The median of a set of numbers is one for which the set contains an equal number of greater and lesser values. Besides $Z$, there are 8 numbers in the set, so that 4 must be greater and 4 lesser than $Z$. The 4 smallest values are 5, 7, 9, and 12. The 4 largest are 16, 18, 23, and 44. So $Z$ must fall between 12 and 16.

**8. A:** There are 4 members of the first set and 4 members of the second set, so there are 4(4) = 16 possible products for $cd$. $cd$ is odd only when both $c$ and $d$ are odd. There are 2 odd numbers in the first set and two in the second set, so 2(2) = 4 products are odd and the probability $cd$ is odd is 4/16 or 1/4.

    A. Correct

    B. Incorrect: 4/12

    C. Incorrect: Probability that $cd$ is even

    D. Incorrect: Number of possible odd products

**9. C:** The given equations form a system of linear equations. Since the first equation is already given in terms of $x$, it will be easier to solve the system using the substitution method. Start by substituting $2y - 3$ for $x$ in the second equation:

$$2x + \frac{1}{2}y = 3$$

$$2(2y - 3) + \frac{1}{2}y = 3$$

Next, solve the resulting equation for $y$. Distribute the 2 and then combine like $y$-terms in the result:

$$4y - 6 + \frac{1}{2}y = 3$$

$$\frac{9}{2}y - 6 = 3$$

Finally, isolate the variable $y$ by adding 6 to both sides and then dividing both sides by the coefficient of $y$, which is $\frac{9}{2}$ (or, equivalently, multiply by 2 and divide by 9):

$$\frac{9}{2}y = 9$$

$$y = 2$$

Copyright © Mometrix Media. You have been licensed one copy of this document for personal use only. Any other reproduction or redistribution is strictly prohibited. All rights reserved. This content is provided for test preparation purposes only and does not imply an endorsement by Mometrix of any particular political, scientific, or religious point of view.

**10. B:** Add the 14 blue, 6 red, 12 green and 8 purple buttons to get a total of 40 buttons. If 25 buttons are removed, there are 15 buttons remaining in the bag. The chance of drawing a red button is now $\frac{1}{3}$. So, you divide 15 into thirds to get 5 red buttons remaining in the bag. The original total of red buttons was 6; so, $6 - 5 = 1$: one red button was removed, choice (B).

**11. D:** The sides of a triangle must all be greater than zero. The sum of the lengths of the two shorter sides must be greater than the length of the third side. Since we are looking for the minimum value of the perimeter, assume the longer of the two given sides, which is 6, is the longest side of the triangle. Then the third side must be greater than $6 - 4 = 2$. Since we are told the sides are all integral numbers, the last side must be 3 units in length. Thus, the minimum length for the perimeter is $4+6+3=13$ units.

**12. A:** A set of six numbers with an average of 4 must have a collective sum of 24. The two numbers that average 2 will add up to 4, so the remaining numbers must add up to 20. The average of these four numbers can be calculated: $20/4 = 5$.

**13. A:** This table shows the numbers of coins added to the first few squares and the equivalent powers of 2:

| Square | 1 | 2 | 3 | 4 |
|---|---|---|---|---|
| Coins | 1 | 2 | 4 | 8 |
| Power of 2 | $2^0$ | $2^1$ | $2^2$ | $2^3$ |

In this series, the number of coins on each is the consecutive powers of 2. The reason is that the number doubles with each consecutive square. However, the series of powers begins with 0 for the first square. For the 64th square, the number of coins will be $2^{63}$.

**14. C:** The correct answer is 8. The total $20 + 13 = 33$, but only 25 cars have been scored. Therefore, $33 - 25$, or 8 cars must have had both a man and a woman inside.

**15. A:** First establish a variable, s, for the length of the smaller square. Since the larger square is 3 feet longer than the smaller one, its length is $s + 3$. Given that the difference between the areas of the two squares is 75, and the area of any square is equal to its side lengths squared, the following equation can be established:

$$(s + 3)^2 - s^2 = 75$$

Simplify the left side of the equation:

$$(s + 3)^2 - s^2 = 75$$

$$(s + 3)(s + 3) - s^2 = 75$$

$$s^2 + 6s + 9 - s^2 = 75$$

$$6s + 9 = 75$$

Isolate the variable and divide both sides by its coefficient to solve for s:

$$6s = 66$$

$$s = 11$$

Copyright © Mometrix Media. You have been licensed one copy of this document for personal use only. Any other reproduction or redistribution is strictly prohibited. All rights reserved.
This content is provided for test preparation purposes only and does not imply an endorsement by Mometrix of any particular political, scientific, or religious point of view.

Therefore, the length of the smaller square is 11 feet.

**16. B:** When the wedges are rearranged into the rectangle, half of the wedge arcs form the top length of the rectangle and the other half of the wedge arcs form the bottom length of the rectangle. Since all of the wedge arcs combine to form the entire circumference of the circle, the length of the rectangle is half of the circumference of the circle. The formula for the circumference of a circle with radius $r$ is $C = 2\pi r$. Half of that circumference is $\left(\frac{1}{2}\right) 2\pi r = \pi r$. Answer C is the width of the rectangle. Answer D is the area of the rectangle.

**17. A:** Setting the cost of shipping equal to the amount received gives us the equation $3{,}000 + 100x = 400x$. Subtract $100x$ from both sides to get $3{,}000 = 300x$, then divide both sides by 300 to see that $x = 10$.

**18. D:** If point $C$ is four times farther from $A$ than from $B$, it means that the ratio of distances from $C$ to $A$ and $B$ is 4:1, respectively. Therefore, the line segment can be broken up into $4 + 1 = 5$ equal segments. The total distance between points $A$ and $B$ is $7 - (-3) = 10$ units. If we divide 10 by 5, each equal segment is 2 units in length. We can then multiply the ratio by 2 to get the actual distances of $C$ from $A$ and $B$, 4(2):1(2) = 8:2. So, $C$ is located 8 units from $A$ and 2 units from $B$. Since $A$ is located at –3, it means that $-3 + 8 = 5$. Answer A is the location if $C$ is four times farther from $B$ than it is from $A$. Answer B is just four units from point $A$. Answer C is just four units from point $B$.

**19. B:** $\frac{x}{8}$ and $\frac{y}{4}$ both equal 4, so consequently:

$$x = 4 \times 8 = 32$$

$$y = 4 \times 4 = 16$$

$$x - y = 32 - 16 = 16$$

**20. C:** This can be solved as two equations with two unknowns. Since the integers are consecutive with $p > n$, we have $p - n = 1$, so that $p = 1 + n$. Substituting this value into $p + n = 15$ gives $1 + 2n = 15$, or $n = \frac{14}{2} = 7$.

**21. D:** You do not know if the values are positive or negative. So, there is not enough information to answer the question.

**22. C:** Solve for $x$:

6x + 7 = 25

Subtract 7 from both sides of the equation:6x = 18

Divide both sides of the equation by 6:x = 3

Column A and Column B are equal.

**23. C:** Since there are 100 cm in a meter, on a 1:100 scale drawing, each centimeter represents one meter. Therefore, an area of one square centimeter on the drawing represents one square meter in actuality. Since the area of the room in the scale drawing is 30 cm$^2$, the room's actual area is 30 m$^2$.

Copyright © Mometrix Media. You have been licensed one copy of this document for personal use only. Any other reproduction or redistribution is strictly prohibited. All rights reserved. This content is provided for test preparation purposes only and does not imply an endorsement by Mometrix of any particular political, scientific, or religious point of view.

Another way to determine the area of the room is to write and solve an equation, such as this one:

$\frac{l}{100} \cdot \frac{w}{100} = 30 \text{ cm}^2$, where $l$ and $w$ are the dimensions of the actual room

$$\frac{lw}{10,000} = 30 \text{ m}^2$$

$$lw = 300,000 \text{ cm}^2$$

$$\text{Area} = 300,000 \text{ cm}^2$$

Since this is not one of the answer choices, convert cm$^2$ to m$^2$: $300,000 \text{ cm}^2 \cdot \frac{1 \text{ m}}{100 \text{ cm}} \cdot \frac{1 \text{ m}}{100 \text{ cm}} = 30 \text{ m}^2$.

**24. B:** In Column A, you will start with the parentheses: (6 - 2) which equals 4. Then, you can divide: $24 \div 4$ which equals 6. So, the number in Column B is greater.

**25. B:** In order to find the measure of $\angle ABC$, we first need to solve for $x$. In the figure, the angles are vertical angles. According to the Vertical Angle Theorem, vertical angles are congruent. Therefore, to solve for $x$, we set up an equation as $4x+12 = 5x-3$. After subtracting $4x$ from both sides and adding 3 to both sides, the equation becomes $15 = x$. Next, substitute the value of $x$ into the expression for the measure of $\angle ABC$: $4(15)+12 = 60+12 = 72°$. To find the measure of $\angle CBE$, you can subtract 72° from 180° which will give you 108°. So, the quantity in Column B is greater.

**26. D:** The information for the cost of a screw is given to you. So, multiply by 10 to get the value of Column A. The cost of a box of nails is also given, but the number of nails in a box is not given. There is not enough information given to determine which column is larger, therefore Choice D is the correct choice.

**27. A:** The median is the value for which an equal number of students have received higher or lower grades and here, $P = 4$. The mode is the most frequently obtained grade, and here, $Q = 3$.

**28. B:** For Column A, $\sqrt[2]{81}$ becomes 9. So, this is 9 x 3 which equals 27. For Column B, 81 x 3 equals 243.

**29. B:** The area of a square is the side squared. Column A yields a square with an area of x². Column B yields a square with an area of 4x². The problem is asking for half the area of Square B, which is 2x². 2x² is larger than x².

**30. D:** Plug in the number 1 for x. Then A is greater than B. But if you plug in (-1), B is greater than A. The answer is Choice D, since neither A nor B is always true.

**31. B:** For Column A, the probability of mutually exclusive events, A or B, occurring may be written as $P(A \text{ or } B) = P(A) + P(B)$. Thus, $P(A \text{ or } B) = \frac{3}{8} + \frac{1}{8}$ or $\frac{1}{2}$. For Column B, the probability of non-mutually exclusive events, A or B, occurring may be written as $P(A \text{ or } B) = P(A) + P(B) - P(A \text{ and } B)$. Thus, $P(A \text{ or } B) = \frac{1}{6} + \frac{4}{6} - \frac{1}{6}$ or $\frac{2}{3}$. So, the correct choice is B which is the larger quantity.

**32. B:** The price that David paid was $19.00 per share. You can divide David's total profit of $22.00 by the number of shares he purchased (200) to find David's profit per share:

$P = \$20.00 \div 200 = \$.10$ per share. So, the price he paid was 10¢ lower than the closing price given in the table. The table shows that Oracle closed at $19.10 per share today. So, the price David

Copyright © Mometrix Media. You have been licensed one copy of this document for personal use only. Any other reproduction or redistribution is strictly prohibited. All rights reserved.
This content is provided for test preparation purposes only and does not imply an endorsement by Mometrix of any particular political, scientific, or religious point of view.

paid was $19.10 - $0.10 = $19.00 per share. Nonetheless, David's profit was a dollar more than the price at which he bought the stock yesterday.

**33. C:** A diagram would help solve this problem:

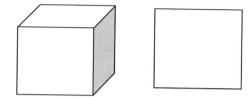

One face of the cube shares an edge with 4 other faces. The number of sides of a square is 4.

**34. C:** Notice that A is simply the factored form of B. There is no need to multiply this out.

**35. C:** The slope of a line is its rate of change, or vertical change over horizontal change. For every 2 the line $P$ moves right, it moves up 1. The slope for line $P$ is $\frac{1}{2}$ and the slope of line $Q$ is also $\frac{1}{2}$. Therefore, the slope of line $P$ is equal to the slope of line $Q$.

**36. A:** For Column A, the probability of mutually exclusive events, A or B, occurring may be written as $P(A \text{ or } B) = P(A) + P(B)$. Thus, $P(A \text{ or } B) = \frac{2}{10} + \frac{5}{10}$ or $\frac{7}{10}$. For Column B, the probability of mutually exclusive events, A or B, occurring may be written as $P(A \text{ or } B) = P(A) + P(B)$. Thus, $P(A \text{ or } B) = \frac{3}{6} + \frac{1}{6}$ or $\frac{2}{3}$. When you give common denominators to these fractions, the fraction of Column A (7/10) is the greater quantity.

**37. A:** The boxplot for data set B shows a larger range between the first and third quartiles. In addition, its median is approximately 25, which is higher than the median of data set A.

## Section 3: Reading Comprehension

**1. D:** This information is all given in the second paragraph.

**2. C:** In the fourth paragraph, the author states that the transient nature of relationships based solely on shared interests is keeping us "socially busy without building the lasting relationships and communities that we want."

**3. B:** The author lists urban sprawl, long work hours, and devotion to television and the internet as causes of problems for American communities.

**4. B:** This is the only one of the answer choices that is not listed in the fifth paragraph as suggestions put forth by the Harvard University study.

**5. D:** The author states in the fifth paragraph that Harvard University School of Government put forth 150 suggestions for increasing social capital.

**6. A:** The author puts this definition in parentheses immediately following his first use of the phrase "social capital."

**7. B:** There is no indication in the passage that the Bennets are interested in becoming friends with Mr. Bingley (choice A), that Mr. Bingley would be a valuable business connection (choice C), or that Mr. Bingley has any prior knowledge of the Bennet daughters (choice D). Mrs. Bennet tells her

Copyright © Mometrix Media. You have been licensed one copy of this document for personal use only. Any other reproduction or redistribution is strictly prohibited. All rights reserved. This content is provided for test preparation purposes only and does not imply an endorsement by Mometrix of any particular political, scientific, or religious point of view.

husband that a new neighbor is moving in: "Mrs. Long says that Netherfield is taken by a young man of large fortune." Mrs. Bennet is sure he will make an excellent husband for one of her daughters: "You must know that I am thinking of his marrying one of them."

**8. A:** Mrs. Bennet feels that Mr. Bingley is likely to marry one of her daughters. She tells her husband that Mr. Bingley is a "single man of large fortune; four or five thousand a year. What a fine thing for our girls!"

**9. C:** Mrs. Bennet wants her husband to be acquainted with Mr. Bingley so that he can introduce Mr. Bingley to their daughters: "But it is very likely that he may fall in love with one of them, and therefore you must visit him as soon as he comes."

**10. A:** Mrs. Bennet remarks to her husband, "But it is very likely that he may fall in love with one of them, and therefore you must visit him as soon as he comes."

**11. B:** Mrs. Bennet is annoyed and fed up with her husband's seeming indifference to Mr. Bingley: "'My dear Mr. Bennet,' replied his wife, 'how can you be so tiresome!'"

**12. D:** Mr. Bennet baits his wife throughout the dialogue: "You want to tell me, and I have no objection to hearing it." Upon hearing about the arrival of Mr. Bingley, he pretends that he doesn't know his wife is looking upon Mr. Bingley as a potential son-in-law: "How so? How can it affect them?" He even asks if Mr. Bingley has the same aim as Mrs. Bennet: "Is that his design in settling here?"

**13. B:** The passage discusses Helen Keller's life beginning with her birth and continuing on into her adulthood.

**14. D:** The passage does mention that Helen graduated from Radcliffe College (choice A), and the passage does tell about Anne's role as Helen's teacher (choice B), but the passage as a whole does not focus on Helen's time at college or Anne's life outside of her role as teacher. The passage does not mention services available for the deaf and blind (choice C). The passage does tell about Helen Keller's life.

**15. C:** The second paragraph explains why Anne Sullivan was crucial to Helen's life, and the third paragraph elaborates on how Anne helped Helen succeed.

**16. C:** The author's use of the phrase "Helen learned at an incredible rate" and the word "remarkable" to describe Helen's life are two examples of the author's admiration.

**17. D:** Although all of the answer choices represent major events in Helen's life, the passage specifies that the advent of Anne Sullivan was the turning point in Helen's life when she began to learn to communicate with other people. "All of that began to change in March 1887 when Anne Sullivan came to live with the Kellers and be Helen's teacher. Anne taught Helen to communicate by forming letters with her fingers held in another person's hand."

**18. A:** The passage does not indicate that Helen's parents were jealous of Anne (choice B), glad to give Anne responsibility for Helen (choice C), or had any preference in their daughter's choice of a college (choice D). The passage does say that Helen's parents loved her and that they brought Anne to their home to be Helen's teacher. This implies that they were frustrated by their own inability to help Helen and were looking for someone who could.

Copyright © Mometrix Media. You have been licensed one copy of this document for personal use only. Any other reproduction or redistribution is strictly prohibited. All rights reserved.
This content is provided for test preparation purposes only and does not imply an endorsement by Mometrix of any particular political, scientific, or religious point of view.

**19. C:** The author points out that just because there is a month focused on African American history, this doesn't mean that African American history must be ignored for the rest of the year.

**20. C:** The author points out in paragraph 3 that the debate about how to meet the need to teach children about African American history can remind parents that this need is not yet fully met.

**21. A:** In paragraph 3, the author states that the material available is rich and varied.

**22. B:** The use of substantial in this sentence has a meaning that is closest to "considerable." The other choices are antonyms of substantial.

**23. B:** Throughout the passage, the author continues to instill hope and encouragement that Black History Month still has a vital role to play in American culture despite opposing attitudes. Therefore, the best choice is emboldening.

**24. C:** Choice A and D cannot be correct because the paragraph contains only a handful of moments that are important to black history which are narrowed further by occurring in February. While the final paragraph contains only men, you should not make the conclusion of choice B. Nowhere in the passage does the author make a distinction between male and female influence in black history. Many women have made a remarkable difference in black history. Rosa Parks, Barbara Jordan, Diane Nash, and Septima Poinsette Clark are only a few. The number of men or women to make a significant impact on black history is not the author's point. Instead, you should conclude that regardless of a person's background, ethnicity, or position in society, there are many vital moments and people that connect to black history and those should be known by every individual.

**25. D:** Foreshadowing is the best choice. Choice (A), first person point of view, does not answer the question and is incorrect because the story is told from the third person point of view. Choice (B) is incorrect because "hyperbole" generally refers to unrealistic exaggeration, but the imagery in this passage is realistic, even if it does describe extreme conditions. Choice (C), onomatopoeia, is incorrect because the passage contains no words like "cluck" or "quack" that sound like what they describe. Choice (D), symbolism, does not adequately answer the question posed.

**26. D:** Choice D is the best answer because the narrator can enter the consciousness of both the man and the dog, making it third person omniscient. Choices (A) and (B) can be ruled out because the narrator does not use the pronouns "I" or "we." Choice (C) does not seem likely because the passage gives us no reason to believe that the narrator's account of this information cannot be trusted.

**27. C:** Only interpretation III fits with the meaning of the passage. The narrator's statement that the man lacked imagination means that he did not have the foresight to realize that he was risking his life. Interpretation I is incorrect because the passage reads, "He was quick and alert in the things of life." Interpretation II is incorrect because the passage contradicts this interpretation.

**28. A:** Choice A offers the best interpretation. The passage refers to immortality and man's place in the universe; the man does not have the imagination to contemplate such issues, and he does not seem to realize the frailty of humans on the planet. Choices (B) and (C) contradict or misinterpret the meaning of the passage. Choice (D) is not really implied by the passage; in fact, the dog's instincts make it seem more intelligent than the man in a certain sense.

**29. C:** It can be supported by the following quotation: "[The dog's] instinct told it a truer tale than was told to the man by the man's judgment." Choice (A) may sound possible, but it does not really capture the narrator's main point of comparison. Choice (B) can be contradicted by the following

Copyright © Mometrix Media. You have been licensed one copy of this document for personal use only. Any other reproduction or redistribution is strictly prohibited. All rights reserved. This content is provided for test preparation purposes only and does not imply an endorsement by Mometrix of any particular political, scientific, or religious point of view.

quotation: "In its brain there was no sharp consciousness of a condition of very cold such as was in the man's brain." Choices (D) can also be contradicted by the preceding quotation.

**30. D:** The best choice is "weakness" as frailty has synonyms of defect, blemish, and fault.

**31. B:** Lincoln begins this speech by discussing the founding of the U.S. and what the original purpose of the U.S. was. Then, he goes on to talk about how the U.S. is currently engaged in a war intended to fracture the nation, and he states that the battle being discussed was one large tragedy that came out of the war. Next, Lincoln says that his speech and even the memorial itself can't truly honor those who died, and that it's up to those who survived to continue the fight to ensure the nation does not break apart. Answer B best communicates this message.

**32. C:** The sentence in which this phrase is found is: The world will little note, nor long remember, what we say here, but can never forget what they did here. In this context, the phrase "the world will little note" means that no one outside of those in attendance or possibly those outside the country will pay attention to the speech or the ceremony. This eliminates all of the answer choices except C.

**33. A:** The ideals of the revolution are addressed in the first paragraph: Four score and seven years ago our fathers brought forth, upon this continent, a new nation, conceived in Liberty, and dedicated to the proposition that all men are created equal. This introduces the point that Lincoln is trying to make about the battle at hand and the war as a whole: the Civil War is threatening the ideas upon which the nation was created.

**34. C:** There is a comparison between the ideas of the Revolution and the Civil War in this speech. To facilitate understanding of this comparison, Lincoln has to set the stage by telling his audience about the past event he is referencing. This establishes the context of his message.

**35. A:** This line directly references the idea in the previous paragraph, which is that the U.S. is a nation that was created to ensure liberty and equality. This sentence talks about how the Civil War is testing whether or not a nation that was created to ensure liberty and equality can really survive.

**36. B:** When President Lincoln argues that the people who died at Gettysburg did not die in vain, he asserts that their passing was not frivolous or unimportant or meaningless.

# Section 4: Mathematics Achievement

**1. A:** To solve, you will need to move the decimal 4 places. Since the scientific notation had a negative power of 10, move the decimal left. If the power of 10 had been positive, you would have needed to move it to the right. In this problem, solve as follows:

$7.4 \times 10^{-4}$

$7.4 \times 0.0001$

$0.00074$

**2. D:** The area of the squares, whose side lengths are the legs of the triangles, are $a^2$ and $b^2$, or in this example, 9 squares and 9 squares. The area of the square whose side lengths are equal to the hypotenuse of the right triangle is $c^2$. If the whole squares, and half squares, in the grid are summed, the area of the square with side length $c$ is 18 squares. The area of the squares whose side

Copyright © Mometrix Media. You have been licensed one copy of this document for personal use only. Any other reproduction or redistribution is strictly prohibited. All rights reserved. This content is provided for test preparation purposes only and does not imply an endorsement by Mometrix of any particular political, scientific, or religious point of view.

lengths are the legs of the triangles, summed, equals the area of the square whose side lengths are the hypotenuse of the triangle.

9 squares + 9 squares = 18 squares, or $a^2 + b^2 = c^2$

Add the area of all three squares together to get the total: 9 + 9 + 18 = 36 square units.

**3. A:** Put this into an algebraic equation:

5 + 6x = 77

Subtract 5 from both sides:

6x = 72

Divide both sides by 6 to get $x = 12$

**4. A:** The sum of two vectors is equal to the sum of their components. Using component-wise addition, $v + w = (4 + (-3), 3 + 4) = (1,7)$. To multiply a vector by a scalar, multiply each component by that scalar. Using component-wise scalar multiplication, $2(1,7) = (2 \cdot 1, 2 \cdot 7) = (2,14)$.

**5. C:** Multiply the first numbers in each of the parentheses to get 6, and add the exponents of the tens. $(2 \times 10^5) \times (3 \times 10^4) = 2 \times 3 \times 10^{5+4} = 6 \times 10^9$.

**6. D:** When the factors, $(x - 4)$ and $(x + 7)$ are multiplied, the $x$-terms sum to $3x$ and the constants produce a product of –28.

**7. B:** Solve the inequality by changing the inequality sign to an equal sign and solve the resulting equation by factoring the left side:

$$x^2 - 7x + 10 = 0$$

$$(x - 2)(x - 5) = 0$$

$$x - 2 = 0 \quad \text{or} \quad x - 5 = 0$$

$$x = 2 \qquad\qquad x = 5$$

Since the original inequality sign was a greater-than-or-equal-to sign (rather than just a greater-than sign), the solution set will include $x = 2$ and $x = 5$.

These two solutions divide the number line into three distinct regions: $x < 2$, $2 < x < 5$, and $x > 5$. To

see which regions are in the solution set, pick one test value from each region and substitute it in the original inequality. If the result is a true inequality, then the whole region is part of the solution set. Otherwise, the whole region is not part in the solution set:

| Region | Test Value | $x^2 - 7x + 10 \geq 0$ | Conclusion |
|--------|-----------|------------------------|------------|
| $x < 2$ | 0 | $(0)^2 - 7(0) + 10 \geq 0$ $7 \geq 0$ | Part of the solution set |

Copyright © Mometrix Media. You have been licensed one copy of this document for personal use only. Any other reproduction or redistribution is strictly prohibited. All rights reserved. This content is provided for test preparation purposes only and does not imply an endorsement by Mometrix of any particular political, scientific, or religious point of view.

| Region | Test Value | $x^2 - 7x + 10 \geq 0$ | Conclusion |
|--------|-----------|------------------------|------------|
| $2 < x < 5$ | 3 | $(3)^2 - 7(3) + 10 \geq 0$ <br> $9 - 21 + 10 \geq 0$ <br> $-2 \geq 0$ | Not part of the solution set |
| $x > 5$ | 6 | $(6)^2 - 7(6) + 10 \geq 0$ <br> $36 - 42 + 10 \geq 0$ <br> $4 \geq 0$ | Part of the solution set |

Therefore, the solution set is $x \leq 2$ or $x \geq 5$.

**8. C:** First write Equation A in slope-intercept form: $y = mx + b$ where m is the slope and b is the y-intercept.

$$5y - 100x = 25$$

$$5y = 100x + 25$$

$$y = 20x + 5$$

Based on the slope-intercept form of Equation A, the slope, m = 20 and the y-intercept, b = 5.

**9. B:** The chart indicates that 40% of the total recycled material is paper. Since 50,000 tons of material are recycled every month, the total amount of paper will be 40% of 50,000 tons, or $\frac{40}{100} \times 50,000 = 20,000$ tons.

**10. C:** The volume of the box is the product of $\sqrt{3}$, $2\sqrt{5}$, and 4. To multiply two or more square root radicals, multiply the coefficients and then multiply the radicands:

$$\sqrt{3} \times 2\sqrt{5} \times 4 = 2\sqrt{15} \times 4$$

$$= 8\sqrt{15}$$

**11. C:** Because both expressions share the factor $10^3$, we can simply factor and add the ones places. $(8 \times 10^3) + (1 \times 10^3) = (1 + 8)(10^3) = 9 \times 10^3$.

**12. B:** The y-intercept of the line is $(0, -1)$. Another point on the line is $(1, 0)$. Slope is the vertical change over horizontal change which is $\frac{1}{1} = 1$. Plugging this information into the slope-intercept form $y = mx + b$, the equation is $y = x - 1$.

**13. C:** When subtracting A from B, the difference matrix can be written as
$\begin{bmatrix} 1-1 & -3-(-3) \\ -4-(-4) & 2-(-2) \end{bmatrix}$, which reduces to $\begin{bmatrix} 0 & 0 \\ 0 & 4 \end{bmatrix}$.

**14. D:** When the dress is marked down by 20%, the cost of the dress is 80% of its original price; thus, the reduced price of the dress can be written as $\frac{80}{100}x$, or $\frac{4}{5}x$, where $x$ is the original price. When discounted an extra 25%, the dress costs 75% of the reduced price, or $\frac{75}{100}\left(\frac{4}{5}x\right)$, or $\frac{3}{4}\left(\frac{4}{5}x\right)$, which simplifies to $\frac{3}{5}x$. So the final price of the dress is three-fifths of the original price.

Copyright © Mometrix Media. You have been licensed one copy of this document for personal use only. Any other reproduction or redistribution is strictly prohibited. All rights reserved. This content is provided for test preparation purposes only and does not imply an endorsement by Mometrix of any particular political, scientific, or religious point of view.

**15. B:** The ratio of correct to incorrect answers is 2:3, giving a whole of 5. It takes 12 sets of 5 questions to total 60 questions. To determine how many correct answers Sam gave, multiply 2 by 12, for a total of 24.

**16. C:** The interquartile range is the spread of the data. Class 3 has the largest interquartile range because it has the largest box.

**17. B:** Use the FOIL method (First, Outer, Inner, Last) to solve this equation:

$(3x + 1) (7x + 10)$

$= (3x)(7x) + (3x)(10) + (1)(7x) + (1)(10)$

$= 21x^2 + 30x + 7x + 10$

Combine like terms to get the answer:

$21x^2 + 37x + 10$

**18. B:** The listed angles are located in the alternate interior angles position. According to the Alternate Interior Angle Theorem, when a transversal cuts across parallel lines, the alternate interior angles are congruent. Since lines $a$ and $b$ are parallel, it means that $2x + 5 = 3x - 25$. After subtracting $2x$ from both sides and adding 25 to both sides, the equation simplifies as $30 = x$. In Answer A, the angles were incorrectly treated as complementary. In Answer C, the angles were incorrectly treated as supplementary. Answer D is the measure of each alternate interior angle, but the question only wanted the value of $x$.

**19. A:** The answer is expanded to simplify the calculations. The total of Choice A is $8.00 + $1.60, which is the same as the total calculated in the problem.

**20. B:** The equation is solved below:

$$6x + 1 = 4x + 9$$

Subtract $4x$ from both sides of the equation

$$2x + 1 = 9$$

Subtract 1 from both sides of the equation

$$2x = 8$$

Divide by 2 on both sides of the equation

$$x = 4$$

Therefore, the equation has only one solution.

**21. D:** In order to determine the number of questions Joshua must answer correctly, consider the number of points he must earn. Joshua will receive 4 points for each question he answers correctly, and x represents the number of questions. Therefore, Joshua will receive a total of 4x points for all the questions he answers correctly. Joshua must earn more than 92 points. Therefore, to determine the number of questions he must answer correctly, solve the inequality $4x > 92$.

Copyright © Mometrix Media. You have been licensed one copy of this document for personal use only. Any other reproduction or redistribution is strictly prohibited. All rights reserved. This content is provided for test preparation purposes only and does not imply an endorsement by Mometrix of any particular political, scientific, or religious point of view.

**22. D:** To solve the equation, first get rid of the denominators by multiplying both sides of the equation by $x(x-3)$ and simplifying the result:

$$\frac{4}{x-3} - \frac{2}{x} = 1$$

$$x(x-3)\left[\frac{4}{x-3} - \frac{2}{x}\right] = x(x-3)\cdot 1$$

$$4x - 2(x-3) = x(x-3)$$

$$4x - 2x + 6 = x^2 - 3x$$

$$2x + 6 = x^2 - 3x$$

The result is a quadratic equation. Move everything to one side and then solve for $x$ by factoring the left side and applying the zero-product rule:

$$x^2 - 5x - 6 = 0$$

$$(x+1)(x-6) = 0$$

$$x + 1 = 0$$

or

$$x - 6 = 0$$

$$x = -1$$

$$x = 6$$

Therefore, the possible solutions are $x = -1$ and $x = 6$. Since neither of these values will cause division by zero when substituted back into the original equation, they are both valid solutions.

**23. C:** A permutation is an arrangement of a set of objects in which the order of the objects does matter. The notation $_nP_k$ gives the number of different permutation you can make if you use a total of $n$ objects to form a group of $k$ objects without using an object more than once. The value of $_nP_k$ can be found using the formula below:

$$_nP_k = \frac{n!}{(n-k)!}$$

In this problem, the committee is electing four people for four separate positions from a pool of 12 people. Thus, to find the number of possible outcomes, calculate $_{12}P_4$:

$$_{12}P_4 = \frac{12!}{(12-4)!}$$

$$= \frac{12\times11\times...\times1}{8\times7\times...\times1}$$

$$= \frac{12\times11\times10\times9}{1}$$

$$= 11,880$$

**141**

Copyright © Mometrix Media. You have been licensed one copy of this document for personal use only. Any other reproduction or redistribution is strictly prohibited. All rights reserved.
This content is provided for test preparation purposes only and does not imply an endorsement by Mometrix of any particular political, scientific, or religious point of view.

Therefore, there are 11,880 ways that the committee can elect the four positions.

**24. A:** First, multiply the numerator and denominator by the denominator's conjugate, $4 + 2i$. Then, simplify the result and write the answer in the form $a + bi$.

$$\frac{2+3i}{4-2i} \cdot \frac{4+2i}{4+2i} = \frac{8+4i+12i+6i^2}{16-4i^2} = \frac{8+16i-6}{16+4} = \frac{2+16i}{20} = \frac{1}{10} + \frac{4}{5}i$$

**25. B:** To divide expressions that contain variables, divide pairs of like variables (or constants) that appear in both the numerator and denominator. For this problem, first divide the constants: $12 \div 3$, then divide the $a$'s: $a^2 \div a$. Since $a^2 \div a$ is equivalent to $\frac{a^2}{a^1}$, use the quotient rule, $\frac{x^a}{x^b} = x^{a-b}$, to simplify it. There is no change to b since the divisor does not contain the variable $b$:

$$\frac{12a^2b}{3a} = \frac{4a^{2-1}b}{1}$$

$$= 4ab$$

**26. C:** "The square of twice the sum of $x$ and three is equal to the product of twenty-four and $x$" is represented by the equation $[2(x+3)]^2 = 24x$. Solve for $x$.

$$[2(x+3)]^2 = 24x$$

$$[2x+6]^2 = 24x$$

$$4x^2 + 24x + 36 = 24x$$

$$4x^2 = -36$$

$$x^2 = -9$$

$$x = \pm\sqrt{-9}$$

$$x = \pm 3i$$

So, $-3i$ is a possible value of $x$.

**27. C:** A reflection is a transformation producing a mirror image. A figure reflected over the $x$-axis will have its vertices in the form $(x, y)$ transformed to $(x, -y)$. The point $W$ at (1,-7) reflects to $W'$ at (1,7). Only Answer C shows $WXYZ$ being carried onto its image $W'X'Y'Z'$ by a reflection across the $x$-axis. Answer A shows a reflection across the line $y = x$. Answer B shows a 90° counterclockwise rotation about the origin. Answer D shows a reflection across the $y$-axis.

**28. B:** If each of the four groups in the class of twenty will contain three boys and two girls, there must be twelve boys and eight girls in the class. The number of ways the teacher can select three boys from a group of twelve boys is $_{12}C_3 = \frac{12!}{3!(12-3)!} = \frac{12!}{3!9!} = \frac{12 \cdot 11 \cdot 10 \cdot 9!}{3!9!} = \frac{12 \cdot 11 \cdot 10}{3 \cdot 2 \cdot 1} = 220$. The number of ways she can select two girls from a group of eight girls is $_8C_2 = \frac{8!}{2!(8-2)!} = \frac{8!}{2!6!} = \frac{8 \cdot 7 \cdot 6!}{2!6!} = \frac{8 \cdot 7}{2 \cdot 1} = 28$. Since each combination of boys can be paired with each combination of girls, the number of group combinations is $220 \cdot 28 = 6,160$.

Copyright © Mometrix Media. You have been licensed one copy of this document for personal use only. Any other reproduction or redistribution is strictly prohibited. All rights reserved. This content is provided for test preparation purposes only and does not imply an endorsement by Mometrix of any particular political, scientific, or religious point of view.

**29. A:** The cosine function is represented by the ratio $\frac{\text{adjacent leg}}{\text{hypotenuse}}$. In $\triangle ABC$, the adjacent leg to $\angle A$ is $AC$ and the hypotenuse is $AB$. Therefore, $\cos A = \frac{AC}{AB}$. Answer B is $\cot A$. Answer C is $\tan A$. Answer D is $\sin A$.

**30. B:** The product is equal to $-14i^2$. Since $i^2 = -1$, the product can be rewritten as $(-14)(-1)$, or 14.

**31. B:** The number of tails he can expect after 6 coin tosses is equal to the product of the probability of getting tails on one coin toss and the number of coin tosses. Thus, the expected value is $\frac{1}{2} \cdot 6$, or 3.

**32. C:** In $\triangle ABC$, the midpoints are marked as $D$, $E$, and $F$. The medians of the triangle are then drawn in as $\overline{AF}$, $\overline{BD}$ and $\overline{CE}$. The medians intersect at a point called the centroid. Based on this intersection, it is the case that $AG = 2GF$, $BG = 2GD$, and $CG = 2GE$. Since we are given that $BG = 6x - 4$ and $GD = 2x + 8$, we can set up the equation as $6x - 4 = 2(2x + 8)$. Simplifying that equation, it becomes $6x - 4 = 4x + 16$. After subtracting $4x$ from both sides and adding 4 to both sides, the equation becomes $2x = 20$. Divide both sides by 2 to get $x = 10$. Then, the length of $\overline{GD}$ is calculated as $2(10) + 8 = 20 + 8 = 28$. Answer A is the value of $x$. Answer B is the length of $\overline{GD}$ if the equation was incorrectly set up as $BG = GD$. Answer D is the length of $\overline{BG}$.

**33. A:** The minimum and maximum values are 7 and 50, respectively. The median is 23, while the first and third quartiles are 15 and 38. The boxplot for Choice A correctly represents these five values.

**34. C:** First solve for the number of questions Matthew must answer correctly. To determine the number of correct answers Matthew needs, solve the following inequality:

$$3x > 96$$
$$x > \frac{96}{3}$$
$$x > 32$$

Therefore, Matthew must correctly answer at more than 32 questions to qualify for varsity sports. Since the test has 40 questions, he must answer less than 8 questions incorrectly. Matthew could also answer 0 questions incorrectly. Hence, the best inequality to describe the number of questions Matthew can answer incorrectly is $0 \leq x < 8$.

**35. C:** Use the formula Volume = length x width x height:

$200 = 5 \times 5 \times h$

$25h = 200$

**36. A:** Matrices can be added or subtracted only if they have the same dimensions. Since these two matrices do, each position of the resulting matrix is the sum of the values of each matrix at the corresponding positions:

$$\begin{bmatrix} 4 & 2 \\ 7 & 12 \end{bmatrix} + \begin{bmatrix} -1 & 15 \\ 3 & -5 \end{bmatrix} = \begin{bmatrix} 4-1 & 2+15 \\ 7+3 & 12-5 \end{bmatrix} = \begin{bmatrix} 3 & 17 \\ 10 & 7 \end{bmatrix}$$

Copyright © Mometrix Media. You have been licensed one copy of this document for personal use only. Any other reproduction or redistribution is strictly prohibited. All rights reserved. This content is provided for test preparation purposes only and does not imply an endorsement by Mometrix of any particular political, scientific, or religious point of view.

**37. B:** First, determine how many miles can be driven on one tank of gas by multiplying the numbers of gallons in a tank by the miles per gallon:

12 gallon/tank x 30 miles/gallon = 360 miles

Next, divide the total miles for the trip by the number of miles driven per tank of gas to determine how many total tanks of gas Robert will need:

1,800 miles ÷ 360 miles/tank = 5 tanks

**38. B:** The slope of a line is a number that represents its steepness. Lines with positive slope go from the bottom-left to the top-right, lines with negative slope go from the top-left to the bottom-right, and horizontal lines have zero slope. You can also think of slope as being $\frac{rise}{run}$. In particular, a slope of 2 (which is equivalent to a slope of 2/1) means that the line rises (goes up) 2 units every time it runs (goes to the right) 1 unit. Looking closely at line $k$, notice that for every 2 units it goes up, it goes to the right 1 unit.

**39. C:** The average time can be represented by the expression, $\frac{3}{4}(16) + \frac{1}{4}(12)$, which equals the sum of 12 and 3, or 15. Thus, the average time overall was 15 seconds.

**40. B:** The events are dependent, since the first marble was not replaced. The sample space of the second draw will decrease by 1 because there will be one less marble to choose. The number of possible red marbles for the second draw will also decrease by 1. Thus, the probability may be written as $P(A \text{ and } B) = \frac{8}{15} \cdot \frac{7}{14}$. The probability he draws a red marble, does not replace it, and draws another red marble is $\frac{4}{15}$.

**41. B:** Start by squaring both sides of the equation and simplifying the result:

$$\left(\sqrt{3x-2}\right)^2 = (x-2)^2$$

$$3x - 2 = x^2 - 4x + 4$$

Next, move everything to one side and factor to find solutions for x:

$$x^2 - 7x + 6 = 0$$

$$(x-1)(x-6) = 0$$

$$x - 1 = 0 \quad \text{or} \quad x - 6 = 0$$

$$x = 1 \qquad x = 6$$

Therefore, the possible solutions are $x = 1$ and $x = 6$. Substitute these solutions into the original equation to see if they are valid solutions:

$$\sqrt{3x-2} = x-2 \qquad\qquad \sqrt{3x-2} = x-2$$

$$\sqrt{3(1)-2} = (1)-2 \qquad \sqrt{3(6)-2} = (6)-2$$

$$\sqrt{1} = 1-2 \qquad\qquad \sqrt{16} = 6-2$$

Copyright © Mometrix Media. You have been licensed one copy of this document for personal use only. Any other reproduction or redistribution is strictly prohibited. All rights reserved. This content is provided for test preparation purposes only and does not imply an endorsement by Mometrix of any particular political, scientific, or religious point of view.

$1 = 1 - 2 \ \text{False}$         $4 = 6 - 2 \ \text{True}$

Since only $x = 6$ leads to a true equality, that is the only solution.

**42. D:** Get all of the variables on one side of the equation and solve.

$7\sqrt{x} + 16 = 79$

Subtract 16 from both sides of the equation:

$7\sqrt{x} = 63$

Divide both sides by 7:

$\sqrt{x} = 9$

Square both sides:

$x = 81$

**43. B:** The product given for Choice B can be written as $27x^3 - 9x^2y + 3xy^2 + 9x^2y - 3xy^2 + y^3$, which reduces to $27x^3 + y^3$.

**44. D:** The expected value is equal to the sum of the products of each card value and its probability. Thus, the expected value is $\left(1 \cdot \frac{1}{5}\right) + \left(2 \cdot \frac{1}{5}\right) + \left(3 \cdot \frac{1}{5}\right) + \left(4 \cdot \frac{1}{5}\right) + \left(5 \cdot \frac{1}{5}\right)$, which equals 3.

**45. D:** If $\frac{1}{4}$ inch represents 8 miles, then 1 inch represents 4 x 8 = 32 miles. Two inches represents 2 x 32 = 64 inches. An $\frac{1}{8}$ of a mile represents 8 ÷ 2 = 4 miles. Then $2\frac{1}{8}$ inches represents 64 + 4 = 68 miles.

**46. C:** To determine the scale factor of the dilation, compare the coordinates of $\Delta J'K'L'$ to the coordinates of $\Delta JKL$. $J$ is at $(-2 \ -3)$ and $J'$ is at $(-4, -6)$, which means that the coordinates of $J$ were multiplied by a scale factor of 2 to get the coordinates of $J'$. $K$ is at $(1, 3)$ and $K'$ is at $(2, 6)$. $L$ is at $(4, -1)$ and $L'$ is at $(8, -2)$. As can be seen, the coordinates of $K$ and $L$ were also multiplied by a scale factor of 2 to get to the coordinates of $K'$ and $L'$. Answer B is the scale factor going from $\Delta J'K'L'$ to $\Delta JKL$. Answer D results if 3 was incorrectly added or subtracted from the $y$-coordinates in points $K$ and $L$ to get $K'$ and $L'$. Answer A is the reciprocal of answer D.

**47. B:** The length of an arc is proportional to the measure of the arc, relative to the circle. Here, the length of arc $\overset{\frown}{AB}$ is in a ratio of 4:48, or 1:12, with the total circle perimeter. Thus, the measure of arc $\overset{\frown}{AB}$ has a ratio of 1:12 with the total circle measure, which is always 360°. To find the unknown arc measure, set up a proportion with the known information as follows: $\frac{1}{12} = \frac{x}{360°}$. Solving for x gives $12x = 360°$, or $x = 30°$.

Copyright © Mometrix Media. You have been licensed one copy of this document for personal use only. Any other reproduction or redistribution is strictly prohibited. All rights reserved. This content is provided for test preparation purposes only and does not imply an endorsement by Mometrix of any particular political, scientific, or religious point of view.

# Practice Test #2

## Section 1 – Verbal Reasoning

*DIRECTIONS: Each of the following questions consists of one word followed by four words. Select the one word whose meaning is closest to the word in capital letters.*

**1. BANISH:**
   a. eject
   b. stamp
   c. atone
   d. ease

**2. RESPECT:**
   a. encourage
   b. expose
   c. relax
   d. revere

**3. HARVEST:**
   a. plague
   b. reap
   c. plant
   d. harass

**4. PETITION:**
   a. apply
   b. pronounce
   c. request
   d. corrupt

**5. SHACKLE:**
   a. chain
   b. exodus
   c. brawl
   d. picket

**6. ELABORATE:**
   a. beaming
   b. effeminate
   c. intricate
   d. alive

**7. DISGUISE:**
   a. detriment
   b. slant
   c. disposal
   d. mask

Copyright © Mometrix Media. You have been licensed one copy of this document for personal use only. Any other reproduction or redistribution is strictly prohibited. All rights reserved. This content is provided for test preparation purposes only and does not imply an endorsement by Mometrix of any particular political, scientific, or religious point of view.

**8. ESSENTIAL:**
  a. substantial
  b. worthy
  c. indispensable
  d. final

**9. DESPAIR:**
  a. violation
  b. cessation
  c. hopelessness
  d. scheme

**10. BURST:**
  a. explode
  b. distract
  c. collide
  d. execute

**11. TIMBER:**
  a. music
  b. current
  c. bond
  d. forest

**12. SIGNIFICANT:**
  a. mournful
  b. noticeable
  c. meaningful
  d. foolish

**13. STUDIO:**
  a. victor
  b. citizen
  c. fashion
  d. workshop

**14. GLEAN:**
  a. emit
  b. gather
  c. bestow
  d. reveal

**15. VIRTUE:**
  a. vision
  b. maiden
  c. peak
  d. quality

Copyright © Mometrix Media. You have been licensed one copy of this document for personal use only. Any other reproduction or redistribution is strictly prohibited. All rights reserved.
This content is provided for test preparation purposes only and does not imply an endorsement by Mometrix of any particular political, scientific, or religious point of view.

### 16. COURIER:

a. goddess
b. messenger
c. inquisitive
d. artist

### 17. SCRUPULOUS:

a. meager
b. shabby
c. subservient
d. honest

### 18. UTENSIL:

a. implement
b. cavity
c. trick
d. chime

### 19. ALOFT:

a. below
b. sufficient
c. well
d. overhead

### 20. OFFENDER:

a. dweller
b. officer
c. employer
d. criminal

*DIRECTIONS:  Select the word(s) that best fit the meaning of each sentence.*

### 21.  He believed that in order to _____ the problem fully, he would need to understand all of its _____.

a. solve...positions
b. comprehend...extreme
c. experience...thoughts
d. address...intricacies

### 22. The author's novel was _____ but she managed to develop numerous _____ fully and enjoyably by its end.

a. thought-provoking...storylines
b. brief...characters
c. uninsightful...answers
d. surprising...plots

Copyright © Mometrix Media. You have been licensed one copy of this document for personal use only. Any other reproduction or redistribution is strictly prohibited. All rights reserved.
This content is provided for test preparation purposes only and does not imply an endorsement by Mometrix of any particular political, scientific, or religious point of view.

23. The rumors were _____ and she welcomed the opportunity to _____ them.
   a. true...repudiate
   b. fabricated...correction
   c. believable...enjoy
   d. odious...refute

24. I was sorry to see her in that _____, she looked so _____.
   a. condition...despondent
   b. situation...arbitrary
   c. state...demure
   d. position...pensive

25. The disarray was _____; the office had to be closed for the day so all the furniture could be placed where it belonged, papers could be re-filed and a general cleaning done.
   a. inconsequential
   b. contemptible
   c. severe
   d. intermittent

26. He told the kids not to be so _____ when he was gone. He was afraid they would _____ the babysitter.
   a. placid...frighten
   b. boisterous...overwhelm
   c. obedient...enraged
   d. truculent...appease

27. It was an _____ house with its vaulted ceilings, obviously expensive furniture and extravagant art covering the walls.
   a. off-kilter
   b. obstreperous
   c. odious
   d. ostentatious

28. They chalked their meeting up to _____; it was the kind of lucky thing that could never have happened by design.
   a. preparation
   b. serendipity
   c. extravagance
   d. peculiarity

29. He was modest in his _____ and did not _____ a promotion to higher levels of responsibility at work.
   a. dreams...refuse
   b. failures...question
   c. habits...necessitate
   d. ambition...pursue

Copyright © Mometrix Media. You have been licensed one copy of this document for personal use only. Any other reproduction or redistribution is strictly prohibited. All rights reserved.
This content is provided for test preparation purposes only and does not imply an endorsement by Mometrix of any particular political, scientific, or religious point of view.

30. History did not feel _____ to her.  Seeking a more _____ major she decided to study economics.
    a.  relevant...topical
    b.  important...literary
    c.  familiar...theatrical
    d.  esoteric...sycophantic

31. She considered herself to be _____ and liked to predict events before they occurred.
    a.  precocious
    b.  prescient
    c.  predated
    d.  prefatory

32. "If the yeti is _____", he asked, "then who made these _____ footprints?"
    a.  genuine...invisible
    b.  dangerous...massive
    c.  imaginary...colossal
    d.  welcoming...cavernous

33. Elijah noticed that the crowd had _____ and it was possible once again to walk around the museum _____.
    a.  thickened...confidently
    b.  intensified...on foot
    c.  vanished...en masse
    d.  dispersed...with ease

34. The trip was very _____ and they vowed to each other that they would not take another for the _____ future.
    a.  enjoyable...near
    b.  unpleasant...so-called
    c.  fruitful...distant
    d.  taxing...foreseeable

35. Because land is limited and the population is constantly growing, real estate _____ typically _____ over time.
    a.  development ... falters
    b.  values ... increase
    c.  brokers ... compromise
    d.  agents ... magnify

36. Infants and toddlers may sometimes have _____ sleep patterns due to growth spurts and rapid changes in their physical development.
    a.  cohesive
    b.  natural
    c.  erratic
    d.  fanciful

Copyright © Mometrix Media. You have been licensed one copy of this document for personal use only. Any other reproduction or redistribution is strictly prohibited. All rights reserved.
This content is provided for test preparation purposes only and does not imply an endorsement by Mometrix of any particular political, scientific, or religious point of view.

**37. The maintenance workers handle quite a range of _____: irrigation repair, plumbing, and general maintenance.**

    a. visitors
    b. flowers
    c. attractions
    d. responsibilities

**38. Natural fibers like organic cotton and bamboo are _____ and _____ without the use of harsh chemicals.**

    a. manufactured ... deployed
    b. woven ... filtered
    c. commissioned ... forgotten
    d. grown ... processed

**39. _____ mattresses contain many toxic substances, such as flame-retardants, adhesives and chemical foams, which are not present in natural latex rubber.**

    a. Conventional
    b. Queen-sized
    c. White
    d. Maximum

**40. A surge protector siphons off _____ voltage in electric circuits that can be _____ to electronic devices.**

    a. electric .. salutary
    b. excess .. harmful
    c. capable .. damaging
    d. considerable .. refractory

Copyright © Mometrix Media. You have been licensed one copy of this document for personal use only. Any other reproduction or redistribution is strictly prohibited. All rights reserved. This content is provided for test preparation purposes only and does not imply an endorsement by Mometrix of any particular political, scientific, or religious point of view.

# Section 2 – Quantitative Reasoning

*DIRECTIONS:  In this section there are four possible answers after each question. Choose which one is best.*

**1. James had $6.50 in his wallet when he left home. He spent $4.25 on drinks and $2.00 on a magazine. Later, his friend repaid him $2.50 that he had borrowed the previous day. How much money does James have in his wallet?**

    a. $12.25
    b. $14.25
    c. $3.25
    d. $2.75

**2. Rachel spent $24.15 on vegetables. She bought 2 lbs of onions, 3 lbs of carrots, and 1 ½ lbs of mushrooms. If the onions cost $3.69 per lb, and the carrots cost $ 4.29 per lb, what is the price per lb of mushrooms?**

    a. $2.60
    b. $2.25
    c. $2.80
    d. $3.10

**3. In an election in Kimball County, Candidate A obtained 36,800 votes. His opponent, Candidate B, obtained 32,100 votes. 2,100 votes went to write-in candidates. What percentage of the vote went to Candidate A?**

    a. 51.8%
    b. 53.4%
    c. 45.2%
    d. 46.8%

**4. If $a$ = -6 and $b$ = 7, then $4a(3b + 5) + 2b$ =?**

    a. -638
    b. -624
    c. -622
    d. -610

**5. Which of the following expressions is equivalent to $x^3x^5$?**

    a. $2x^8$
    b. $x^{15}$
    c. $x^2$
    d. $x^8$

**6. If $\frac{12}{x} = \frac{30}{6}$, what is the value of $x$?**

    a. 3.6
    b. 2.4
    c. 3.0
    d. 2.0

Copyright © Mometrix Media. You have been licensed one copy of this document for personal use only. Any other reproduction or redistribution is strictly prohibited. All rights reserved. This content is provided for test preparation purposes only and does not imply an endorsement by Mometrix of any particular political, scientific, or religious point of view.

**7. Which of the following statements is true?**

 a. Perpendicular lines have opposite slopes
 b. Perpendicular lines have the same slopes
 c. Perpendicular lines have reciprocal slopes
 d. Perpendicular lines have opposite reciprocal slopes

**8. Arrange the following numbers in order from the least to greatest $2^3, 4^2, 6^0, 9, 10^1$.**

 a. $2^3, 4^2, 6^0, 9, 10^1$
 b. $6^0, 9, 10^1, 2^3, 4^2$
 c. $10^1, 2^3, 6^0, 9, 4^2$
 d. $6^0, 2^3, 9, 10^1, 4^2$

**9. Which of the following expressions is equivalent to $(a + b)(a - b)$?**

 a. $a^2 - b^2$
 b. $(a + b)^2$
 c. $(a - b)^2$
 d. $ab(a - b)$

**10. Which of the following expressions represents the ratio of the area of a circle to its circumference?**

 a. $\pi r^2$
 b. $\frac{\pi r^2}{2\pi}$
 c. $\frac{2\pi r}{r^2}$
 d. $\frac{r}{2}$

**11. Which of the following are complementary angles?**

 a. $71°$ and $19°$
 b. $18°$ and $18°$
 c. $90°$ and $90°$
 d. $90°$ and $45°$

**12. A man decided to buy new furniture from Futuristic Furniture for $2600. Futuristic Furniture gave the man two choices: pay the entire amount in one payment with cash, or pay $1000 as a down payment and $120 per month for two full years in the financial plan. If the man chooses the financial plan, how much more would he pay?**

 a. $1480 more
 b. $1280 more
 c. $1600 more
 d. $2480 more

Copyright © Mometrix Media. You have been licensed one copy of this document for personal use only. Any other reproduction or redistribution is strictly prohibited. All rights reserved.
This content is provided for test preparation purposes only and does not imply an endorsement by Mometrix of any particular political, scientific, or religious point of view.

### 13. Find the area of the rectangle.

5ft

7 ft

a. 5 ft²
b. 12 ft²
c. 24 ft²
d. 35 ft²

### 14. Which of the following choices expresses 5/8 as a percentage?

a. 40%
b. 58%
c. 62.5%
d. 65%

### 15. In the following figure, angle b = 120°. What is the measurement of angle a?

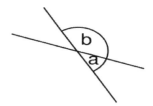

a. 40°
b. 60°
c. 90°
d. 100°

### 16. What is the perimeter of the following figure?

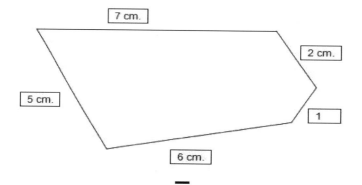

7 cm.

2 cm.

5 cm.

1

6 cm.

a. 15cm
b. 18cm
c. 21 cm
d. 36cm

Copyright © Mometrix Media. You have been licensed one copy of this document for personal use only. Any other reproduction or redistribution is strictly prohibited. All rights reserved.
This content is provided for test preparation purposes only and does not imply an endorsement by Mometrix of any particular political, scientific, or religious point of view.

**17. AC is a straight line. Angle BEC is 45°. What is the measure for angle AEB?**

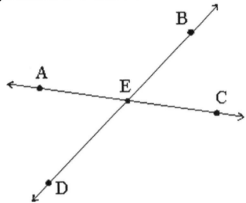

  a.  Angle BEC is 90°
  b.  Angle BEC is 115°
  c.  Angle BEC is 135°
  d.  Angle BEC is 180°

**18. Which of the following demonstrates 25,125,652 in proper scientific notation?**

  a.  $2,512,565.2 \times 10^1$
  b.  $251256.52 \times 10^2$
  c.  $25,125.652 \times 10^3$
  d.  $2.5125652 \times 10^7$

**19. To begin making her soup, Jennifer added four containers of chicken broth with 1 liter of water into the pot. Each container of chicken broth contains 410 milliliters. How much liquid is in the pot?**

  a.  1.64 liters
  b.  2.64 liters
  c.  5.44 liters
  d.  6.12 liters

**20. Find the sum.**

$(3x^2 + x + 3) + 8x^2 + 5x + 16$

  a.  $7x^2 + 29 \, x2$
  b.  $11x2 + 6x + 19$
  c.  $30x + 19$
  d.  $(3x2 + 3x) + 13x^2 + 16$

Copyright © Mometrix Media. You have been licensed one copy of this document for personal use only. Any other reproduction or redistribution is strictly prohibited. All rights reserved.
This content is provided for test preparation purposes only and does not imply an endorsement by Mometrix of any particular political, scientific, or religious point of view.

DIRECTIONS:  In questions 21–35, note the given information, if any, and then compare the quantity in Column A to the quantity in Column B. Answer as follows:

A   if the quantity in Column A is greater

B   if the quantity in Column B is greater

C   if the two quantities are equal

D   if the relationship cannot be determined from the information given

**21. Before Esther paid for the cab, she had 17 percent more money in her wallet than Stella had in hers. After Esther paid for the cab she had 17      percent less money in her wallet than she had before paying.**

| Column A | Column B |
|---|---|
| The amount Stella has in her wallet | The amount Esther has in her wallet after paying for the cab |

**22.**

| Column A | Column B |
|---|---|
| $-(|-6|-1)$ | 5 |

**23. $ds \neq 0$**

| Column A | Column B |
|---|---|
| The time required to travel d miles at s miles per hour | The time required to travel d/3 miles at 3s miles per hour |

**24.**

$x = 3y - 4$
$x = 2$

| Column A | Column B |
|---|---|
| Y | X |

**25.**

| Column A | Column B |
|---|---|
| The number of hours in 5 days | The number of days in 17 weeks |

**26.**

| Column A | Column B |
|---|---|
| $4^8$ | 66,000 |

**27.**

| Column A | Column B |
|---|---|
| $5^3$ | $3^5$ |

**28.  m > n > 0**

| Column A | Column B |
|---|---|
| 4mn/m | 4mn/n |

Copyright © Mometrix Media. You have been licensed one copy of this document for personal use only. Any other reproduction or redistribution is strictly prohibited. All rights reserved.
This content is provided for test preparation purposes only and does not imply an endorsement by Mometrix of any particular political, scientific, or religious point of view.

**29.  t and u are positive integers and t < u**

| Column A | Column B |
|---|---|
| 7/9 | t/u |

**30.**

| Column A | Column B |
|---|---|
| 1 – 1/32 | 7/8 + 1/56 |

**31.  x does not = 0**

| Column A | Column B |
|---|---|
| $|x|/x$ | 1 |

**32.  2x + 3y < 7**

| Column A | Column B |
|---|---|
| 3x + 2y | 14 |

**33.  d = 3.01763 and $\boxed{d}$ is the decimal expression for d rounded to the nearest thousandth.**

| Column A | Column B |
|---|---|
| The number of decimal places where d and $\boxed{d}$ differ. | 2 |

**34.**

| Column A | Column B |
|---|---|
| The surface area of a box with a length of 8, height of 4 and width of 3 | 136 |

**35.**

| Column A | Column B |
|---|---|
| The volume of a cylindrical tank with a height of 20 ft and a diameter of 1 ft | 20 ft$^3$ |

Copyright © Mometrix Media. You have been licensed one copy of this document for personal use only. Any other reproduction or redistribution is strictly prohibited. All rights reserved.
This content is provided for test preparation purposes only and does not imply an endorsement by Mometrix of any particular political, scientific, or religious point of view.

## Section 3 – Reading Comprehension

*DIRECTIONS: Read each passage carefully and then answer the questions pertaining to it. For each question, decide on the basis of the passage which one of the choices best answers the question.*

*Questions 1 to 4 pertain to the following passage:*

It is most likely that you have never had diphtheria. You probably don't even know anyone who has suffered from this disease. In fact, you may not even know what diphtheria is. Similarly, diseases like whooping cough, measles, mumps, and rubella may all be unfamiliar to you. In the nineteenth and early twentieth centuries, these illnesses struck hundreds of thousands of people in the United States each year, mostly children, and tens of thousands of people died. The names of these diseases were frightening household words. Today, they are all but forgotten. That change happened largely because of vaccines.

You probably have been vaccinated against diphtheria. You may even have been exposed to the bacterium that causes it, but the vaccine prepared your body to fight off the disease so quickly that you were unaware of the infection. Vaccines take advantage of your body's natural ability to learn how to combat many disease-causing germs, or microbes. What's more, your body remembers how to protect itself from the microbes it has encountered before. Collectively, the parts of your body that remember and repel microbes are called the immune system. Without the proper functioning of the immune system, the simplest illness—even the common cold—could quickly turn deadly.

On average, your immune system needs more than a week to learn how to fight off an unfamiliar microbe. Sometimes, that isn't enough time. Strong microbes can spread through your body faster than the immune system can fend them off. Your body often gains the upper hand after a few weeks, but in the meantime you are sick. Certain microbes are so virulent that they can overwhelm or escape your natural defenses. In those situations, vaccines can make all the difference.

Traditional vaccines contain either parts of microbes or whole microbes that have been altered so that they don't cause disease. When your immune system confronts these harmless versions of the germs, it quickly clears them from your body. In other words, vaccines trick your immune system in order to teach your body important lessons about how to defeat its opponents.

## 1. What is the main idea of the passage?
   a. The nineteenth and early twentieth centuries were a dark period for medicine.
   b. You have probably never had diphtheria.
   c. Traditional vaccines contain altered microbes.
   d. Vaccines help the immune system function properly.

Copyright © Mometrix Media. You have been licensed one copy of this document for personal use only. Any other reproduction or redistribution is strictly prohibited. All rights reserved. This content is provided for test preparation purposes only and does not imply an endorsement by Mometrix of any particular political, scientific, or religious point of view.

## 2. Which statement is *not* a detail from the passage?

a. Vaccines contain microbe parts or altered microbes.
b. The immune system typically needs a week to learn how to fight a new disease.
c. The symptoms of disease do not emerge until the body has learned how to fight the microbe.
d. A hundred years ago, children were at the greatest risk of dying from now-treatable diseases.

## 3. What is the meaning of the word *virulent* as it is used in the third paragraph?

a. tiny
b. malicious
c. contagious
d. annoying

## 4. What is the author's primary purpose in writing the essay?

a. to entertain
b. to persuade
c. to inform
d. to analyze

*Questions* 5 to 8 pertain to the following passage:

In the American Southwest of the late 1800s, the introduction of barbed wire fencing led to fierce disputes between ranchers and farmers, both eager to protect their rights and their livelihood. The farmers were the clear winners of the two groups, and the barbed wire fences stayed and proliferated. Barbed wire proved to be ideal for use in western conditions; it was cheaper and easier to use than the alternatives of wood fences, stone walls or hedges. Within a few decades all the previously open range land became fenced-in private property. This change was so dramatic to the western culture that some consider the introduction of barbed wire fencing to be the event that ended the Old West period of our history.

## 5. According to the author, which group supported the use of barbed wire fences?

a. the ranchers
b. the farmers
c. both the ranchers and the farmers
d. neither the ranchers nor the farmers

## 6. According to the author, what do some believe the introduction of barbed wire ended?

a. the disputes between the farmers and the ranchers
b. the controversy over whether wood fences or stone walls were better
c. the Old West period of our history
d. the livelihood of the farmers

## 7. Which of the following did the author **not** imply would have been found in the Old West prior to the introduction of barbed wire fencing?

a. no fencing in some places
b. wood fences
c. hedges
d. brick walls

Copyright © Mometrix Media. You have been licensed one copy of this document for personal use only. Any other reproduction or redistribution is strictly prohibited. All rights reserved.
This content is provided for test preparation purposes only and does not imply an endorsement by Mometrix of any particular political, scientific, or religious point of view.

8. **According to the author, when did the introduction of barbed wire fencing occur?**
   a. the late 16th century
   b. the late 17th century
   c. the late 18th century
   d. the late 19th century

*Questions 9 to 16 pertain to the following passage:*

Heart palpitations are an extremely common symptom and are generally not associated with life threatening cardiac disturbances. Palpitations are the sensation that the heart is pounding or racing, often accompanied by an unpleasant awareness of one's own heartbeat. The heart's rhythm may be normal or abnormal, with a sensation of skipped beats or of periods of rapid, irregular beats. Palpitations may be felt in the chest, throat, or neck.

Normal cardiac contraction rates at rest are in the range 60 - 100 beats per minute. It may be substantially lower for athletes – even dropping to less than 55 beats per minute. Certain medications are intended to lower the heart rate and may also bring it below the average range.

Several clinical conditions impact the resting heart rate: tachycardia is a condition in which it is very rapid and may exceed 100 beats per minute. Bradycardia is the opposite: an unusually slow heart rate. Extrasystole, moreover, is a condition in which occasional extra heart beats may occur.

Although patients may find them to be extremely frightening, heart palpitations are usually not serious. However, the sensations may be indicative of an abnormal heart rhythm—arrhythmia—which is more likely in patients with known heart conditions at the time the palpitations begin or with significant risk factors for heart disease, an abnormal heart valve, or an electrolyte abnormality in the blood -- for example, a low potassium level.

Among the most common causes of palpitations are physical factors such as exercise, anxiety and stress, hyperventilation, physical conditions such as fever, low levels of blood oxygen, anemia or overactive thyroid. Other causes include substances such as caffeine, nicotine, cocaine or other drugs, including medications like thyroid pills, beta blockers, asthma drugs and anti-arrhythmics. It is worth noting that medications used to treat irregular heart rhythms may cause the emergence of different rhythmic irregularities. Finally, heart palpitations may indicate heart disease and are especially indicative of mitral valve prolapse, a condition in which the valve separating the left atrium and ventricle fails to close completely.

Reducing caffeine intake will often significantly reduce heart palpitations. Reducing stress and anxiety can help lessen their frequency and intensity. Breathing exercises or deep relaxation have been successfully employed to reduce the severity of episodes. Practicing yoga or tai chi on a regular basis can also reduce the frequency of palpitations.

Copyright © Mometrix Media. You have been licensed one copy of this document for personal use only. Any other reproduction or redistribution is strictly prohibited. All rights reserved. This content is provided for test preparation purposes only and does not imply an endorsement by Mometrix of any particular political, scientific, or religious point of view.

Patients should be encouraged to keep a record of how often palpitations occur, when they happen, how long they last, and heart rate at the time of the episode. This information may help to evaluate their seriousness and their underlying cause.

Emergency medical care is needed if the patient loses consciousness, experiences shortness of breath, chest pain, unusual sweating, dizziness, or lightheadedness. A physician should be contacted if the extra heartbeats are frequent (more than a half dozen per minute, if the pulse increases to more than 100 beats per minute, or if the pattern of palpitations changes suddenly. Medical consultation is also indicated in patients with risk factors for heart disease, such as high cholesterol, diabetes, or high blood pressure.

**9. Heart palpitations**

    a.  do not indicate a life-threatening heart condition
    b.  may indicate a serious heart condition
    c.  are a common sensation that may safely be ignored
    d.  are always associated with an abnormal heart rhythm

**10. The purpose of this article is to**

    a.  describe the treatment of heart palpitations
    b.  encourage people to exercise, in order to control heart palpitations
    c.  give a general description of a medical condition
    d.  show that smoking is a primary cause of heart disease

**11. The normal heart rate for patients at rest**

    a.  may be lowered by exercise
    b.  must be in the range 60-100 beats per minute
    c.  can be felt in the neck
    d.  is called bradycardia

**12. Which of the following groups should consult a physician if they feel heart palpitations?**

    a.  People with high caffeine intake
    b.  Athletes
    c.  People with fever
    d.  People with cardiac conditions

**13. Mitral valve prolapse is**

    a.  a leading cause of heart palpitations
    b.  caused by excessive caffeine intake
    c.  a heart condition that causes palpitations
    d.  used in diagnosing heart palpitations

**14. Which of these terms does NOT signify an abnormality of heart rhythm?**

    a.  bradycardia
    b.  arrhythmia
    c.  electrolyte abnormality
    d.  extrasystole

Copyright © Mometrix Media. You have been licensed one copy of this document for personal use only. Any other reproduction or redistribution is strictly prohibited. All rights reserved.
This content is provided for test preparation purposes only and does not imply an endorsement by Mometrix of any particular political, scientific, or religious point of view.

**15. Which of the following is recommended to manage a heart palpitation condition?**
   a. bed rest
   b. beta blockers
   c. tachycardia
   d. breathing exercises

**16. Which of the following may indicate a more serious condition in an individual experiencing heart palpitations?**
   a. tachycardia
   b. extrasystole
   c. fever
   d. hyperventilation

*Questions 17 to 24 pertain to the following passage:*

It is tempting to think that your eyes are simply mirrors that reflect whatever is in front of them. Researchers, however, have shown that your brain is constantly working to create the impression of a continuous, uninterrupted world.

For instance, in the last ten minutes, you have blinked your eyes around 200 times. You have probably not been aware of any of these interruptions in your visual world. Something you probably have not seen in a long time without the aid of a mirror is your nose. It is always right there, down in the bottom corner of your vision, but your brain filters it out so that you are not aware of your nose unless you purposefully look at it.

Nor are you aware of the artery that runs right down the middle of your retina. It creates a large blind spot in your visual field, but you never notice the hole it leaves. To see this blind spot, try the following: Cover your left eye with your hand. With your right eye, look at the O on the left. As you move your head closer to the O, the X will disappear as it enters the blind spot caused by your optical nerve.

O                                                                X

Your brain works hard to make the world look continuous!

**17. The word <u>filters</u>, as used in this passage, most nearly means:**
   a. Alternates
   b. Reverses
   c. Ignores
   d. Depends

**18. The word <u>retina</u>, as used in this passage, most nearly means:**
   a. Optical illusion
   b. Part of the eye
   c. Pattern
   d. Blindness

Copyright © Mometrix Media. You have been licensed one copy of this document for personal use only. Any other reproduction or redistribution is strictly prohibited. All rights reserved.
This content is provided for test preparation purposes only and does not imply an endorsement by Mometrix of any particular political, scientific, or religious point of view.

**19. Which of the following statements can be inferred from this passage?**

 a. Not all animals' brains filter out information.
 b. Visual perception is not a passive process.
 c. Blind spots cause accidents.
 d. The eyes never reflect reality.

**20. What is the author's purpose for including the two letters in the middle of the passage?**

 a. To demonstrate the blind spot in the visual field.
 b. To organize the passage.
 c. To transition between the last two paragraphs of the passage.
 d. To prove that the blind spot is not real.

**21. What is the main purpose of this passage?**

 a. To persuade the reader to pay close attention to blind spots.
 b. To explain the way visual perception works.
 c. To persuade the reader to consult an optometrist if the O and X disappear.
 d. To prove that vision is a passive process.

**22. Based on the passage, which of the following statements is true?**

 a. The brain cannot accurately reflect reality.
 b. Glasses correct the blind spot caused by the optical nerve.
 c. Vision is the least important sense.
 d. The brain fills in gaps in the visual field.

**23. The author mentions the nose to illustrate what point?**

 a. The brain filters out some visual information.
 b. Not all senses work the same way.
 c. Perception is a passive process.
 d. The sense of smell filters out information.

**24. Which of the following statements can be inferred from the second paragraph?**

 a. The brain filters out the sound created by the shape of the ears.
 b. The brain does not perceive all activity in the visual field.
 c. Closing one eye affects depth perception.
 d. The brain evolved as a result of environmental factors.

*Questions 25 to 33 pertain to the following passage:*

The United States has always been a <u>pluralistic</u> society, meaning it has always embraced many points of view and many groups with different identities. That is not to say that these groups have always seen eye to eye. The first political parties developed in the United States as a result of conflicting visions of the American identity. Many politicians believed that wealthy merchants and lawyers represented the country's true identity, but many others saw <u>it</u> in the farmers and workers who formed the country's economic base.

The event that brought this disagreement to the surface was the creation of the Bank of the United States in 1791. The bank set out to rid the country of the debts it had accumulated during the American Revolution. Until then, each state was responsible for its own debts. The Bank of the United States, however, wanted to

Copyright © Mometrix Media. You have been licensed one copy of this document for personal use only. Any other reproduction or redistribution is strictly prohibited. All rights reserved.
This content is provided for test preparation purposes only and does not imply an endorsement by Mometrix of any particular political, scientific, or religious point of view.

assume these debts and pay them off itself. While many people considered this offer to be a good financial deal for the states, many states were uncomfortable with the arrangement because they saw it as a power play by the federal government. If a central bank had control over the finances of individual states, the people who owned the bank would profit from the states in the future. This concern was the basis of the disagreement: Who should have more power, the individual states or the central government?

The Democratic-Republican Party developed to protest the bank, but it came to represent a vision of America with power spread among states. The Federalist Party was established in defense of the bank, but its ultimate vision was of a strong central government that could help steer the United States toward a more <u>competitive</u> position in the world economy.

These different points of view—central government versus separate states—would not be resolved easily. These same disagreements fueled the tension that erupted into the Civil War over half a century later.

**25. According to the passage, the word "pluralistic" most nearly means:**
   a. Divisive
   b. Conservative
   c. Tolerant
   d. Liberty

**26. What is the author's purpose in writing this passage?**
   a. To persuade the reader to accept the Federalist Party's point of view.
   b. To explain the disagreements between early American political parties.
   c. To explain the importance of a strong central government.
   d. To criticize the founders of the Bank of the United States.

**27. The word "competitive" is used in the passage to mean:**
   a. Inferior
   b. Stronger
   c. Partisan
   d. Identity

**28. Which of the following best describes the main idea of the passage?**
   a. Political parties should emphasize areas of agreement instead of disagreement.
   b. The earliest political parties in the U.S. reflected conflicting interests.
   c. The Federalist Party had a better plan for America's interests abroad.
   d. The Bank of the United States was not a secure financial institution.

**29. In the last sentence of the first paragraph, the pronoun "it" refers to which of the following?**
   a. The country's identity.
   b. The future of the country.
   c. State's rights.
   d. A political party.

Copyright © Mometrix Media. You have been licensed one copy of this document for personal use only. Any other reproduction or redistribution is strictly prohibited. All rights reserved.
This content is provided for test preparation purposes only and does not imply an endorsement by Mometrix of any particular political, scientific, or religious point of view.

**30. Which of the following statements can be inferred from the second paragraph?**

   a. The formation of the Bank of the United States should not have created so much conflict.

   b. Individual states believed that they should not have to share their profits with the central government.

   c. The bank was attempting to swindle the states.

   d. The states were not willing to listen to reason.

**31. Which of the following statements best fits with the viewpoint of the Federalist Party?**

   a. The U.S. should be a confederacy of individual states with equal power.

   b. The government should not meddle in the affairs of states.

   c. States should not have any rights.

   d. The stronger the central government, the stronger the country.

**32. Which of the following statements best fits with the viewpoint of the Democratic-Republican Party?**

   a. The federal government should not have too much power.

   b. The Bank of the United States would never be able to repay the states' debts.

   c. The states should not have too much power.

   d. The constitution must be revised to give the government more power.

**33. Which of the following statements can be inferred from the final paragraph?**

   a. The Civil War was fought between the Federalist and the Democratic-Republican Parties.

   b. The different interests reflected by the first two political parties were not easily reconciled.

   c. The Civil War could have been avoided if the Bank of the United States had not been created.

   d. The Bank of the United States is a direct cause of the Civil War.

*Questions 34 to 40 pertain to the following passage:*

Easily the most recognizable constellation in the night sky, the Big Dipper has captured the imaginations of people of every culture and every historical period. Not all people have seen the shape of a dipper, though. In fact, the Big Dipper is only part of a larger constellation called Ursa Major. The seven stars that make up the handle and pan of the Big Dipper are just a few of the eighteen stars that make up Ursa Major, a name the Greeks gave the constellation that means "The Great Bear."

Native Americans also saw the constellation as a bear, but they saw the bear in the cup of the dipper. Some Native American groups saw the stars of the handle as three warriors hunting the bear; others saw them as three cubs following their mother. In England the cluster of stars is thought to resemble a plow, but in Scandinavia it is known as a wagon. In ancient Mayan astronomy, it was called a spoon. Arabic astronomers saw the bowl as a coffin and the three stars in the handle as mourners at a funeral. Others have seen it as a bull's thigh, or even a governmental organization.

American slaves sang a song called "Follow the Drinking Gourd." On one level, the song sounded like it was about the cup the slaves used to drink water, but it also worked as a <u>code</u> to teach slaves who wanted their freedom to escape to the north by following the Big Dipper when traveling by night.

The Big Dipper is <u>circumpolar</u>, so it can be seen all night long. This reason may account in part for its easy visibility among the constellations.

Copyright © Mometrix Media. You have been licensed one copy of this document for personal use only. Any other reproduction or redistribution is strictly prohibited. All rights reserved. This content is provided for test preparation purposes only and does not imply an endorsement by Mometrix of any particular political, scientific, or religious point of view.

**34. As used in the passage, the word "circumpolar" most nearly means:**
   a. Seasonal
   b. Stays in the sky all night
   c. Stationary
   d. Bright

**35. Which statement best describes the author's purpose in writing this passage?**
   a. To present correct and incorrect interpretations of the Big Dipper.
   b. To explain the secret codes of American slaves.
   c. To persuade the reader to spend more time viewing the night skies.
   d. To inform the reader of different interpretations of the Big Dipper.

**36. Which statement can be inferred from the third paragraph?**
   a. Stars can be used to navigate unknown areas.
   b. Slavery was an immoral institution.
   c. All old spirituals contain secret messages.
   d. Slaves adopted the Native American interpretation of the Big Dipper.

**37. Which of the following statements is true of the Native American interpretation of the Big Dipper?**
   a. The handle was interpreted as mourners at a funeral.
   b. Their interpretation was inherited from the Mayan civilization.
   c. Some groups interpreted the three stars of the handle differently.
   d. They also used the stars to navigate their way to freedom from slavery.

**38. Which of the following statements seems true based on the passage?**
   a. No two cultures share the same interpretation of the Big Dipper.
   b. Navigating by the stars has largely been replaced by technology.
   c. The stars have inspired the imaginations of many cultures.
   d. Myths are often based in truth.

**39. According to the passage, the word "code" most nearly means:**
   a. Cipher
   b. Interpretation
   c. Secret message
   d. Slang

**40. According to the passage, which one of the following statements is true of the constellations?**
   a. Seen from another galaxy, constellations would not appear the same.
   b. Some stars are closer to the Earth than others.
   c. The light from some stars takes billions of years to arrive on the Earth.
   d. Many different cultures are compelled to connect individual stars to others and form constellations.

Copyright © Mometrix Media. You have been licensed one copy of this document for personal use only. Any other reproduction or redistribution is strictly prohibited. All rights reserved.
This content is provided for test preparation purposes only and does not imply an endorsement by Mometrix of any particular political, scientific, or religious point of view.

## Section 4 – Mathematics Achievement

*DIRECTIONS: In this section there are four possible answers after each question. Choose which one is best.*

**1.  If $a=3$ and $b=-2$, what is the value of $a^2+3ab-b^2$?**

    a.  5
    b.  -13
    c.  -4
    d.  - 20

**2.  32 is what percent of 80?**

    a.  25%
    b.  32%
    c.  40%
    d.  44%

**3.  Jack and Kevin play in a basketball game.  If the ratio of points scored by Jack to points scored by Kevin is 4 to 3, which of the following could NOT be the total number of points scored by the two boys?**

    a.  7
    b.  14
    c.  16
    d.  28

**4. Factor the following expression: $x^2 + x - 12$**

    a.  $(x - 4)\,(x + 4)$
    b.  $(x - 2)\,(x + 6)$
    c.  $(x + 6)\,(x - 2)$
    d.  $(x + 4)\,(x - 3)$

**5.  The average of six numbers is 4.  If the average of two of those numbers is 2, what is the average of the other four numbers?**

    a.  5
    b.  6
    c.  7
    d.  8

**6.  What is the next-highest prime number after 67?**

    a.  68
    b.  69
    c.  71
    d.  73

**7.  Solve: $0.25 \times 0.03 =$**

    a.  75
    b.  0.075
    c.  0.75
    d.  0.0075

Copyright © Mometrix Media. You have been licensed one copy of this document for personal use only. Any other reproduction or redistribution is strictly prohibited. All rights reserved.
This content is provided for test preparation purposes only and does not imply an endorsement by Mometrix of any particular political, scientific, or religious point of view.

**8.** Dean's Department Store reduces the price of a $30 shirt by 20%, but later raises it again by 20% of the sale price. What is the final price of the shirt?

    a. $24.40
    b. $32
    c. $30
    d. $28.80

**9.** How many 3-inch segments can a 4.5-yard line be divided into?

    a. 15
    b. 45
    c 54
    d. 64

**10.** Sheila, Janice, and Karen, working together at the same rate, can complete a job in 3 1/3 days. Working at the same rate, how much of the job could Janice and Karen do in one day?

    a. 1/5
    b. 1/4
    c. 1/3
    d. 1/9

**11.** Dave can deliver four newspapers every minute. At this rate, how many newspapers can he deliver in 2 hours?

    a. 80
    b. 160
    c. 320
    d. 480

**12.** $4^6 \div 2^8$

    a. 2
    b. 8
    c. 16
    d. 32

**13.** If $a = 4$, $b = 3$, and $c = 1$, then $\frac{a(b-c)}{b(a+b+c)}$

    a. 4/13
    b. 1/3
    c. 1/4
    d. 1/6

**14.** What is 20% of $\frac{12}{5}$, expressed as a percentage?

    a. 48%
    b. 65%
    c. 72%
    d. 76%

Copyright © Mometrix Media. You have been licensed one copy of this document for personal use only. Any other reproduction or redistribution is strictly prohibited. All rights reserved. This content is provided for test preparation purposes only and does not imply an endorsement by Mometrix of any particular political, scientific, or religious point of view.

**15.** Archie's gas tank is 1/3 full. If Archie adds 3 gallons of gas to the tank, it will be ½ full. What is the capacity in gallons of Archie's tank?

    a.  28
    b.  12
    c.  20
    d.  18

**16.** Which mixed fraction is equivalent to the expression $7\frac{2}{3} + 4\frac{1}{2} + 1\frac{1}{9}$?

    a.  $12\frac{4}{15}$
    b.  $13\frac{5}{18}$
    c.  $13\frac{2}{54}$
    d.  $13\frac{4}{54}$

**17.** What is the value of $x$, if $\frac{x}{2} + \frac{3}{8} = 7$?

    a.  53
    b.  $\frac{28}{3}$
    c.  $\frac{53}{4}$
    d.  $\frac{56}{3}$

**18.** The figure below shows an isosceles triangle. If the side AC is equal to 7 inches, what is the length of the side BC?

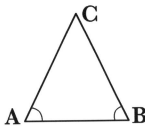

    a.  7 inches
    b.  $\sqrt{7}$ inches
    c.  $2\sqrt{7}$ inches
    d.  $\frac{2\sqrt{7}}{3}$ inches

**19.** For which value of $x$ is the following algebraic equation true?
$$(x^2 - 9) = 0$$

    a.  x = 9
    b.  x = 4
    c.  x = -9
    d.  x = -3

Copyright © Mometrix Media. You have been licensed one copy of this document for personal use only. Any other reproduction or redistribution is strictly prohibited. All rights reserved. This content is provided for test preparation purposes only and does not imply an endorsement by Mometrix of any particular political, scientific, or religious point of view.

**20. A patient in a hospital runs up a bill that is partially paid for by his insurance. The deductible on his policy is $500 and the policy pays 80% of the remaining bill. If the total bill is $8500, what are the patient's out-of-pocket expenses?**

   a. $7200
   b. $3200
   c. $2100
   d. $500

**21. $(-12) + 4 + \left(\frac{1}{3}\right) - \left(-\frac{2}{3}\right)$ is equal to**

   a. $-7$
   b. $-8\frac{1}{3}$
   c. $-7\frac{1}{3}$
   d. $-7\frac{2}{3}$

**22. Which of the following sets of angle measurements forms an equilateral triangle?**

   a. $40°, 40°, 40°$
   b. $40°, 40°, 100°$
   c. $40°, 70°, 70°$
   d. $60°, 60°, 60°$

**23. To determine if a person is overweight, a body mass index (BMI) is computed. BMI is given by $BMI = w/h^2 \times 703$, where $w$ is the patient's weight in lbs and $h$ is the patient's height in inches. A 100-lb patient is 5 feet tall. What is the patient's approximate BMI?**

   a. 18
   b. 7.03
   c. 19.5
   d. 11.7

**24. Which of the following is the multiplicative inverse of 5?**

   a. $\frac{1}{2}$
   b. 0.2
   c. 0.5
   d. 0.25

**25. Which of the following is a prime factor of 60?**

   a. 6
   b. 10
   c. 8
   d. 3

**26. Which of the following expressions is equal to $x^{mn}$?**

   a. $(x^m)^n$
   b. $x^{m+n}$
   c. $x^m x^n$
   d. $nx^m$

Copyright © Mometrix Media. You have been licensed one copy of this document for personal use only. Any other reproduction or redistribution is strictly prohibited. All rights reserved.
This content is provided for test preparation purposes only and does not imply an endorsement by Mometrix of any particular political, scientific, or religious point of view.

**27. A right triangle is inscribed within a circle of radius $R$, as shown in the figure, such that the apex of the triangle is at the center of the circle. What is the length of the hypotenuse?**

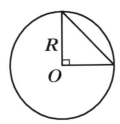

 a.  $\pi r^2$
 b.  $\sqrt{2}R$
 c.  $\sqrt{2}R^2$
 d.  $2R$

**28. Which of the following expressions means the same thing as 8.25 x 10⁴?**

 a.  8,250
 b.  82,500
 c.  825,000
 d.  8,250,000

**29. If $\frac{1}{x} + \frac{1}{10} = 0$, what is the value of $x$?**

 a.  10
 b.  −10
 c.  $-\dfrac{1}{10}$
 d.  0.01

**30. A fair coin is tossed three times. What is the probability that it will land heads up on both the first and third tosses?**

 a.  $\dfrac{1}{2}$
 b.  $\dfrac{1}{4}$
 c.  $\dfrac{1}{8}$
 d.  $\dfrac{1}{12}$

**31. If 12 is 15% of a number, what is 35% of the same number?**

 a.  28
 b.  24
 c.  30
 d.  32

Copyright © Mometrix Media. You have been licensed one copy of this document for personal use only. Any other reproduction or redistribution is strictly prohibited. All rights reserved.
This content is provided for test preparation purposes only and does not imply an endorsement by Mometrix of any particular political, scientific, or religious point of view.

32. If $2 \times \sqrt[3]{x} = 4$, then $x = ?$

    a.  2
    b.  4
    c.  6
    d.  8

33. The square of a number is subtracted from six times that number. The result is 9. What is the number?

    a.  2
    b.  3
    c.  4
    d.  6

34. In the figure below, a rectangle is inscribed within a circle such that one side coincides with the diameter. Radius OF intersects the rectangle at point E. This radius is drawn so that the angle $\angle COF$ is 50°. What is the magnitude of angle $\angle FEB$?

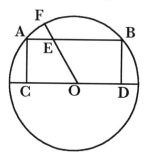

    a.  140°
    b.  130°
    c.  120°
    d.  110°

35. Which of the following statements is true?

    a.  A circle and its tangent have two points in common
    b.  A circle and its tangent have one point in common
    c.  A tangent is a line that intersects a circle
    d.  A tangent is a line that passes through the center of a circle

36. What is the value of $y$ if $x = 7$ and $y = 3x^2 - 2x + 4$?

    a.  137
    b.  431
    c.  11
    d.  165

Copyright © Mometrix Media. You have been licensed one copy of this document for personal use only. Any other reproduction or redistribution is strictly prohibited. All rights reserved. This content is provided for test preparation purposes only and does not imply an endorsement by Mometrix of any particular political, scientific, or religious point of view.

37. A rectangle has a width of $\sqrt{\frac{w}{8}}$ feet and a length of $\sqrt{\frac{w}{4}}$ feet. What is the area of the rectangle in square feet?

    a. $\frac{w^2}{\sqrt{3}}$

    b. $\frac{w}{4\sqrt{2}}$

    c. $\frac{\sqrt{w}}{12}$

    d. $\frac{w}{12}$

38. A surgeon draws two surgical gloves at random from a bag containing 6 blue and 6 green gloves. What is the probability that both gloves will be of the same color?

    a. 1 in 6

    b. 1 in 12

    c. 1 in 2

    d. 5 in 11

39. If $3 + \frac{1}{q} = 0$, then what is the value of $6 + 6q$?

    a. $-\frac{2}{3}$

    b. -4

    c. 0

    d. 4

40. If $m > 0$ and $n < 0$, which of the following statements is true?

    a. The sum m + n is always negative.

    b. The quotient $\frac{m}{n}$ is always negative.

    c. The product mn is always positive.

    d. The difference m – n is always positive.

41. If $x = 16$, $x^{-\frac{1}{2}} = ?$

    a. $\frac{1}{2}$

    b. $\frac{1}{4}$

    c. $-\frac{1}{4}$

    d. $-4$

Copyright © Mometrix Media. You have been licensed one copy of this document for personal use only. Any other reproduction or redistribution is strictly prohibited. All rights reserved. This content is provided for test preparation purposes only and does not imply an endorsement by Mometrix of any particular political, scientific, or religious point of view.

**42. What is the slope of the line shown in the figure below?**

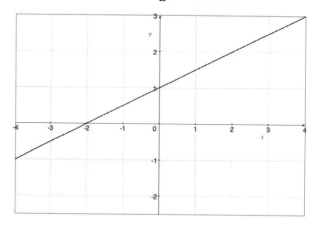

   a.   $-2$
   b.   $2$
   c.   $-\dfrac{1}{2}$
   d.   $\dfrac{1}{2}$

**43. $0.81 \times \dfrac{1}{\sqrt{9}}$?**

   a.   0.9
   b.   0.09
   c.   0.21
   d.   0.27

**44. The volume of blood in a human body can be predicted by the equation: $V = 0.07w$, where $V$ is the volume in pints and $w$ is the weight of the body in pounds. The average person's body contains 12 pints of blood. According to the relationship given, what is the average person's weight?**

   a.   162.3 lbs
   b.   168.5 lbs
   c.   171.4 lbs
   d.   178.3 lbs

**45. What is 0.819 rounded to the nearest hundredth?**

   a.   0.81
   b.   0.9
   c.   0.82
   d.   0.8

Copyright © Mometrix Media. You have been licensed one copy of this document for personal use only. Any other reproduction or redistribution is strictly prohibited. All rights reserved.
This content is provided for test preparation purposes only and does not imply an endorsement by Mometrix of any particular political, scientific, or religious point of view.

## Section 5 – Essay

*DIRECTIONS: Write an essay on the following prompt on the paper provided. Your essay should NOT exceed 2 pages and must be written in ink. Erasing is not allowed.*

**Prompt: <u>Climate change is constant and natural</u>.**

Support your position with specific examples from personal experience, the experience of others, current events, history, or literature.

Copyright © Mometrix Media. You have been licensed one copy of this document for personal use only. Any other reproduction or redistribution is strictly prohibited. All rights reserved.
This content is provided for test preparation purposes only and does not imply an endorsement by Mometrix of any particular political, scientific, or religious point of view.

# Answers and Explanations for Test #2

## Section 1 – Verbal Reasoning

**1. A:** To banish is to eject by force from a country, state, or sovereignty.

**2. D:** To respect is to hold in esteem or honor – to revere.

**3. B:** To harvest is to gather, or reap, a crop.

**4. C:** To petition is to request earnestly, often through some formal channel of communication.

**5. A:** A shackle is a fastening device that confines the legs or arms to prevent unrestricted movement – a chain.

**6. C:** Something elaborate is marked by complexity of detail – intricate.

**7. D:** A disguise is something intended for concealment of identity, character, or quality – a mask.

**8. C:** Something essential is absolutely necessary or indispensable.

**9. C:** Despair is a state of hopelessness.

**10. A:** To burst is to explode or break open.

**11. D:** Timber is sometimes used to refer to a wooded land, such as a forest.

**12. C:** Something significant is meaningful or important.

**13. D:** A studio, also called a workshop, is a place for an artist to create, experiment, and perform other related artistic tasks.

**14. B:** To glean is to gather something slowly and through effort.

**15. D:** A virtue is a good or admirable quality or property.

**16. B:** A courier is a messenger.

**17. D:** To be scrupulous is to be honest or principled.

**18. A:** A utensil is an implement or tool that serves a useful purpose.

**19. D:** Something that is aloft is high up or overhead.

**20. D:** An offender is someone who breaks a law – a criminal.

**21. D:** Answer (a) is incorrect because it is not logically correct to speak of a problem's "positions." Answer (b) is incorrect because "all of its extreme" is not grammatically correct. Answer (c) is incorrect because it is not logically correct to speak of a problem's "thoughts." Answer (d) is the better answer.

**22. B:** Answers (a) and (d) are incorrect because the conjunction "but" in the sentence suggests that the second half happened despite the first half; in this answer, it doesn't logically make sense to say

**176**

Copyright © Mometrix Media. You have been licensed one copy of this document for personal use only. Any other reproduction or redistribution is strictly prohibited. All rights reserved. This content is provided for test preparation purposes only and does not imply an endorsement by Mometrix of any particular political, scientific, or religious point of view.

that numerous storylines were developed despite the thought-provoking nature of the book, that numerous plots were developed despite the surprising nature of the book, or that numerous chapters were developed despite the long-winded nature of the book. Answer (c) is incorrect because the second word, "answers," does not make sense in the context of the sentence. Answer (b) correctly links the two halves of the sentence: despite the brevity of the book, the author was able to develop numerous characters.

**23. D:** Answer (a) is incorrect because one would not repudiate true rumors. Answer (b) is incorrect; the phrase "to correction them" is not grammatically correct. Answer (c) is grammatically correct but does not make as much logical sense as answer (d).

**24. A:** Answer (b) is incorrect because one does not "look" arbitrary or abstruse. Answers (c) and (d) are grammatically correct, but answer (a) is the better answer because it explains why the speaker was sorry to see the object of the sentence: because she was despondent.

**25. C:** Answer (a) is incorrect because it suggests the disarray was minor; the opposite of the meaning suggested by the rest of the sentence. Answers (b) and (d) are incorrect because they offer information about the disarray that is not relevant to the rest of the sentence.

**26. B:** Answers (a) and (c) are incorrect because placid and obedient children are easy to care for, and would not logically be expected to frighten or enrage caretakers. Similarly, answer (d) is incorrect because truculent children might be difficult to care for and would not logically be expected to appease themselves to caretakers.

**27. D:** All the adjectives describing the house and the things in the house suggest a showy and grandiose home; ostentatious is the only answer choice that fits this meaning.

**28. B:** The word sought is one that describes something lucky that does not happen through design. Answer (b), serendipity, fits this meaning. Answer (a) is incorrect as it means the opposite of the word sought. Answers (c) and (d) do not relate to the rest of the sentence.

**29. D:** Answer (a) is incorrect because the second word suggests he didn't *deny* a promotion when offered him, while the word that best fits the meaning of the sentence will be one that indicates that he didn't *seek* a promotion. Answer (c) refers to habits not ambition. Answer (b) is wrong because it is not logically correct to say he was modest in his failures.

**30. A:** Answers (b), (c) and (d) are incorrect as they all provide words that do not make logical sense describing an economic major ("literary," "theatrical," and "sycophantic").

**31. B:** prescient, which means able to anticipate the course of events. Answer (a) means early in development and is incorrect. Answer (c) means proceeding in time and is incorrect. Answer (d) means related to a preface or located in front and is incorrect.

**32. C:** Answer (a) is incorrect because there is no context in the sentence for someone to discuss invisible footprints; additionally if the footprints were, despite invisibility, known of then it would be possible that the yeti had made them and the question wouldn't make sense. Answers (b), (d) are incorrect because there is no conflict between the words dangerous and massive, nor welcoming and cavernous, and the sentence requires such conflict to make sense. Answer (c) is correct because the sentence appropriately poses the conflict of what could make such colossal footprints if the yeti does not exist.

Copyright © Mometrix Media. You have been licensed one copy of this document for personal use only. Any other reproduction or redistribution is strictly prohibited. All rights reserved.
This content is provided for test preparation purposes only and does not imply an endorsement by Mometrix of any particular political, scientific, or religious point of view.

**33. D:** The words sought are something a crowd does that then allows for an individual to walk in a certain way. Answers (a) and (b) are incorrect because a crowd thickening or intensifying does not lead to an individual being able to walk more confidently or on foot. Answer (c) is wrong because if the crowd has vanished, an individual is unable to walk en masse.

**34. D:** The part of the sentence provided indicates that the trip was such as to make the takers of it vow not to take another for some part of the future. Thus the first word should indicate that the trip was not a pleasant one; for this reason, answers (a) and (c) are incorrect. Answer (b) is incorrect because the second word, so-called, does not logically complete the sentence.

**35. B:** The word "because" at the beginning of the sentence indicates that a reason is being given for the condition described in the second clause. Answer B logically completes the sentence: increasing demand for a limited resource leads to an increase in its value.

**36. C:** The second part of the sentence suggests that growth spurts and rapid physical changes disturb sleep patterns, so they are not likely to be "natural." Of the remaining choices, only "erratic" makes sense, and it provides a good description of a disturbed pattern.

**37. D:** The list that follows clearly describes tasks for which maintenance workers may be responsible as part of their jobs.

**38. D:** The sentence describes the advantages of natural organic fibers for the consumer.

**39. A:** The sentence contrasts the properties of typical, or "conventional", mattresses with natural latex rubber ones. The properties listed obviously have no connection with mattress size or color.

**40. B:** A surge protector protects against excess voltage that could harm electronic devices. The other choices make no sense.

## Section 2 – Quantitative Reasoning

**1. D:** James had $2.75 after all the transactions described. To solve this problem, first subtract $4.25 and $2.00 from the initial sum of $6.50, leaving $0.25. Then add $2.50, arriving at the final answer of $2.75.

**2. A:** Begin by determining the total cost of the onions and carrots, since these prices are given. This will equal (2 x $3.69) + (3 x $4.29) = $20.25. Next, this sum is subtracted from the total cost of the vegetables to determine the cost of the mushrooms: $24.15 - $20.25 = $3.90. Finally, the cost of the mushrooms is divided by the quantity (lbs) to determine the cost per pound:

$$\text{Cost per lb} = \frac{\$3.90}{1.5} = \$2.60$$

**3. A:** Candidate A's vote ratio is the number of votes that he obtained divided by the total number of votes cast. Then, multiply that decimal by 100 to convert the decimal into a percentage. Therefore, Candidate A's Vote is: $\text{Percentage} = \frac{36,800}{36,800+32,100+2,100} \times 100 = 51.8\%$

**4. D:** First, compute the value enclosed by the parentheses, $3b + 5 = 3 \times 7 + 5 = 26$. Next, compute $4a = -24$. Note that $a$ is negative, so that this product is negative as well. The product $4a(3b + 5)$ will therefore be negative as well, and equals -624. Finally, add the value of $2b$, or 2 x 7 =14, to -624, to get the final answer $-624 + 14 = -610$.

Copyright © Mometrix Media. You have been licensed one copy of this document for personal use only. Any other reproduction or redistribution is strictly prohibited. All rights reserved. This content is provided for test preparation purposes only and does not imply an endorsement by Mometrix of any particular political, scientific, or religious point of view.

Substitute the given values for the variables into the expression

4·-6 (3 · 7 +5) + 2· 7

Using order of operations, compute the expression in the parentheses first.

Remember that first you must multiply 3 by 7, then add 5 in order to follow order of operations

=4·-6 (21 +5) + 2· 7    Next add the values in the parenthesis.

= 4·-6 (26) + 2· 7    Simplify by multiplying the numbers outside the parenthesis.

=-24(26) +14    Multiply -24 by 26

=-624 +14    Add.

=-610

**5. D:** In order to multiply two powers that have the same base, add their exponents. Therefore, $x^3 x^5 = x^{3+5} = x^8$.

Also note that $x^3$=x·x·x; therefore the expression equals x·x·x · x·x·x·x·x

**6. B:** A proportion such as this can be solved by taking the cross product of the numerators and denominators from either side.

$$\frac{12}{x} = \frac{30}{6}$$    Take the cross product by cross multiplication

$30x = 6 \times 12$    Multiply 6 by 12

$30x = 72$    Divide each side by 30.

$x = 2.4$

**7. D:** The slopes of perpendicular lines are reciprocals of opposite sign. For example, in the figure below, line A has a slope of -1/2, while line B has a slope of 2.

**8. D:** When a number is raised to a power, it is multiplied by itself as many times as the power indicates. For example, $2^3 = 2 \times 2 \times 2 = 8$. A number raised to the power of 0 is always equal to 1, so $6^0$ is the smallest number shown. Similarly, for the other numbers: $9 = 9^1 = 9$; $10^1 = 10$; $4^2 = 4 \times 4 = 16$.

**9. A:** Compute the product using the FOIL method, in which the *First* term, then the *Outer* terms, the *Inner* terms, and finally the *Last* terms are figured in sequence of multiplication. As a result,

$$(a + b)(a - b) = a^2 + ba - ab - b^2$$

Since *ab* is equal to *ba*, the middle terms cancel each other which leaves $a^2 - b^2$.

Copyright © Mometrix Media. You have been licensed one copy of this document for personal use only. Any other reproduction or redistribution is strictly prohibited. All rights reserved.
This content is provided for test preparation purposes only and does not imply an endorsement by Mometrix of any particular political, scientific, or religious point of view.

**10. D:** The area of the circle is πr² while the circumference is 2πr. Taking the ratio of these two expressions and reducing gives: $Ratio = \frac{\pi r^2}{2\pi r} = \frac{r}{2}$.

**11. A:** Complementary angles are two angles that add to 90°.

**12. B:** Multiply $120 by 24 months (a full two years) to get $2880. Add the thousand dollars for the down payment to get $3880. Find the difference between the entire amount all at once ($2600) and the amount paid in the plan ($3880). To find the difference, you subtract. The difference shows that $1280 more is paid with the installment plan.

**13. D:** Area = length × width

A = 7 × 5

A = 35

**14. C:** Solve as follows:

5/8 = x/100

5 · 100 ÷ 8 = x

x = 62.5

**15. B:** These are supplementary angles. That means that the two angles will add up to a total of 180°, which is the angle of a straight line. To solve, subtract as follows:

b = 180° - 120°

b = 60°

**16. C:** To find perimeter, add the sides. 5 + 7 + 2 + 1 + 6 = 21 cm

**17. C:** A straight line is 180°. Subtract to solve: 180° - 45° = 135°

**18. D:** Scientific notation uses powers of ten to represent values in simplified form. There will be a non-zero digit in the ones place and possibly some digits to the right of the decimal multiplied by a power of ten. If you carry out the multiplication, you would be left with the original number.

**19. B:** 410 ml x 4 containers = 1640 ml

Change to liters: 1640 ÷ 1000 = 1.64

Add the liter that was already in the pot: 1.64 + 1 = 2.64 liters

**20. B:** To solve, line up the like terms, as follows:

$$3x^2 + \ \ x + \ \ 3$$
$$+ \ \ \ \ \ \ \ 8x^2 + \ 5x + 16$$
$$11x^2 + 6x + 19$$

Copyright © Mometrix Media. You have been licensed one copy of this document for personal use only. Any other reproduction or redistribution is strictly prohibited. All rights reserved. This content is provided for test preparation purposes only and does not imply an endorsement by Mometrix of any particular political, scientific, or religious point of view.

**21. A:** Let x stand for the amount of money in Stella's wallet. Before paying for the cab, Esther has 17 percent more money than Stella, or 1.17x. After paying for the cab, Esther has 17 percent less than before paying. Since 100 – 17 = 83, Esther now has 83 percent of what she started with, or .83 (1.17x), or .9711x, which is less than x, the amount of money Stella has.

**22. B:** The vertical bars indicate absolute value, which has the effect of turning negative numbers positive. So |–6| = 6, which means |–6| – 1 = 5. This gives us –5 in column A, which is less than positive 5.

**23. A:** Let $t_A$ be the time required to travel d miles at s miles per hour, or $t_A = \frac{d}{s}$. Likewise let $t_B$ stand for the time required to travel $\frac{d}{3}$ miles at 3s miles per hour, or $t_B = \frac{d}{9s}$. Since B has a larger denominator, A is always larger.

**24. C:** Substituting $x = 2$ into the first equation yields $2 = 3y - 4$, or $y = 2$.

**25. A:** There are 24 hours in one day, so in 5 days there are $5 \times 24 = 120$ hours. There are seven days in one week, so in 17 weeks, there are $17 \times 7 = 119$ days.

**26. B:** $4^8 = 65{,}536$, which is less than 66,000.

**27. B:** $5^3 = 125$, whereas $3^5 = 243$.

**28. B:** The rational expression $\frac{4mn}{m}$ reduces to 4n, and the rational expression $\frac{4mn}{n}$ reduces to 4m. Because both m and n are positive and $n < m$, we know that $4n < 4m$.

**29. D:** With the information given, all that can be concluded about the value in column B is that it is between 0 and 1.

**30. A:** Although this can also be solved by finding the exact values of columns A and B, there is an easier way to determine the relative values. Column A is 1 – 1/32 or 31/32. 7/8 is equal to 28/32, so since 1/56 is less than 3/32, column A must be larger.

**31. D:** Without knowing whether x is positive or negative, we cannot determine whether the expression in Column A is equal to 1 or –1.

**32. D:** Since the values for *x* and *y* are never stated in absolute terms, we cannot tell which column is larger without more information.

**33. A:** Rounded to the nearest thousandth, the number is 3.01800. This differs from the original value of d in three decimal places.

**34. C:** The surface area of a rectangular solid is the sum of the areas of the sides. This box has two sides with area $8 \times 4 = 32$, two sides with area $8 \times 3 = 24$, and two sides with area $4 \times 3 = 12$. The sum is $2(32) + 2(24) + 2(12) = 136$.

**35. B:** The volume of a cylinder is $\pi r^2 h$, where r is the radius of the cylinder and h is the height. In this case the volume is $\pi \left(\frac{1}{2}\right)^2 (20) = 20 \left(\frac{\pi}{4}\right)$ cubic feet. Since $\left(\frac{\pi}{4}\right)$ is less than 1, column B is larger.

Copyright © Mometrix Media. You have been licensed one copy of this document for personal use only. Any other reproduction or redistribution is strictly prohibited. All rights reserved.
This content is provided for test preparation purposes only and does not imply an endorsement by Mometrix of any particular political, scientific, or religious point of view.

# Section 3 – Reading Comprehension

**1. D:** The main idea of this passage is that vaccines help the immune system function properly. One of the common traps that many test-takers fall into is assuming that the first sentence of the passage will express the main idea. Although this will be true for some passages, often the author will use the first sentence to attract interest or to make an introductory, but not central, point. On this question, if you assume that the first sentence contains the main idea, you will incorrectly choose answer B. Finding the main idea of a passage requires patience and thoroughness; you cannot expect to know the main idea until you have read the entire passage. In this case, a diligent reading will show you that answer choices A, B, and C express details from the passage, but only answer choice D is a comprehensive summary of the author's message.

**2. C:** This passage does not state that the symptoms of disease will not emerge until the body has learned to fight the disease. In this question, the details expressed in answer choices A, B, and D are all explicit in the passage. The passage never states, however, that the symptoms of disease do not emerge until the body has learned how to fight the disease-causing microbe. On the contrary, the passage implies that a person may become quite sick and even die before the body learns to effectively fight the disease.

**3. B:** In the third paragraph, the word *virulent* means "malicious." In some cases, you may already know the basic definition of the word. Nevertheless, you should always go back and look at the way the word is used in the passage. The exam may include answer choices that are legitimate definitions for the given word, but which do not express how the word is used in the passage. For instance, the word *virulent* could in some circumstances mean contagious. However, since the passage is not talking about transfer of the disease, but the effects of the disease once a person has caught it, malicious is the more appropriate answer.

**4. C:** The author's primary purpose in writing this essay is to inform. If the passage took an objective look at the pros and cons of various approaches to fighting disease, we would say that the passage was a piece of analysis. Because the purpose of this passage is to present new information to the reader in an objective manner, it is clear that the author's intention is to inform.

**5. B**

**6. C**

**7. D**

**8. D**

**9. B:** Although heart palpitations are usually not serious, as indicated in the first paragraph, they can be symptoms of a more serious underlying cardiac condition.

**10. C:** The article is a general introduction to the phenomenon of heart palpitations, describing symptoms and causes. While it does list treatments for palpitations, it does not go into detail on treatment options, as that is not the main purpose of the article.

**11. A:** The text tells us that, in people who exercise routinely, the normal resting heart rate may be lowered from the range of 60 to 100 beats per minute to less than 55 beats per minute.

**12. D:** According to the article, heart palpitations are not usually serious and therefore a doctor's care is not normally required. Among the normal causes are exercise, fever, and consumption of

Copyright © Mometrix Media. You have been licensed one copy of this document for personal use only. Any other reproduction or redistribution is strictly prohibited. All rights reserved. This content is provided for test preparation purposes only and does not imply an endorsement by Mometrix of any particular political, scientific, or religious point of view.

caffeine. However, they may indicate a serious condition in patients with heart disease so that, for those people, further investigation is warranted.

**13. C:** The fifth paragraph tells us that prolapse of the heart's mitral valve is a condition in which the valve separating the left atrium and ventricle fails to close completely. It is not a leading cause of heart palpitations, because these are more often caused by benign factors such as exercise, but it frequently causes palpitations among those who are afflicted with it.

**14. C:** Electrolyte abnormality refers to an unusual blood composition. The other terms are described in the text: bradycardia is a slow heart rhythm, arrhythmia is an irregular rhythm, and extrasystole is the occurrence of extra beats of the heart.

**15. D:** Breathing exercises are among the treatments listed in the sixth paragraph.

**16. A:** Tachycardia is defined in the third paragraph as a very rapid heartbeat, over 100 beats per minute. The last paragraph of the text tells us that a physician should be contacted if the pulse increases to more than 100 beats per minute in a person experiencing palpitations.

**17. C:** Choice C is the best answer. The sentence reads, "Your brain <u>filters</u> [your nose] out," which means your brain ignores it.

**18. B:** Only choice B reflects the meaning of the term "retina," which is a part of the eye's anatomy.

**19. B:** The final sentence reads, "Your brain works hard to make the world look continuous." It follows that visual perception is an active process, not a passive one, making choice B the best answer.

**20. A:** If the reader follows the instructions given in the paragraph, the O and X in the middle of the passage can be used to demonstrate the blind spot in the visual field. Choice A is the best answer.

**21. B:** The passage explains the way that visual perception works. Choice B is the best answer.

**22. D:** Much of the information in the passage is provided to show examples of how the brain fills in gaps in the visual field. Choice D is the best answer.

**23. A:** The author of the passage mentions the nose to demonstrate how the brain filters information out of the visual field. Choice A is the best answer.

**24. B:** Choice B can be inferred from the second paragraph. The paragraph states that the brain filters out information, which means that the brain does not perceive all activity in the visual field.

**25. C:** The passage states that a pluralistic society means one that embraces "many points of view," which is closest in meaning to choice C, "tolerant."

**26. B:** This passage does not choose one point of view on the issue, so only choice B is in keeping with the passage's purpose, which is to explain the disagreements between the earliest political parties in the US.

**27. B:** The word <u>competitive</u> means that the country would be able to compete financially with other countries. Choice B, stronger, is the best choice.

**28. B:** The passage explains the conflicting interests the Democratic-Republican Party and the Federalist Party represent. Choice B best reflects that point.

Copyright © Mometrix Media. You have been licensed one copy of this document for personal use only. Any other reproduction or redistribution is strictly prohibited. All rights reserved.
This content is provided for test preparation purposes only and does not imply an endorsement by Mometrix of any particular political, scientific, or religious point of view.

**29. A:** It refers to the noun "identity." Choice A is the best choice.

**30. B:** Since the passage does not choose to argue a particular point of view, the best choice would be the most neutral statement, choice B.

**31. D:** Choice D best reflects the true position of the Federalist Party.

**32. A:** Choice A best represents the Democratic-Republican Party's perspective.

**33. B:** The final paragraph mentions the Civil War only to show that these differing perspectives would not be easily reconciled. Choice B is the best answer.

**34. B:** The meaning of this term can be found in the context of the sentence. Choice B, "stays in the sky all night," is closest in meaning to the statement "so it can be seen all night long."

**35. D:** This passage's purpose is to inform the reader of different interpretations of this group of stars. Choice D is the best choice.

**36. A:** Only choice A can be correctly inferred from the third paragraph.

**37. C:** Only choice C is consistent with the meaning of the passage.

**38. C:** Choice C is closest to the meaning of the passage.

**39. C:** Choice C best captures the way the passage uses the term code.

**40. D:** Though several of these statements are true, only choice D is directly related to the passage itself.

## Section 4 – Mathematics Achievement

**1. B:** Substitute the given values for $a$ and $b$ and perform the required operations:

$$a^2 + 3ab - b^2 = 3^2 + 3(3)(-2) - (-2)^2$$
$$= 9 - 18 - 4$$
$$= -13$$

**2. C:** This problem is solved by finding $x$ in this equation: $\frac{32}{80} = \frac{x}{100}$.

**3. C:** Every possible combination of scores is a multiple of 7, since the two terms of the ratio have a sum of seven.

**4. D:** Recall that the general form of a quadratic expression is $ax^2 + bx + c$. A great way to factor quadratic expression like this, where $a = 1$ and all the answer choices are integer factors, would be

Copyright © Mometrix Media. You have been licensed one copy of this document for personal use only. Any other reproduction or redistribution is strictly prohibited. All rights reserved. This content is provided for test preparation purposes only and does not imply an endorsement by Mometrix of any particular political, scientific, or religious point of view.

to consider the factors of the last term, $c$. Specifically, any two factors of $c$ that would add to $b$. Essentially: $f_1 \times f_2 = -12$ and $f_1 + f_2 = 1$. We can check the factors of $-12$:

| $f_1$ | $f_2$ | $f_1 + f_2$ |
|-------|-------|-------------|
| 12 | -1 | 11 |
| 6 | -2 | 4 |
| 4 | -3 | 1 |
| 3 | -4 | -1 |
| 2 | -6 | -4 |
| 1 | -12 | -11 |

From this it is clear that the only option that works is 4 and $-3$.

**5. A:** A set of six numbers with an average of 4 must have a collective sum of 24. The two numbers that average 2 will add up to 4, so the remaining numbers must add up to 20. The average of these four numbers can be calculated: $20/4 = 5$.

**6. C:** Prime numbers are those that are only evenly divisible by one and themselves.

**7. D:** This is multiplication with decimals. It is often easiest to perform the multiplication on the numbers without the decimals and then figure out where to put the decimal in the final result. To do this, convert the decimals to fractions and then multiply:

$$0.25 \times 0.03 = \frac{25}{100} \times \frac{3}{100} = \frac{25 \times 3}{100 \times 100} = \frac{25 \times 3}{10000} \qquad \begin{array}{r} {}^{+1} \\ 25 \\ \times \quad 3 \\ \hline 75 \end{array} \qquad \frac{75}{10000} = 0.0075$$

**8. D:** Multiply 30 by 0.2 and subtract this from the original price of the shirt to find the sale price: $24. Then multiply 24 by 0.2 and add the product to the sale price to find the final price.

**9. C:** For this problem there are 3 inches in each segment, 12 inches in a foot, and 3 feet in a yard. Set up a conversion problem and simplify:

$$4.5 \text{ yd} \times \frac{3 \text{ ft}}{1 \text{ yd}} \times \frac{12 \text{ in}}{1 \text{ ft}} \times \frac{1 \text{ segment}}{3 \text{ in}} = 4.5 \times 12 \text{ segments} = 54 \text{ segments}$$

**10. A:** If it takes 3 people 3 1/3 days to do the job, then it would take one person 10 days: $3 \times 3\frac{1}{3} = 10$. Thus, it would take 2 people 5 days, and one day of work for two people would complete 1/5 of the job.

**11. D:** There are 60 minutes in an hour, so Dave can deliver 240 newspapers every hour. In 2 hours, then, he can deliver 480 papers.

**12. C:** Since 4 is the same as $2^2$, $4^6 = 2^{12}$. When dividing exponents with the same base, simply subtract the exponent in the denominator from the exponent in the numerator.

$$2^{12} \div 2^8 = 2^{12-8} = 2^4 = 16$$

**13. B:** Substitute the given values and solve. Resolve the parenthetical operations first.

**14. A:** Convert 20% to the fraction 1/5, then multiply by 12/5. The resulting fraction, 12/25, must have both numerator and denominator multiplied by 4 to become a percentage.

Copyright © Mometrix Media. You have been licensed one copy of this document for personal use only. Any other reproduction or redistribution is strictly prohibited. All rights reserved. This content is provided for test preparation purposes only and does not imply an endorsement by Mometrix of any particular political, scientific, or religious point of view.

**15. D:** This problem can be solved with the following equation, in which $x$ is the total capacity of the tank: $\frac{1}{2}x = \frac{1}{3}x + 3$.

**16. B:** To add the fractional part of mixed fractions, convert to the same denominator before adding the fractions and simplifying. The integers may be added separately. To convert the fractions, first determine the least common denominator. In this case, the LCD is 2 x 9 = 18. The expression is equivalent to: $7\frac{12}{18} + 4\frac{9}{18} + 1\frac{2}{18} = 12\frac{23}{18} = 13\frac{5}{18}$.

**17. C:** To solve for a variable, separate the terms containing the variable and those without on opposite sides of the equal sign. This gives: $\frac{x}{2} = 7 - \frac{3}{8} = \frac{56}{8} - \frac{3}{8} = \frac{53}{8}$.

Multiplying both sides of this equation by 2 yields $x = \frac{53}{4}$.

**18. A:** In an isosceles triangle, two of the three sides are equal. Because side AC equals 7 inches, side BC is also equal to 7 inches.

**19. D:** The product of two negative numbers is a positive number. Because $x^2 = (x)(x)$, then, if $x = -3$, we have $x^2 = (-3)(-3) = 9$. The algebraic sentence becomes (9 – 9), which equals zero.

**20. C:** The patient pays the first $500, which is the deductible. Then, the policy pays 80% of the remainder. The patient is responsible for the remaining 20% of the remainder. Since this is in addition to the deductible, the patient's total expense is $1600+$500 = $2100.

**21. A:** Subtraction of a negative number is equivalent to addition.

**22. D:** An equilateral triangle is one in which all of the sides are equal, and therefore all of the angles are equal. Because the internal angles of a triangle must add up to 180°, choice a is incorrect, as the angles will not form a triangle.

**23. C:** Since there are 12 inches in a foot, the patient is 5 x 12 = 60 inches tall.

**24. B:** The product of a number and its multiplicative inverse is 1. Therefore, the inverse of a number $x$ is $\frac{1}{x}$, because $x = \frac{1}{\frac{1}{x}} = \frac{x}{x} = x$. The inverse of 5 is equal to $\frac{1}{5}$, which equals 0.2.

**25. D:** A prime number is one which is wholly divisible only by itself and by 1. Although all of the numbers shown, except for choice c, are factors of 60, only choice d is prime.

**26. A:** To determine the power of a power, multiply the exponents. This example presents the reverse case: the product of exponents is equivalent to the power of a power. For example, $2^{2\cdot3} = 2^6 = 64 = (2^2)^3 = 4^3$.

**27. B:** Because both sides of the triangle extending from the center of the circle are radii, both will be equal to $R$. By the Pythagorean theorem, the square of the hypotenuse is equal to the sum of the squares of the two other sides, or $h^2 = R^2 + R^2 = 2R^2$. The hypotenuse itself is equal to the square root of this number, or $\sqrt{2}R$.

**28. B:** In scientific notation, the first number is called the coefficient and the second term is called the base. The exponent of the base indicates the number of positions to move the decimal of the coefficient to the right (if it is positive), or to the left (if it is negative). In this case, move the decimal 4 positions to the right, so that 8.25 becomes 82,500.

Copyright © Mometrix Media. You have been licensed one copy of this document for personal use only. Any other reproduction or redistribution is strictly prohibited. All rights reserved.
This content is provided for test preparation purposes only and does not imply an endorsement by Mometrix of any particular political, scientific, or religious point of view.

**29. B:** Isolate the variable on one side of the equal sign by subtracting from each side of the equation. Then, this equation can be solved by performing a cross product: multiply each fraction by the denominator of the other, yielding – $x = 10$, or $x = -10$.

**30. B:** Even though the coin is tossed three times, the results of the second toss have no bearing on the result, because we make no specification as to whether this toss should come up heads (H) or tails (T). The results of the first and third tosses are independent of one another, and for each, the probability that the result will be H is 50%, or ½. The probability of two independent events is the product of their individual probabilities,

**31. A:** First, determine what 1% of the number must be. Then, multiply by 35 to find that 35% of the same number is 0.8 x 35 = 28.

**32. D:** Divide both sides of the equation by 2, yielding $\sqrt[3]{x} = 2$. Eliminate the cube root in this equation by elevating both sides to the third power. This yields the equivalent equation, $x = 2^3 = 8$.

**33. B:** Write an algebraic equation to express the problem. If $n$ is the number described in the problem, then $6n - n^2 = 9$. Rearranging this equation yields $0 = n^2 - 6n + 9$. The expression to the right of the equality sign is a perfect square and is readily factored to yield $0 = (n - 3)^2$. This equation is valid if the expression inside the brackets is equal to zero, that is, if $x - 3 = 0$, or if $x = 3$.

**34. B:** Because the lines AB and CD are the sides of a rectangle, they must be parallel. Therefore, the angle $\angle$AEF is equal to the angle $\angle$COF and is 50°. As AB is a straight line segment, angles $\angle$AEF and $\angle$FEB must total 180°: that is, they are supplementary. Therefore, $\angle$FEB = 180° - 50° = 130°.

**35. B:** A tangent is a line that touches, but does not intersect, a circle or arc. It will have a single point in common with the figure.

**36. A:** Substitute the value 7 for $x$ in the equation. This yields $y = 3(7^2) - 2(7) + 4 = 3(49) - 14 + 4 = 137$.

**37. B:** The area of a rectangle is the product of the width and length. The product of two fractions is the product of the numerators divided by the product of the denominators. The square root of a fraction is the square root of the numerator over that of its denominator. Combining these observations, we have for the area: $\frac{w}{4\sqrt{2}}$.

**38. D:** The surgeon may draw either color the first time. Whichever color he draws first, the situation for the second draw is the same. Eleven gloves remain in the bag, of which 5 are of the same color drawn the first time, and 6 are of the other color. Therefore, the chance of drawing the matching color on the second draw is 5 out of 11.

Copyright © Mometrix Media. You have been licensed one copy of this document for personal use only. Any other reproduction or redistribution is strictly prohibited. All rights reserved.
This content is provided for test preparation purposes only and does not imply an endorsement by Mometrix of any particular political, scientific, or religious point of view.

**39. D:** Isolate the variable in the first equation by subtracting 3 from both sides. This yields $\frac{1}{q} = -3 = -\frac{3}{1}$. Inverting both sides of this equation solves for $q$: $q = -\frac{1}{3}$. Substitute this value into the second expression to determine its value: $6 + 6\left(-\frac{1}{3}\right) = 6 - \frac{6}{3} = 6 - 2 = 4$.

**40. B:** The conditions given in the problem mean that $m$ is positive and that $n$ is negative. The quotient of a positive number and a negative number is always negative.

**41. B:** A fractional exponent indicates a radical. Thus, $x^{\frac{1}{2}} = \sqrt{x}$, $x^{\frac{1}{3}} = \sqrt[3]{x}$, etc. A negative exponent indicates a quantity placed in the denominator. Therefore, $x^{-\frac{1}{2}} = \frac{1}{x^{\frac{1}{2}}} = \frac{1}{\sqrt{x}}$. Substituting 16 for $x$ yields $\frac{1}{\sqrt{16}} = \frac{1}{4}$

**42. D:** The slope of a line is equal to the increase in the $y$ dimension divided by the increase in the $x$ dimension (the *rise* divided by the *run*). Find an interval on the graph with a defined increase in $x$. For example, from $x = 0$ to $x = 2$, $x$ increases *by* 2 units. Measure the increase in $y$ over the same interval: it goes from 1 at $x = 0$ to 2 at $x = 2$, therefore the change in $y$ is 1 unit over that interval. Then, divide $\frac{\text{rise}}{\text{run}} = \frac{\Delta y}{\Delta x} = \frac{1}{2}$.

**43. D:** Since $\sqrt{9} = 3$, the expression is equivalent to $\frac{0.81}{3} = 0.27$.

**44. C:** Solve the equation for $w$ by dividing both sides by the factor 0.07. This yields $w = \frac{V}{0.07}$. Substituting for $V$ yields the solution: $w = \frac{12}{0.07} = 171.4$ lbs.

**45. C:** The hundredth part of a unit is represented by the figure two places to the right of the decimal point, so that rounding to the nearest hundredth means truncating the number at that position. If the last digit is greater than 5, it is rounded upwards. Otherwise, it is rounded downwards. As the last digit in this case is 9 (which represents thousandths of a unit), it is closer to 10 than it is to 0 and is thus rounded upwards.

Copyright © Mometrix Media. You have been licensed one copy of this document for personal use only. Any other reproduction or redistribution is strictly prohibited. All rights reserved. This content is provided for test preparation purposes only and does not imply an endorsement by Mometrix of any particular political, scientific, or religious point of view.

# Practice Test #3

## Section 1 – Verbal Reasoning

*DIRECTIONS: Each of the following questions consists of one word followed by four words. Select the one word whose meaning is closest to the word in capital letters.*

**1. GIMMICK:**

    a. grant
    b. attribute
    c. sign
    d. ploy

**2. HEAVE:**

    a. cure
    b. launch
    c. mound
    d. weigh

**3. LULL:**

    a. calm
    b. bait
    c. bedtime
    d. haul

**4. WRY:**

    a. bread
    b. intent
    c. irate
    d. cynical

**5. CLIMAX:**

    a. hindrance
    b. culmination
    c. enigma
    d. closure

**6. ARROGANT:**

    a. proud
    b. intelligible
    c. dominant
    d. erect

**7. INAUGURATION:**

    a. president
    b. induction
    c. stimulus
    d. grade

189

Copyright © Mometrix Media. You have been licensed one copy of this document for personal use only. Any other reproduction or redistribution is strictly prohibited. All rights reserved.
This content is provided for test preparation purposes only and does not imply an endorsement by Mometrix of any particular political, scientific, or religious point of view.

**8. MAUDLIN:**
 a. immature
 b. pragmatic
 c. gaunt
 d. sentimental

**9. PIOUS:**
 a. pathetic
 b. shrill
 c. snide
 d. devout

**10. RESUSCITATE:**
 a. revere
 b. breathe
 c. revive
 d. answer

**11. vehement:**
 a. troubled
 b. intense
 c. changeable
 d. obstinate

**12. diatribe:**
 a. criticism
 b. apology
 c. commend
 d. merit

**13. cogitate:**
 a. surprise
 b. endanger
 c. confuse
 d. deliberate

**14. invidious:**
 a. offensive
 b. pleasant
 c. ornate
 d. infectious

**15. hyperbole:**
 a. reference
 b. amendment
 c. exaggeration
 d. demarcation

Copyright © Mometrix Media. You have been licensed one copy of this document for personal use only. Any other reproduction or redistribution is strictly prohibited. All rights reserved. This content is provided for test preparation purposes only and does not imply an endorsement by Mometrix of any particular political, scientific, or religious point of view.

# Mometrix

**16. innocuous:**
  a. harmful
  b. innocent
  c. scandalous
  d. hidden

**17. capricious:**
  a. steady
  b. unpredictable
  c. pleasant
  d. violent

**18. intermittent:**
  a. occasional
  b. intense
  c. frequent
  d. bursts

**19. SOLITARY:**
  a. single
  b. solid
  c. sturdy
  d. stoic

**20. precipitous:**
  a. rugged
  b. dangerous
  c. steep
  d. wet

*DIRECTIONS: Select the word(s) that best fit the meaning of each sentence.*

**21. Anne felt that taking vitamin supplements daily would have a _____ effect, that is, it would promote health and well-being.**
  a. cognitive
  b. mercurial
  c. salubrious
  d. loquacious

**22. Hanley's race car produced a _____ amount of noise, more than any of the other vehicles.**
  a. prodigal
  b. redundant
  c. quantitative
  d. prodigious

191

Copyright © Mometrix Media. You have been licensed one copy of this document for personal use only. Any other reproduction or redistribution is strictly prohibited. All rights reserved. This content is provided for test preparation purposes only and does not imply an endorsement by Mometrix of any particular political, scientific, or religious point of view.

**23.** Most of us did not feel that Carmen was cut out to be a trial lawyer, given her _____ for _____ any kind of confrontation.

    a. ambition .. influencing
    b. regard .. negotiating
    c. habit .. protesting
    d. penchant .. avoiding

**24.** Samantha had a _____ appetite and went through all the food we had brought in one night.

    a. fragile
    b. minute
    c. voracious
    d. fastidious

**25.** She had many reasons for choosing to _____ a year of her life putting her _____ variety of skills to work for others.

    a. donate .. immense
    b. lose .. single
    c. summarize .. cavernous
    d. fashion .. industrial

**26.** Anthony was a _____ individual, whose _____ eyes always gave the impression that he had recently lost something dear to him.

    a. gleeful .. laughing
    b. hot-headed .. flashing
    c. tall .. glinting
    d. lugubrious .. mournful

**27.** He could not understand Della's _____, her constant locking of doors and windows as if to protect herself from some _____ threat.

    a. paranoia .. unspecified
    b. glee .. manifest
    c. actions .. global
    d. kindness .. imminent

**28.** Jeremy was considered _____ child by his teachers because he was noisy and often stubbornly defiant.

    a. a model
    b. a capricious
    c. an obstreperous
    d. a saturnine

**29.** Nesting from sea level to 2000 feet, willow flycatchers favor open or bushy areas over heavily _____ habitats.

    a. closeted
    b. timbered
    c. rainy
    d. mountainous

Copyright © Mometrix Media. You have been licensed one copy of this document for personal use only. Any other reproduction or redistribution is strictly prohibited. All rights reserved. This content is provided for test preparation purposes only and does not imply an endorsement by Mometrix of any particular political, scientific, or religious point of view.

**30. Solar flare activity is notoriously variable: _____ flare-ups may continue for days, only to be followed by lengthy periods of _____.**

   a. huge..discharge
   b. prolix..irruption
   c. violent..quiescence
   d. magma..dissolution

**31. A man of questionable morals, he had such a reputation for _____ that I gave _____ to nothing that he told me.**

   a. duplicity..credence
   b. sapience..payment
   c. incisiveness..doubt
   d. rapaciousness..contrition

**32. After the election, the winning candidate took a _____ tone in his remarks about his _____ rival.**

   a. cathartic..malignant
   b. conciliatory..defeated
   c. verbose..barnstorming
   d. laudatory..victorious

**33. When she was angry, she would sit quietly at the back of the room, _____ at everyone.**

   a. nictating
   b. flinching
   c. ruminating
   d. glowering

**34. The ____ of the rainbow were ____ against the bright blue sky.**

   a. Textures, Clear
   b. Hues, Vivid
   c. Alabaster, Bright
   d. Line, Dark

**35. The president has a ____ of ____ around him when he makes public appearances.**

   a. Catalyst, Individuals
   b. Barrier, Contrast
   c. Hedge, Protection
   d. Derrick, Protection

**36. The books subject matter was ____ to the ____, and it did not sell.**

   a. Attractive, Masses
   b. Limited, People
   c. Loathsome, Masses
   d. Colorful, Individual

Copyright © Mometrix Media. You have been licensed one copy of this document for personal use only. Any other reproduction or redistribution is strictly prohibited. All rights reserved.
This content is provided for test preparation purposes only and does not imply an endorsement by Mometrix of any particular political, scientific, or religious point of view.

**37. The kitten was soaked to the _____ from the ___.**

    a.   Skin, Abyss
    b.   Skin, Craven
    c.   Skin, Storm
    d.   Hide, Abyss

**38. The French exchange student spoke English as if it were her first language. She was**

    a.   Dandy
    b.   Fluent
    c.   Caustic
    d.   Talented

**39. The prescription plan did not cover name brand drugs if there was a _____ substitute available.**

    a.   Generic
    b.   Reasonable
    c.   Compatible
    d.   Complete

**40. The siblings found _____ in each other as they ___ the good times with their father.**

    a.   Happiness, Prepared
    b.   Sorrow, Committed
    c.   Solace, Remembered
    d.   Sorrow, Limited

Copyright © Mometrix Media. You have been licensed one copy of this document for personal use only. Any other reproduction or redistribution is strictly prohibited. All rights reserved.
This content is provided for test preparation purposes only and does not imply an endorsement by Mometrix of any particular political, scientific, or religious point of view.

## Section 2 – Quantitative Reasoning

*DIRECTIONS: In this section there are four possible answers after each question. Choose which one is best.*

**1. 11/12 – 1/6 =**

    a.  1/4
    b.  1/2
    c.  3/4
    d.  5/6

**2. Kate got a 56 on her first math test. On her second math test, she raised her grade by 12%. What was her grade?**

    a.  62.7
    b.  67.2
    c.  68.0
    d.  72.3

**3. If one side of a square has a length of 56 cm, what is its perimeter?**

    a.  112 cm
    b.  224 cm
    c.  448 cm
    d.  3136 cm

**4. Four people decide to adopt a dog and take turns caring for it. Person A thinks he can take care of the dog 1/4 of the time; person B thinks she can handle 1/8; person C thinks he can take care of the dog 1/2 of the time. What part is left for the fourth person to cover?**

    a.  1/8
    b.  1/4
    c.  1/3
    d.  1/2

**5. A skyscraper is 548 meters high. The building's owners decide to increase its height by 3%. How high would the skyscraper be after the increase?**

    a.  551 meters
    b.  555 meters
    c.  562 meters
    d.  564 meters

**6. 275 – (-64) – 32 =**

    a.  179
    b.  243
    c.  307
    d.  371

Copyright © Mometrix Media. You have been licensed one copy of this document for personal use only. Any other reproduction or redistribution is strictly prohibited. All rights reserved.
This content is provided for test preparation purposes only and does not imply an endorsement by Mometrix of any particular political, scientific, or religious point of view.

**7.** $9x – 3y + 8xy – 3$

    If $x = 10$ and $y = -2$, what is the value of this expression?

    a.  -67
    b.  -61
    c.  -79
    d.  241

**8. Simplify the following:** $9x (3x^2 + 2x - 9)$

    a.  $27x^2 + 18x - 81$
    b.  $27x^3 + 18x^2 – 81x$
    c.  $12x^3 + 11x^2 - x$
    d.  $27x^3 + 18x^2 – 18x$

**9. Evaluate the following expression, if $x = 3$.**

    $x^5 x^2 + y^0 =$

    a.  59,049
    b.  59,050
    c.  2,187
    d.  2,188

**10.** $x^2 + 12x + 36 = 0$

What is the value of $x$?

    a.  $x = 6$
    b.  $x = -6$
    c.  $x = 6, -6$
    d.  $x = 0, 6$

**11. Simplify the following expression.**

$$\frac{64x^4 + 8x^3 - 4x^2 + 16x}{8x}$$

    a.  $56x^3 – 12x^2 + 8$
    b.  $8x^3 + x^2 – (1/2)x + 2$
    c.  $8x^4 + x^3 – (1/2)x^2 + 2x$
    d.  $8x^3 + x^2 – 2x + 2$

**12. Factor the following expression.**

    $9x^2y - 18xy - 27y$

    a.  $9(x^2y – 2xy – 3y)$
    b.  $9y(x + 3)(x + 1)$
    c.  $9y(x - 3)(x+1)$
    d.  $9y(x + 3)(x – 1)$

Copyright © Mometrix Media. You have been licensed one copy of this document for personal use only. Any other reproduction or redistribution is strictly prohibited. All rights reserved.
This content is provided for test preparation purposes only and does not imply an endorsement by Mometrix of any particular political, scientific, or religious point of view.

13. Simplify the following expression.

$$\sqrt{3}(5\sqrt{3} - \sqrt{12} + \sqrt{10})$$

   a. $9 + \sqrt{30}$
   b. $15 - \sqrt{15} + \sqrt{13}$
   c. $15\sqrt{3} - 3\sqrt{12} + 3\sqrt{10}$
   d. $3 - \sqrt{13}$

14. A line passes through points A (-3, 18) and B (5, 2). What is the slope of the line?

   a. 2
   b. -2
   c. 1/2
   d. -1/2

15. What is the midpoint of points A (-20, 8) and B (5, 3)?

   a. (5.5, 7.5)
   b. (7.5, 5.5)
   c. (5.5, -7.5)
   d. (-7.5, 5.5)

16. A rectangle is twice as long as it is wide. If the width is 3 meters, what is the area in m²?

   a. 12 m²
   b. 6 m²
   c. 9 m²
   d. 18 m²

17. There are an equal number of boys and girls in Mrs. McCarthy's class. The average height of the boys is 110 cm. The average height of the entire class is 105 cm. What is the average height, in centimeters, of the girls in Mrs. McCarthy's class?

   a. 90 cm
   b. 95 cm
   c. 100 cm
   d. 105 cm

18. Examine (a), (b), and (c) and select the best answer.

   (a) $\frac{3}{5}$     (b) $\frac{40}{50}$     c) $\frac{8}{50}$

   a. a > b > c
   b. a = b = c
   c. a < b > c
   d. a < b < c

19. What number subtracted from 80 leaves one-third the product of 5 and 12?

   a. 25
   b. 35
   c. 40
   d. 60

Copyright © Mometrix Media. You have been licensed one copy of this document for personal use only. Any other reproduction or redistribution is strictly prohibited. All rights reserved.
This content is provided for test preparation purposes only and does not imply an endorsement by Mometrix of any particular political, scientific, or religious point of view.

**20. Examine (a), (b), and (c) and find the best answer. Consider only the magnitude of each measurement.**

       (a) The perimeter of a rectangle with length of 6 cm and width of 4 cm
       (b) The perimeter of a square with sides 4 cm long
       (c) The area of a square with sides 4 cm long

   a.  (b) > (c)
   b.  = (b) = (c)
   c.  (b) = (c)
   d.  (b) < (c)

*DIRECTIONS: In questions 21–35, note the given information, if any, and then compare the quantity in Column A to the quantity in Column B. Answer as follows:*

*A  if the quantity in Column A is greater*

*B  if the quantity in Column B is greater*

*C  if the two quantities are equal*

*D  if the relationship cannot be determined from the information given*

**21.**

| Column A | Column B |
| --- | --- |
| The number of minutes in 3.5 hours | The number of days in 30 weeks |

**22.**

| Column A | Column B |
| --- | --- |
| $4^8$ | $8^4$ |

**23.**

| Column A | Column B |
| --- | --- |
| Probability of selecting a given name out of a hat containing 17 names | 0.07 |

**24.**

| Column A | Column B |
| --- | --- |
| $-\lvert -9 \rvert - 2$ | 7 |

**25. x is a positive integer**

    $x/y = 1/6$

| Column A | Column B |
| --- | --- |
| $y$ | 6 |

**26. Before the Smiths added on to their house, their square footage was 25% less than that of the Wilsons. After the Smiths added on to their house, their square footage was 25% more than it had been.**

| Column A | Column B |
| --- | --- |
| Square footage of the Smiths' house | Square footage of the Wilsons' house |

Copyright © Mometrix Media. You have been licensed one copy of this document for personal use only. Any other reproduction or redistribution is strictly prohibited. All rights reserved.
This content is provided for test preparation purposes only and does not imply an endorsement by Mometrix of any particular political, scientific, or religious point of view.

**27.** x < y < -1

| Column A | Column B |
|---|---|
| $(2x - 2y)(4x + 4y)$ | $x^2 - y^2$ |

**28. s and t are integers**

$2|s| = 2t$

| Column A | Column B |
|---|---|
| s | t |

**29. x and y are positive**

$x/y > 4$

| Column A | Column B |
|---|---|
| y | 0.2x |

**30.**

| Column A | Column B |
|---|---|
| $-2^6$ | $(-2)^6$ |

**31. Turtle travels at 3 mph; Rabbit travels at 25 mph**

| Column A | Column B |
|---|---|
| Time for turtle to travel 15 miles | Time for rabbit to travel 100 miles |

**32.** $n^2 = 25$

| Column A | Column B |
|---|---|
| n | 5 |

**33. The calories in 6 cups of coffee, each with 3 spoons of sugar equals the calories of 4 cups of coffee, each with 5 spoons of sugar**

| Column A | Column B |
|---|---|
| calories in a cup of coffee | calories in a spoon of sugar |

**34.** *x < 0*

| Column A | Column B |
|---|---|
| $x^2$ | $x^3$ |

**35. The sum of three consecutive integers is 114**

| Column A | Column B |
|---|---|
| 39 | The smallest number of the three |

Copyright © Mometrix Media. You have been licensed one copy of this document for personal use only. Any other reproduction or redistribution is strictly prohibited. All rights reserved.
This content is provided for test preparation purposes only and does not imply an endorsement by Mometrix of any particular political, scientific, or religious point of view.

## Section 3 – Reading Comprehension

*DIRECTIONS: Read each passage carefully and then answer the questions pertaining to it. For each question, decide on the basis of the passage which one of the choices best answers the question.*

*Questions 1 to 6 pertain to the following passage:*

The immune system is a network of cells, tissues, and organs that defends the body against attacks by foreign invaders. These invaders are primarily microbes—tiny organisms such as bacteria, parasites, and fungi—that can cause infections. Viruses also cause infections, but are too primitive to be classified as living organisms. The human body provides an ideal environment for many microbes. It is the immune system's job to keep the microbes out or destroy them.

The immune system is amazingly complex. It can recognize and remember millions of different enemies, and it can secrete fluids and cells to wipe out nearly all of them. The secret to its success is an elaborate and dynamic communications network. Millions of cells, organized into sets and subsets, gather and transfer information in response to an infection. Once immune cells receive the alarm, they produce powerful chemicals that help to regulate their own growth and behavior, enlist other immune cells, and direct the new recruits to trouble spots.

Although scientists have learned much about the immune system, they continue to puzzle over how the body destroys invading microbes, infected cells, and tumors without harming healthy tissues. New technologies for identifying individual immune cells are now allowing scientists to determine quickly which targets are triggering an immune response. Improvements in microscopy are permitting the first-ever observations of living B cells, T cells, and other cells as they interact within lymph nodes and other body tissues.

In addition, scientists are rapidly unraveling the genetic blueprints that direct the human immune response, as well as those that dictate the biology of bacteria, viruses, and parasites. The combination of new technology with expanded genetic information will no doubt reveal even more about how the body protects itself from disease.

### 1. What is the main idea of the passage?
 a. Scientists fully understand the immune system.
 b. The immune system triggers the production of fluids.
 c. The body is under constant invasion by malicious microbes.
 d. The immune system protects the body from infection.

### 2. Which statement is *not* a detail from the passage?
 a. Most invaders of the body are microbes.
 b. The immune system relies on excellent communication.
 c. Viruses are extremely sophisticated.
 d. The cells of the immune system are organized.

Copyright © Mometrix Media. You have been licensed one copy of this document for personal use only. Any other reproduction or redistribution is strictly prohibited. All rights reserved. This content is provided for test preparation purposes only and does not imply an endorsement by Mometrix of any particular political, scientific, or religious point of view.

**3. What is the meaning of the word *ideal* as it is used in the first paragraph?**
   a. thoughtful
   b. confined
   c. hostile
   d. perfect

**4. Which statement is *not* a detail from the passage?**
   a. Scientists can now see T cells.
   b. The immune system ignores tumors.
   c. The ability of the immune system to fight disease without harming the body remains mysterious.
   d. The immune system remembers millions of different invaders.

**5. What is the meaning of the word *enlist* as it is used in the second paragraph?**
   a. call into service
   b. write down
   c. send away
   d. put across

**6. What is the author's primary purpose in writing the essay?**
   a. to persuade
   b. to analyze
   c. to inform
   d. to entertain

*Questions 7 to 14 pertain to the following passage:*

Plastics have long been considered one of the great conveniences of the modern era, but evidence is mounting to indicate that these conveniences have come at an incredible cost. The <u>chief</u> benefit of plastics is their <u>durability</u>, but this benefit turns out to be the same reason plastic has become a significant problem: It takes between *two and four hundred years* to decompose. All of this plastic has accumulated into a catastrophic mess and has also caused disease in humans.

Between Hawaii and Japan, a giant mass of plastic twice the size of Texas slowly swirls with the currents of the Pacific Ocean. This area has come to be known as the Great Pacific Garbage Patch, and its effects on the ecology of the ocean are unimaginable. According to United Nations researchers, a hundred thousand sea mammals and a million seabirds die each year. They are found with cigarette lighters, syringes, and other plastics that they mistake for food in their stomachs. Evidence also indicates that the plastic we store our food in poses health risks. For instance, phthalates (pronounced "THEY-lates") have been shown to have detrimental effects on the reproductive system, yet they are found in many plastic products—including baby bottles and water bottles. They have also been linked to various forms of cancer. Additionally, a chemical called bisphenol A that is found in many plastics can <u>mimic</u> the effects of the hormone estrogen, which can also affect the reproductive system.

In short, plastics may turn out to be a lot less convenient than they seem!

Copyright © Mometrix Media. You have been licensed one copy of this document for personal use only. Any other reproduction or redistribution is strictly prohibited. All rights reserved. This content is provided for test preparation purposes only and does not imply an endorsement by Mometrix of any particular political, scientific, or religious point of view.

**7. Which of the following best describes the author's purpose in writing this passage?**

    a. To persuade readers to accept the author's point of view.
    b. To explain the benefits of plastic.
    c. To explain the risks of plastic bottles.
    d. To inform the reader of the effects of phthalates in plastics.

**8. As used in this passage, the word "chief" most nearly means:**

    a. Main
    b. Least likely
    c. Benefit
    d. Leader of a Native American tribe

**9. Which of the following statements can be inferred from paragraph two?**

    a. The Great Pacific Garbage Patch is not a significant threat to humans.
    b. No one has determined why sea mammals and seabirds are dying at an alarming rate.
    c. The Great Pacific Garbage Patch is too large to be cleaned up by one country.
    d. Ocean currents carry the plastic to the middle of the ocean.

**10. Which of the following statements best summarizes the main idea of this passage?**

    a. The benefits of plastics outweigh their risks.
    b. Plastics pose a significant threat to humans and other living creatures.
    c. Phthalates should not be used in baby bottles.
    d. Plastics decompose very slowly.

**11. As used in this passage, the word "mimic" most nearly means:**

    a. Reduce
    b. Cancerous
    c. Intensify
    d. Resemble

**12. What particular risk does the author say the Great Pacific Garbage Patch poses to marine animals?**

    a. It affects yearly temperature averages.
    b. Animals accidentally ingest the plastics and die.
    c. The animals' habitat is poisoned by phthalates.
    d. Seabirds cannot get to the fish below the garbage.

**13. Why does this passage not discuss more of plastics' benefits?**

    a. Plastics have no benefits.
    b. The passage emphasizes the dangers over the benefits in order to prove that plastics are harmful.
    c. The passage devotes a significant amount of attention to the benefits of plastics.
    d. Discussing the benefits would contradict the author's point that plastics are a necessary evil.

**14. According to the passage, the word "durability" most nearly means:**

    a. Decomposition
    b. Permanence
    c. Coloration
    d. Poisonous

Copyright © Mometrix Media. You have been licensed one copy of this document for personal use only. Any other reproduction or redistribution is strictly prohibited. All rights reserved.
This content is provided for test preparation purposes only and does not imply an endorsement by Mometrix of any particular political, scientific, or religious point of view.

*Questions 15 to 23 pertain to the following passage:*

Daylight Saving Time (DST) is the practice of changing clocks so that afternoons have more daylight and mornings have less. Clocks are adjusted forward one hour in the spring and one hour backward in the fall. The main purpose of the change is to make better use of daylight.

DST began with the goal of conservation. Benjamin Franklin suggested it as a method of saving on candles. It was used during both World Wars to save energy for military needs. Although DST's potential to save energy was a primary reason behind its implementation, research into its effects on energy conservation are contradictory and unclear.

Beneficiaries of DST include all activities that can benefit from more sunlight after working hours, such as shopping and sports. A 1984 issue of *Fortune* magazine estimated that a seven-week extension of DST would yield an additional $30 million for 7-Eleven stores. Public safety may be increased by the use of DST: some research suggests that traffic fatalities may be reduced when there is additional afternoon sunlight.

On the other hand, DST complicates timekeeping and some computer systems. Tools with built-in time-keeping functions such as medical devices can be affected negatively. Agricultural and evening entertainment interests have historically opposed DST.

DST can affect health, both positively and negatively. It provides more afternoon sunlight in which to get exercise. It also impacts sunlight exposure; this is good for getting vitamin D, but bad in that it can increase skin cancer risk. DST may also disrupt sleep.

Today, daylight saving time has been adopted by more than one billion people in about 70 countries. DST is generally not observed in countries near the equator because sunrise times do not vary much there. Asia and Africa do not generally observe it. Some countries, such as Brazil, observe it only in some regions.

DST can lead to peculiar situations. One of these occurred in November, 2007 when a woman in North Carolina gave birth to one twin at 1:32 a.m. and, 34 minutes later, to the second twin. Because of DST and the time change at 2:00 a.m., the second twin was officially born at 1:06, 26 minutes earlier than her brother.

## 15. According to the passage, what is the main purpose of DST?
   a. To increase public safety
   b. To benefit retail businesses
   c. To make better use of daylight
   d. To promote good health

## 16. Which of the following is NOT mentioned in the passage as a negative effect of DST?
   a. Energy conservation
   b. Complications with time keeping
   c. Complications with computer systems
   d. Increased skin cancer risk

Copyright © Mometrix Media. You have been licensed one copy of this document for personal use only. Any other reproduction or redistribution is strictly prohibited. All rights reserved.
This content is provided for test preparation purposes only and does not imply an endorsement by Mometrix of any particular political, scientific, or religious point of view.

**17. The article states that DST involves:**

   a. Adjusting clocks forward one hour in the spring and the fall.
   b. Adjusting clocks backward one hour in the spring and the fall.
   c. Adjusting clocks forward in the fall and backward in the spring.
   d. Adjusting clocks forward in the spring and backward in the fall.

**18. Which interests have historically opposed DST, according to the passage?**

   a. retail businesses and sports
   b. evening entertainment and agriculture
   c. 7-Eleven and health
   d. medical devices and computing

**19. According to the article, increased sunlight exposure:**

   a. is only good for health.
   b. is only bad for health.
   c. has no effect on health.
   d. can be both good and bad for health.

**20. The article states that DST is observed only in some regions in which of the following?**

   a. The equator
   b. Asia
   c. Africa
   d. Brazil

**21. What is an example given in the passage of a peculiar situation that DST has caused?**

   a. sleep disruption
   b. driving confusion
   c. twin birth order complications
   d. countries with DST only in certain regions

**22. According to the passage, a 1984 magazine article estimated that a seven-week extension of DST would provide 7-Eleven stores with an extra $30 million. Approximately how much extra money is that per week of the extension?**

   a. 42,000
   b. 420,000
   c. 4,200,000
   d. 42,000,000

**23. For what purpose did Benjamin Franklin first suggest DST?**

   a. to save money for military needs
   b. to save candles
   c. to reduce traffic fatalities
   d. to promote reading

*Questions 24 to 35 pertain to the following passage:*

We don't usually think of coins as works of art, and most of them really do not invite us to do so. The study of coins, their development and history, is termed *numismatics*. Numismatics is a topic of great interest to archeologists and anthropologists, but not usually from the perspective of visual delectation. The coin

Copyright © Mometrix Media. You have been licensed one copy of this document for personal use only. Any other reproduction or redistribution is strictly prohibited. All rights reserved. This content is provided for test preparation purposes only and does not imply an endorsement by Mometrix of any particular political, scientific, or religious point of view.

is intended, after all, to be a utilitarian object, not an artistic one. Many early Greek coins are aesthetically pleasing as well as utilitarian, however, and not simply because they are the earliest examples of coin design. Rather, Greek civic individualism provides the reason. Every Greek political entity expressed its identity through its coinage.

The idea of stamping metal pellets of a standard weight with an identifying design had its origin on the Ionian Peninsula around 600 B.C. Each of the Greek city-states produced its own coinage adorned with its particular symbols. The designs were changed frequently to commemorate battles, treaties, and other significant occasions. In addition to their primary use as a pragmatic means of facilitating commerce, Greek coins were clearly an expression of civic pride. The popularity of early coinage led to a constant demand for new designs, such that there arose a class of highly skilled artisans who took great pride in their work, so much so that they sometimes even signed it. As a result, Greek coins provide us not only with an invaluable source of historical knowledge, but also with a genuine expression of the evolving Greek sense of form. These minuscule works reflect the development of Greek sculpture from the sixth to the second century B.C. as dependably as do larger works made of marble. And since they are stamped with the place and date of their production, they provide an historic record of artistic development that is remarkably dependable and complete.

**24. What is the purpose of this passage?**
   a. To attract new adherents to numismatics as a pastime.
   b. To show how ancient Greeks used coins in commerce.
   c. To teach the reader that money was invented in Greece.
   d. To describe ancient Greek coinage as an art form

**25. What is meant by the phrase "most of them really do not invite us to do so," as used in the first sentence?**
   a. Money is not usually included when sending an invitation.
   b. Most coins are not particularly attractive.
   c. Invitations are not generally engraved onto coins.
   d. Coins do not speak.

**26. What is a synonym for "delectation", as used in the third sentence?**
   a. Savoring
   b. Choosing
   c. Deciding
   d. Refusing

**27. What is meant by the term numismatics?**
   a. The study of numbers
   b. Egyptian history
   c. Greek history
   d. The study of coins

Copyright © Mometrix Media. You have been licensed one copy of this document for personal use only. Any other reproduction or redistribution is strictly prohibited. All rights reserved.
This content is provided for test preparation purposes only and does not imply an endorsement by Mometrix of any particular political, scientific, or religious point of view.

28. **According to the text, how do ancient Greek coins differ from most other coinage?**
    a. They are different simply because they were the first coins.
    b. Each political entity made its own coins.
    c. They were made of precious metals.
    d. They were designed with extraordinary care.

29. **How often were new coins designed in ancient Greece?**
    a. Monthly
    b. Not very often.
    c. Whenever there was a significant occasion to commemorate.
    d. When the old ones wore out.

30. **What is indicated by the fact that the artisans who designed the coins sometimes signed them?**
    a. They took pride in their work.
    b. They were being held accountable for their work.
    c. The signature certified the value of the coin.
    d. The Greeks had developed writing.

31. **What is meant by the term *pragmatic, as used in the fourth sentence of the second paragraph*?**
    a. Valuable
    b. Monetary
    c. Useful
    d. Practical

32. **According to the passage, how are Greek coins similar to Greek sculpture?**
    a. Some sculptures were made of metal.
    b. The coins were smaller.
    c. Shapes were stamped into the coins.
    d. Coin designs evolved along with the Greek sense of form.

33. **Why is it significant that new coin designs were required frequently?**
    a. This indicates that there was a lot of commercial activity going on.
    b. This gave the designers a lot of practice.
    c. There were a lot of things to commemorate.
    d. The Greeks needed to find new sources of precious metals.

34. **Why is it significant that the coins were dated, according to the passage?**
    a. The dates contributed to the designs
    b. The age of the designers could be determined.
    c. It allows historians to track the evolution of Greek artistic styles.
    d. It allows historians to know when battles and treaties took place.

35. **What was the primary purpose of the Greek coin?**
    a. To commemorate treaties and battles.
    b. To provide minuscule works of art.
    c. They were used as adornments.
    d. To facilitate commerce.

Copyright © Mometrix Media. You have been licensed one copy of this document for personal use only. Any other reproduction or redistribution is strictly prohibited. All rights reserved.
This content is provided for test preparation purposes only and does not imply an endorsement by Mometrix of any particular political, scientific, or religious point of view.

*Questions 36 to 40 pertain to the following passage:*

The phylum Annelida, named for the Latin word *anellus*, meaning "ring", includes earthworms, leeches, and other similar organisms. In their typical form, these animals exhibit bilateral symmetry, a cylindrical cross section, and an elongate body divided externally into segments (*metameres*) by a series of rings (*annuli*). They are segmented internally as well, with most of the internal organs repeated in series in each segment. This organization is termed *metamerism*. Metameric segmentation is the distinguishing feature of this phylum, and provides it with a degree of evolutionary plasticity in that certain segments can be modified and specialized to perform specific functions. For example, in some species certain of the locomotor *parapodia*, or feet, may be modified for grasping, and some portions of the gut may evolve digestive specializations.

The gut is a straight, muscular tube that functions independently of the muscular activity in the body wall. The Annelida resemble the nematodes, another worm phylum, in possessing a fluid-filled internal cavity separating the gut from the body wall. In both phyla, this cavity is involved in locomotion. However, in the annelids, this space is formed at a much later time during the development of the embryo, and presumably evolved much later as well. This fluid-filled internal space is called a true *coelom*.

The annelid excretory and circulatory systems are well developed, and some members of the phylum have evolved respiratory organs. The nervous system offers a particular example of metameric specialization. It is concentrated anteriorly into enlarged cerebral ganglia connected to a ventral nerve cord that extends posteriorly and is organized into repeating segmental ganglia.

This phylum includes members bearing adaptations required for aquatic (marine or freshwater) or terrestrial habitats. They may be free-living entities or exist as parasites. Among the best known are the earthworm *Lumbricus*, the water leech *Hirudo*, and the marine worm *Nereis*.

**36. What is the purpose of this passage?**
   a.  To describe the annelid nervous system.
   b.  To describe the annelid digestive system.
   c.  To introduce distinctive features of annelid anatomy.
   d.  To define metamerism.

**37. What is meant by the term *metamerism*?**
   a.  Segmentation of the anatomy
   b.  A series of rings
   c.  Bilateral symmetry
   d.  Evolutionary plasticity

**38. What is meant by the term *parapodia*?**
   a.  Specialization
   b.  Appendages
   c.  Locomotion
   d.  Metameres

Copyright © Mometrix Media. You have been licensed one copy of this document for personal use only. Any other reproduction or redistribution is strictly prohibited. All rights reserved.
This content is provided for test preparation purposes only and does not imply an endorsement by Mometrix of any particular political, scientific, or religious point of view.

39. **Which of the following is one evolutionary advantage of segmentation?**
   a.  segmented animals have many feet.
   b.  segmented animals have a fluid-filled coelom.
   c.  parts of some segments can become specialized to perform certain functions.
   d.  segments can evolve.

40. **A group of worms other than the Annelida are called**
   a.  Lumbricus
   b.  Nematodes
   c.  Leeches
   d.  Parapodia

Copyright © Mometrix Media. You have been licensed one copy of this document for personal use only. Any other reproduction or redistribution is strictly prohibited. All rights reserved. This content is provided for test preparation purposes only and does not imply an endorsement by Mometrix of any particular political, scientific, or religious point of view.

## Section 4 – Mathematics Achievement

*DIRECTIONS: In this section there are four possible answers after each question. Choose which one is best.*

**1. Two even integers and one odd integer are multiplied together. Which of the following could be their product?**

    a.  3.75
    b.  9
    c.  16.2
    d.  24

**2. If $520 \div x = 40n$, then which of the following is equal to $nx$?**

    a.  13
    b.  40nx
    c.  26
    d.  40

**3. Linda had 76 books at her yard sale. She had 16 customers. If 12 books remain unsold, what is the average number of books purchased by each customer?**

    a.  2
    b.  4
    c.  6
    d.  8

**4. Class starts at 9:00 a.m. John arrives 26 minutes early. The teacher arrives 30 minutes later. What time does the teacher arrive at class?**

    a.  9:04 p.m.
    b.  8:34 a.m.
    c.  9:34 a.m.
    d.  9:04 a.m.

**5. Which of the following is NOT less than .33?**

    a.  4/15
    b.  13/45
    c.  26/81
    d.  4/9

**6. If $a - 16 = 8b + 6$, what does $a + 3$ equal?**

    a.  b + 3
    b.  8b + 9
    c.  8b + 22
    d.  8b + 25

Copyright © Mometrix Media. You have been licensed one copy of this document for personal use only. Any other reproduction or redistribution is strictly prohibited. All rights reserved.
This content is provided for test preparation purposes only and does not imply an endorsement by Mometrix of any particular political, scientific, or religious point of view.

7. In the figure below, angles *b* and *d* are equal. What is the degree measure of angle *d*?

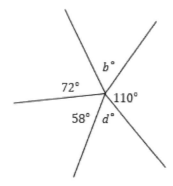

a. 240°
b. 120°
c. 80°
d. 60°

8. A man walked continuously across a desert at 2.5 miles per hour for 3 days. How many miles did he walk?

a. 180 miles
b. 120 miles
c. 90 miles
d. 12 miles

9. Janice weighs *x* pounds. Elaina weighs 23 pounds more than Janice. June weighs 14 pounds more than Janice. In terms of *x*, what is the sum of their weights minus 25 pounds?

a. 3x + 37
b. 3x + 12
c. x + 12
d. 3x - 25

10. A bag contains 14 blue, 6 red, 12 green and 8 purple buttons. 25 buttons are removed from the bag randomly. How many of the removed buttons were red if the chance of drawing a red button from the bag is now $1/3$?

a. 0
b. 1
c. 3
d. 5

11. A washing machine makes 85 revolutions per minute on the spin cycle. If the washing machine spends 15 minutes on the spin cycle per wash, how many washes will it take to reach 100,000 revolutions (rounded to the nearest whole number)?

a. 1,275
b. 1,175
c. 100
d. 78

Copyright © Mometrix Media. You have been licensed one copy of this document for personal use only. Any other reproduction or redistribution is strictly prohibited. All rights reserved.
This content is provided for test preparation purposes only and does not imply an endorsement by Mometrix of any particular political, scientific, or religious point of view.

12. Solve the following equation:  $(y + 1)(y + 2)(y + 3)$

    a.  $y^3 + y^2 + 3y + 2$
    b.  $y^3 + 3y^2 + 6y + 3$
    c.  $y^3 + 6y^2 + 11y + 6$
    d.  $8y^3 + 6y + 8$

13. What is the area of the parallelogram in the figure below?

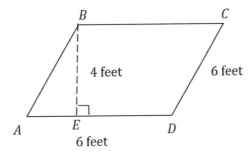

    a.  10 square feet
    b.  12 square feet
    c.  16 square feet
    d.  24 square feet

14. 50 students are enrolled in both English and Math. 90 students are enrolled in either English or Math. If 25 students are enrolled in English, but not Math, how many students are enrolled in Math but not English?

    a.  15
    b.  25
    c.  50
    d.  65

15. If a savings account earns 3.75% simple interest, how much interest will a deposit of $2,500 earn in one month?

    a.  $93.75
    b.  $666.67
    c.  $2,503.75
    d.  $2,593.75

Copyright © Mometrix Media. You have been licensed one copy of this document for personal use only. Any other reproduction or redistribution is strictly prohibited. All rights reserved.
This content is provided for test preparation purposes only and does not imply an endorsement by Mometrix of any particular political, scientific, or religious point of view.

**16.** In the figure below, *AD* = 5 and *AB* = 12.  What is the length of *AC* (not shown)?

   a.  10
   b.  13
   c.  17
   d.  60

**17.** Convert 12.5% to a fraction.
   a.  1/3
   b.  1/8
   c.  3/8
   d.  5/8

**18.** Rick scores 95%, 68%, 86%, 83%, 64%, 92%, and 79% on his math tests over the semester. When calculating students' semester averages, Rick's teacher disregards each student's highest and lowest score. What is Rick's average test score?
   a.  57.71%
   b.  75.5%
   c.  80.8%
   d.  81.6%

**19.** Five dice are rolled together one time. What is the probability of rolling five 6s?
   a.  $1/6$
   b.  1/30
   c.  5/6
   d.  1/7,776

**20.** Simplify the following equation:  $4(6 - 3)^2 - (-2)$
   a.  34
   b.  38
   c.  42
   d.  48

**21.** On a highway map, the scale indicates that 1 inch represents 45 miles. If the distance on the map is 3.2 inches, how far is the actual distance?
   a.  45 miles
   b.  54 miles
   c.  112 miles
   d.  144 miles

Copyright © Mometrix Media. You have been licensed one copy of this document for personal use only. Any other reproduction or redistribution is strictly prohibited. All rights reserved.
This content is provided for test preparation purposes only and does not imply an endorsement by Mometrix of any particular political, scientific, or religious point of view.

22. In the figure below, find the value of *x*:

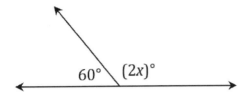

$60°$ $(2x)°$

a. 30
b. 60
c. 100
d. 120

23. In the number 6,502,104.9738, what digit is in the thousandths place?

a. 3
b. 5
c. 6
d. 8

24. Tim can make 5 pies with 2 pounds of flour. If he needs to make 7 pies, how many pounds of flour does he need?

a. 2 1/2
b. 2 4/5
c. 3
d. 3 3/8

25. Solve for *n* in the following equation:  $4n - p = 3r$

a. 3r/4 - p
b. p + 3r
c. p - 3r
d. 3r/4 + p/4

26. A square and an equilateral triangle have the same perimeter. If one side of the triangle measures 4 inches, how long is one side of the square?

a. 10
b. 8
c. 6
d. 3

27. Which of the following fractions, when entered into the triangle, makes the statement true?

$3/8 < \Delta < 13/24$

a. 7/8
b. 5/8
c. 5/12
d. 1/3

Copyright © Mometrix Media. You have been licensed one copy of this document for personal use only. Any other reproduction or redistribution is strictly prohibited. All rights reserved.
This content is provided for test preparation purposes only and does not imply an endorsement by Mometrix of any particular political, scientific, or religious point of view.

**28.** Find the value of *x* in the figure below:

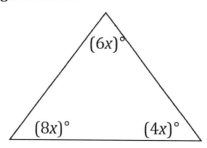

a. 10
b. 16
c. 18
d. 60

**29.** Susan works 24 hours per week at an hourly rate of $9.75. Her employer gives her a raise, increasing her weekly pay to $244.80. On an hourly basis, how much was her raise?

a. $.35
b. $.40
c. $.45
d. $.50

**30.** There are 6 blue marbles, 3 red marbles, and 5 yellow marbles in a bag. What is the probability of selecting a blue or red marble on the first draw?

a. 1/3
b. 4/7
c. 8/14
d. 9/14

**31.** What is a good estimate of the circumference of the circle in the figure below?

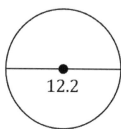

12.2

a. 6
b. 12
c. 24
d. 36

Copyright © Mometrix Media. You have been licensed one copy of this document for personal use only. Any other reproduction or redistribution is strictly prohibited. All rights reserved.
This content is provided for test preparation purposes only and does not imply an endorsement by Mometrix of any particular political, scientific, or religious point of view.

**32. Using the chart below, which equation describes the relationship between x and y?**

| X | y |
|---|---|
| 2 | 6 |
| 3 | 9 |
| 4 | 12 |
| 5 | 15 |

   a.  x = 3y
   b.  y = 3x
   c.  y = 1/3x
   d.  x/y = 3

**33. What is the product of four squared and six?**

   a.  22
   b.  28
   c.  55
   d.  96

**34. Because of its lower gravity, a 180-pound man would weigh only 30 pounds on the moon. If horse weighed 200 pounds on the moon, what would be its weight on Earth?**

   a.  1,200 pounds
   b.  1,000 pounds
   c.  600 pounds
   d.  66 pounds

**35. Solve the following equation:  $(y + 2)(y + 3)(y + 4)$**

   a.  y2 + 3y + 2
   b.  3y2 + 6y + 3
   c.  y3 + 9y2+ 26y + 24
   d.  8y3 + 6y + 8

**36. A gas tank containing 15 gallons of gas is three-quarters full. What is the capacity of the tank?**

   a.  15 gallons
   b.  18 gallons
   c.  14 gallons
   d.  20 gallons

**37. The distance between two towns is 275 miles. A truck driver must leave one town and arrive at the other at 9:30 p.m. If the trucker drives at an average rate of 55 miles per hour, at what time should the trucker depart?**

   a.  4:00 p.m.
   b.  4:30 p.m.
   c.  5:00 p.m.
   d.  4:00 a.m.

Copyright © Mometrix Media. You have been licensed one copy of this document for personal use only. Any other reproduction or redistribution is strictly prohibited. All rights reserved.
This content is provided for test preparation purposes only and does not imply an endorsement by Mometrix of any particular political, scientific, or religious point of view.

**38. Find the value of *x* in the figure below:**

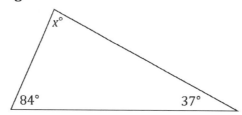

a. 239°
b. 120°
c. 78°
d. 59°

**39. Thirty-five boys went out for the soccer team. Of these, $\frac{5}{7}$ made the team. Of the boys who made the team, $\frac{4}{5}$ showed up for practice on Wednesday. How many boys were at the Wednesday practice?**

a. 18
b. 20
c. 22
d. 25

**40. Evaluate $x^2 - (2y - 3)$ if $x = 4$ and $y = 3$.**

a. 12
b. 13
c. 10
d. 8

**41. During a 60 minute television show, the entertainment portion lasted 15 minutes less than 4 times the advertising portion. How long was the entertainment portion?**

a. 30 minutes
b. 40 minutes
c. 45 minutes
d. 50 minutes

**42. Which number is missing in the numerical sequence 18, 15, ___, 9, 6 ?**

a. 12
b. 14
c. 10
d. 8

**43. Morgan plans to replace the floor in his bedroom with square tiles that have a side of 12 inches. The bedroom is 15 feet wide and 18 feet long, and Morgan can lay 9 tiles per hour. How long will the job take?**

a. 30 hours
b. 18 hours
c. 10.5 hours
d. 12 hours

Copyright © Mometrix Media. You have been licensed one copy of this document for personal use only. Any other reproduction or redistribution is strictly prohibited. All rights reserved.
This content is provided for test preparation purposes only and does not imply an endorsement by Mometrix of any particular political, scientific, or religious point of view.

**44.** The first three members of a 4-man swimming team swim their laps in 22.4 seconds, 23.8 seconds, and 21.9 seconds, respectively. How fast must the fourth man swim his lap for the team to average 22 seconds?

 a. 21.0 seconds
 b. 19.9 seconds
 c. 19.5 seconds
 d. 20.2 seconds

**45.** Evaluate the following expression if $u = 3$ and $v = 4$: $\frac{1}{3}u^2 + \frac{3v}{4} =$

 a. 21
 b. 18
 c. 12
 d. 6

Copyright © Mometrix Media. You have been licensed one copy of this document for personal use only. Any other reproduction or redistribution is strictly prohibited. All rights reserved.
This content is provided for test preparation purposes only and does not imply an endorsement by Mometrix of any particular political, scientific, or religious point of view.

## Section 5 – Essay

*DIRECTIONS: Write an essay on the following prompt on the paper provided. Your essay should NOT exceed 2 pages and must be written in ink. Erasing is not allowed.*

**Prompt:** Internet socializing by teenagers should be restricted

Support your position with specific examples from personal experience, the experience of others, current events, history, or literature.

Copyright © Mometrix Media. You have been licensed one copy of this document for personal use only. Any other reproduction or redistribution is strictly prohibited. All rights reserved. This content is provided for test preparation purposes only and does not imply an endorsement by Mometrix of any particular political, scientific, or religious point of view.

# Answers and Explanations for Test #3

## Section 1 – Verbal Reasoning

**1. D:** A gimmick is a ploy, trick, or ruse designed to draw attention.

**2. B:** To heave something is to launch or throw it.

**3. A:** To lull is to soothe, quiet, or calm.

**4. D:** To be wry is to be dryly humorous, often with a touch of irony or bitterness – to be cynical.

**5. B:** A climax is the highest or most intense point in the development or resolution of something – the culmination.

**6. A:** To be arrogant is to have or display an overbearing sense of self-worth or self-importance – to be proud.

**7. B:** An inauguration is a formal induction into office.

**8. D:** To be maudlin is to be excessively or foolishly sentimental.

**9. D:** To be pious is to show an eager desire to fulfill religious duties – to be devout.

**10. C:** To resuscitate is to restore consciousness, vigor, or life – to revive.

**11. B:** Vehement most closely means the same thing as intense.

**12. A:** Diatribe most closely means the same thing as criticism.

**13. D:** Cogitate most closely means the same thing as deliberate.

**14. A:** Invidious most closely means the same thing as offensive.

**15. C:** Hyperbole most closely means the same thing as exaggeration.

**16. B:** Innocuous most closely means the same thing as innocent.

**17. B:** The word "capricious" means "unpredictable" or "changeable."

**18. A:** The word "intermittent" also means "occasional" or "discontinuous."

**19. A:** Solitary can mean a number of different things, but one meaning is single. For example, if you said there was a solitary tree in a yard, you would mean that there was a single tree.

**20. C:** The word "precipitous" means "steep."

**21. C:** The definition of "salubrious", which means "promoting health", is given in the sentence.

**22. D:** "Prodigious" means "a great deal." Of the other choices, note that "quantitative" means "pertaining to the measurement of quantity" and that the sentence does not deal with measurement.

219

Copyright © Mometrix Media. You have been licensed one copy of this document for personal use only. Any other reproduction or redistribution is strictly prohibited. All rights reserved.
This content is provided for test preparation purposes only and does not imply an endorsement by Mometrix of any particular political, scientific, or religious point of view.

**23. D:** Since trial lawyers are regularly involved in confrontation, Carmen seems unsuited because she has a tendency (penchant) for avoiding such interactions.

**24. C:** "Voracious" means "craving or consuming large quantities."

**25. A:** Only choice A makes sense in both blanks.

**26. D:** The words "lugubrious" and "mournful", which have similar meanings, are appropriate for a description of someone who seems to have just suffered a loss.

**27. A:** A "paranoia" is an unjustified fear, so it makes sense that the threat was unspecified. The other choices are inconsistent with the locking of doors and response to a threat.

**28. C:** *Obstreperous* is defined as noisy, clamorous, or difficult to control. *Saturnine* or *brooding* children are moody. *Capricious* ones are simply hard to predict.

**29. B:** A *timbered* area is one with a lot of forest cover, here contrasted to the open or shrub-covered landscape favored by the birds. Since their favored elevation has already been specified, choice D is incorrect. The other choices make no sense.

**30. C:** *Quiescence* means calm: here, periods of violent eruptions are followed by periods with little or no flare activity.

**31. A:** *Duplicity* indicates lack of truthfulness, and *credence* is belief in what one is told.

**32. B:** A *conciliatory* tone is one that seeks to reconcile with someone. Choice D is incorrect because the rival could not have been victorious since the sentence describes activities of the winning candidate.

**33. D:** To *glower* is to stare in a sullen, disapproving manner.

**34. B:**

**35. C:**

**36. C:**

**37. C:**

**38. B:**

**39. A:**

**40. C:**

# Section 2 – Quantitative Reasoning

**1. C:** Explanation: Multiply 1/6 by 2 to get a common denominator.

$1/6 \times 2 = 2/12$

Then calculate $11/12 - 2/12 = 9/12$

Reduce this fraction by dividing both numerator and denominator by 3.

Copyright © Mometrix Media. You have been licensed one copy of this document for personal use only. Any other reproduction or redistribution is strictly prohibited. All rights reserved. This content is provided for test preparation purposes only and does not imply an endorsement by Mometrix of any particular political, scientific, or religious point of view.

$(9 \div 3) / (12 \div 3) = 3/4$

**2. A:** First, calculate 12% of 56.

$56 \times 0.12 = 6.72$

Then, add this value (the increase) to the original value of 56.

$56 + 6.72 = 62.72$

Rounding off, we get 62.7

**3. B:** Explanation: One side of a square is 56cm. All of its sides are equal, and the perimeter is the sum of all sides.

Therefore, the perimeter equals 56cm+56cm+56cm+56cm

The perimeter is 224cm.

**4. A:** Explanation: There are three fractions: 1/4, 1/8, and 1/2.

To answer the question, they have to be added. The common denominator is 8.

$2/8 + 1/8 + 4/8 = 7/8$

Among just the first three people, the dog is being taken care of 7/8 of the time.

Now, the time that is left over must be calculated.

Using the common denominator of 8, we know that $1 = 8/8$

Therefore, to calculate the proportion of time the fourth person will have to care for the dog:

$8/8 - 7/8 = 1/8$

**5. D:** Explanation: First, calculate 3% of 548 meters.

548 meters $\times$ 0.03 = 16.44 meters.

Then, add it to the original height.

548 meters + 16.44 meters = 564.44 meters

Rounding off, we get 564 meters.

**6. C:** Explanation: $275 - (-64) - 32 =$

When a negative number is subtracted from a value, it becomes a positive:

$275 - (-64) - 32 =$

$275 + 64 - 32 =$

$339 - 32 = 307$

Copyright © Mometrix Media. You have been licensed one copy of this document for personal use only. Any other reproduction or redistribution is strictly prohibited. All rights reserved. This content is provided for test preparation purposes only and does not imply an endorsement by Mometrix of any particular political, scientific, or religious point of view.

**7. A:** Explanation: Since we know the value of $x$ and $y$, it is simply a matter of substituting them into the expression:

$9x - 3y + 8xy - 3$

$9(10) - 3(-2) + 8(10)(-2) - 3$

$90 + 6 - 160 - 3$

$96 - 163 = -67$

**8. B:** Explanation: $9x (3x^2 + 2x - 9)$

To simplify, multiply the value outside of the brackets ($9x$) by the values inside of the brackets.

$9x \cdot 3x^2 + 9x \cdot 2x - 9x \cdot 9$

$27x^3 + 18 x^2 - 81x$

**9. D:** Explanation: $x^5 x^2 + y^0 =$

We know that $x = 3$.

Therefore, we can find the value of $x^5 x^2$

$3^5 3^2$

$243 \cdot 9 = 2,187$

We don't know the value of $y$, but any value to the power of zero is equal to one.

Therefore, $2,187 + 1 = 2,188$

**10. B:** Explanation: $x^2 + 12x + 36 = 0$

To solve for $x$, this equation must be factored.

$(x + 6)(x + 6)$

Then, solve for $x$.

$x + 6 = 0$

$x = -6$

**11. B:** Explanation: $\dfrac{64x^4 + 8x^3 - 4x^2 + 16x}{8x}$

To simplify, each term in the numerator can be divided by $8x$ to eliminate the denominator. When variables with an exponent are divided by one another, the exponent in the denominator is subtracted from the exponent in the numerator. When there is no exponent listed, it is assumed to be $x^1$.

We are left with: $8x^3 + x^2 - 1/2x + 2$

**12. C:** $9x^2y - 18xy - 27y$

222

Copyright © Mometrix Media. You have been licensed one copy of this document for personal use only. Any other reproduction or redistribution is strictly prohibited. All rights reserved. This content is provided for test preparation purposes only and does not imply an endorsement by Mometrix of any particular political, scientific, or religious point of view.

$9y$ is contained in all parts of this expression. Therefore, $9y$ can be factored out.

$9y(x^2 – 2x – 3)$

$(x^2 – 2x – 3)$ can also be factored.

$(x – 3)(x + 1)$

We end up with $9y(x – 3)(x + 1)$

**13. A:** Explanation: $\sqrt{3}(5\sqrt{3} - \sqrt{12} + \sqrt{10})$

To simplify, all terms inside the brackets must be multiplied by $\sqrt{3}$

$5\sqrt{3} \times \sqrt{3} - \sqrt{3} \times \sqrt{12} + \sqrt{10} \times \sqrt{3}$

According to the order of operations, multiplication is completed first.

$5\sqrt{9} - \sqrt{36} + \sqrt{30}$

Since the square root of 9 and 36 are whole numbers, this expression can be further simplified.

$5 \times 3 – 6 + \sqrt{30}$

$15 – 6 + \sqrt{30}$

$9 + \sqrt{30}$

**14. B:** Explanation: To calculate the slope of a line, we simply have to figure out the change in $y$ over the change in $x$.

$\underline{18 - 2}$

$-3 - 5$

$\underline{16} = -2$

$-8$

-2 is the slope of the line.

**15. D:** Explanation: To find a midpoint, simply calculate the average of the two sets of points.

For $x$, the midpoint is calculated in the following manner:

$(-20 + 5)/2 = -7.5$

For $y$, the midpoint is calculated in the following manner:

$(8 + 3)/2 = 5.5$

The midpoint is (-7.5, 5.5)

**16. D:** The area of a rectangle is calculated as the product of the width and length. If the length is twice the width of 3 m, it must be 6 m long. Then, 3 x 6 = 18 m².

Copyright © Mometrix Media. You have been licensed one copy of this document for personal use only. Any other reproduction or redistribution is strictly prohibited. All rights reserved.
This content is provided for test preparation purposes only and does not imply an endorsement by Mometrix of any particular political, scientific, or religious point of view.

**17. C:** The average is computed by dividing the sum of all the measurements by the number of measurements. Let $B$ = the average height of the boys, $G$ = the average height of the girls, and $C$ = the average height of the class. Since the number of boys and the number girls are equal, then $(B + G)/2 = C$. Then $B + G = 2C$. Substituting the known values, $110 + G = 2 \times 105$ and $110 + G = 210$. Subtracting 110 from each side of the equation, $G = 100$.

**18. C:** Multiply both the numerator and denominator of fraction (a) by 10 to convert to the same denominator as the other two fractions. Then compare the numerators: $\frac{30}{50} < \frac{40}{50} > \frac{8}{50}$.

**19. D:** Since $\frac{5 \times 12}{3} = \frac{60}{3} = 20$, and $80 - 60 = 20$, D is the correct answer.

**20. C:** The perimeter of a rectangle of length 6 and width 4 equals $2(6 + 4) = 20$. The perimeter of a square of side 4 equals $4 + 4 + 4 + 4 = 16$. And the area of a square of side 4 equals $4 \times 4 = 16$. Although the units for the measurement of area differ from those of the perimeters, the magnitude of the measurements for (b) and (c) are the same.

**21. C:** There are 60 minutes in an hour, so in 3.5 hours there are $60 \times 3.5 = 2106$ minutes. There are 7 days in a week, so in 30 weeks there are $7 \times 30 = 210$ days.

**22. A:** $4^8 = (2^2)^8 = 2^{16}$, whereas $8^4 = (2^3)^4 = 2^{12}$.

**23. B:** The probability of selecting a given name out of a hat containing 17 names is $\frac{1}{17}$, or approximately 0.059.

**24. B:** The absolute value of –9 is 9. So $-|-9| = -9$; $-9 - 2 = -11$, which is less than 7.

**25. D:** Knowing the proportional value of $\frac{x}{y}$ does not tell us anything about the exact value of either variable. We know that y must be positive because x is positive, but we cannot get any more precise than that.

**26. B:** Let x stand for the square footage of the Wilsons' house. Then before adding on, the square footage of the Smiths' house would have been $100 - 25 = 75$ percent of that number. We express this as 0.75x. After adding on, the Smiths' house had 25% more square feet than it had had before. This is expressed as $1.25(0.75x)$, or 0.9375x, which is still smaller than the Wilsons' house.

**27. A:** The expression in Column A can be factored as follows: $(2x - 2y)(4x - 4y) = 2(x - y) \cdot 4(x + y) = 8(x - y)(x + y)$, which multiplies out to be $8(x^2 - y^2)$. We know that x and y are both less than –1, and that x is farther away from zero than y is. This means that $x^2$ and $y^2$ are both positive, and that $x^2$ is greater than $y^2$. Therefore $x^2 - y^2$ is a positive number, which means that $8(x^2 - y^2)$ is a larger positive number.

**28. D:** Because of the absolute value sign, s could be positive, negative, or zero, so we have no way of knowing whether it is equal to or less than t.

**29. D:** The given information is enough to tell us that 0.2x is greater than 0.8y, but y itself could still be any positive real number, and there is no way to tell if it is greater or less than 0.2x.

**30. B:** The order of operations dictates that when there are no parentheses, exponents are calculated before negative signs. Thus $-2^6$ could be rewritten: $-(2^6)$, a negative number. On the other hand, $(-2)^6$ is a positive number because any negative taken to an even power will be positive.

Copyright © Mometrix Media. You have been licensed one copy of this document for personal use only. Any other reproduction or redistribution is strictly prohibited. All rights reserved. This content is provided for test preparation purposes only and does not imply an endorsement by Mometrix of any particular political, scientific, or religious point of view.

**31. A:** The turtle, moving at 3 mph, will take 5 hours to travel the required distance while the rabbit, which is moving at 25 mph, will require only 4 hours to reach its destination.

**32. D:** Because n is squared in the information we are given, we do not know whether n is equal to 5 or –5.

**33. C:** Let x stand for the number of calories in a cup of coffee, and let y stand for the number of calories in a spoon of sugar. Then the given information can be expressed as $6(x + 3y) = 4(x + 5y)$, which reduces to $6x + 18y = 4x + 20y$. Subtract 4x from both sides to get $2x + 18y = 20y$, then subtract 18y from both sides to get $2x = 2y$, which means that x and y are equal.

**34. A:** When x is a negative number, $x^3$ is also negative. On the other hand, $x^2$ will always be positive.

**35. A:** We can express any three consecutive integers as x, x +1, and x +2. Thus their sum is $x + (x + 1) + (x + 2)$, or $3x + 3$. Setting this equal to 114, we have $3x + 3 = 114$. Subtract 3 from both sides to get $3x = 111$, then divide both sides by 3 to get $x = 37$, which means the three integers are 37, 38, and 39.

## Section 3 – Reading Comprehension

**1. D:** The main idea of the passage is that the immune system protects the body from infection. The author repeatedly alludes to the complexity and mystery of the immune system, so it cannot be true that scientists fully understand this part of the body. It is true that the immune system triggers the production of fluids, but this description misses the point. Similarly, it is true that the body is under constant invasion by malicious microbes; however, the author is much more interested in the body's response to these microbes. For this reason, the best answer choice is D.

**2. C:** The passage never states that viruses are extremely sophisticated. In fact, the passage explicitly states the opposite. However, in order to know this you need to understand the word *primitive*. The passage says that viruses are too primitive, or early in their development, to be classified as living organisms. A primitive organism is simple and undeveloped—exactly the opposite of sophisticated. If you do not know the word *primitive*, you can still answer the question by finding all three of the answer choices in the passage.

**3. D:** In the first paragraph, the word *ideal* means "perfect." Do not be confused by the similarity of the word *ideal* to *idea* and mistakenly select answer choice A. Take a look at the context in which the word is used. The author is describing how many millions of microbes can live inside the human body. It would not make sense, then, for the author to be describing the body as a *hostile* environment for microbes. Moreover, whether or not the body is a confined environment would not seem to have much bearing on whether it is good for microbes. Rather, the paragraph suggests that the human body is a perfect environment for microbes.

**4. B:** The passage never states that the immune system ignores tumors. Indeed, at the beginning of the third paragraph, the author states that scientists remain puzzled by the body's ability to fight tumors. This question is a little tricky, because it is common knowledge that many tumors prove fatal to the human body. However, you should not take this to mean that the body does not at least try to fight tumors. In general, it is best to seek out direct evidence in the text rather than to rely on what you already know.

**5. A:** In the second paragraph, the word *enlist* means "call into service." The use of this word is an example of figurative language, the use of a known image or idea to elucidate an idea that is

Copyright © Mometrix Media. You have been licensed one copy of this document for personal use only. Any other reproduction or redistribution is strictly prohibited. All rights reserved.
This content is provided for test preparation purposes only and does not imply an endorsement by Mometrix of any particular political, scientific, or religious point of view.

perhaps unfamiliar to the reader. In this case, the author is describing the efforts of the immune system as if they were a military campaign. The immune system *enlists* other cells, and then directs these *recruits* to areas where they are needed. You are probably familiar with *enlistment* and *recruitment* as they relate to describe military service. The author is trying to draw a parallel between the enlistment of young men and women and the enlistment of immune cells. For this reason, "call into service" is the best definition for *enlist*.

**6. C:** The author's primary purpose in writing this essay is to inform. In this case, the passage is written in a clear, declarative style with no obvious prejudice on the part of the author. The primary intention of the passage seems to be providing information about the immune system to a general audience.

**7. A:** This passage attempts to persuade readers to accept its point of view. While some of the other choices are true of particular statements found in the passage, only choice A is true of the passage as a whole.

**8. A:** Choice A is best. The <u>chief</u> benefit, in this context, means the main benefit.

**9. D:** Only choice D can be correctly inferred from the second paragraph.

**10. B:** Choice B best represents the passage as a whole.

**11. D:** To <u>mimic</u> is to resemble. Choice D is best.

**12. B:** The passage mentions the plastics found in the stomachs of dead birds, so choice B is best.

**13. B:** Choice B best answers the question: The author excludes discussion of plastics' benefits in order to focus on their dangers.

**14. B:** <u>Durability</u> in this sense means permanence.

**15. C:** The first paragraph states that the main purpose of DST it to make better use of daylight.

**16. A:** Energy conservation is discussed as a possible benefit of DST, not a negative effect of it.

**17. D:** The first paragraph states that DST involves setting clocks forward one hour in the spring and one hour backward in the fall.

**18. B:** The last sentence in paragraph four notes that agricultural and evening entertainment interests have historically been opposed to DST.

**19. D:** The passage gives examples of both good and bad effects extra daylight can have on health.

**20. D:** The sixth paragraph notes that DST is observed in only some regions of Brazil.

**21. C:** The last paragraph of the passage notes that DST can lead to peculiar situations, and relays an anecdote about the effect of DST on the birth order of twins.

**22. C:** If $30,000,000 is gained over 7 weeks, each week has a gain of 1/7 of that, or $4,200,000.

**23. B:** In the second paragraph, the author asserts that Benjamin Franklin suggested DST as a way to save candles.

Copyright © Mometrix Media. You have been licensed one copy of this document for personal use only. Any other reproduction or redistribution is strictly prohibited. All rights reserved.
This content is provided for test preparation purposes only and does not imply an endorsement by Mometrix of any particular political, scientific, or religious point of view.

**24. D:** The passage describes the artistry of ancient Greek coins and gives the reasons why so much effort went into designing them.

**25. B:** The first sentence indicates that coins are utilitarian objects, and few are designed well enough to be worth considering them as anything more.

**26. A:** "Delectation" means to savor or to enjoy the flavor or beauty of something, in this case the design of the coins.

**27. D:** The word is defined in the second sentence of the passage.

**28. D:** The passage describes the coins as artistic objects, not simply because they were the first coins, but also because of the historical situation which is described, and which led to their being designed with great care and pride.

**29. C:** The text states that new coins were developed frequently, to commemorate battles, treaties, etc.

**30. A:** The text tells us that the designers were highly skilled and that they were so proud of their work that they signed it.

**31. D:** The sentence contrasts the artistic content of the coins with their use as a practical means of commercial exchange.

**32. D:** The text tells us that coin designs changed along with larger sculptures to reflect changing Greek artistic tastes.

**33. B:** The frequent need for new designs meant that the artisans who did the work had ample opportunity to perfect their skills.

**34. C:** The text tells us that the dated coins provide a dependable record of Greek artistic development.

**35. D:** Coins were developed as a means of commercial exchange, and the text tells us that this was their main use.

**36. C:** The passage describes several distinctive features of annelid anatomy and tells how some of them differ from other worms.

**37. A:** The term is defined in the text as an organization of the anatomy into segments.

**38. B:** The term is defined in the text between commas.

**39. C:** The text gives the example of feet specializing into grasping organs to illustrate this evolutionary advantage of segmental plasticity.

**40. B:** *Nematodes* differ from the annelids in the structure of the coelom. *Lumbricus* and leeches are both members of the Annelida.

## Section 4 – Mathematics Achievement

**1. D:** Integers include all positive and negative whole numbers and the number zero. The product of three integers must be an integer, so you can eliminate any answer choice that is not a whole

Copyright © Mometrix Media. You have been licensed one copy of this document for personal use only. Any other reproduction or redistribution is strictly prohibited. All rights reserved. This content is provided for test preparation purposes only and does not imply an endorsement by Mometrix of any particular political, scientific, or religious point of view.

number: choices (A) and (C). The product of two even integers is even. The product of even and odd integers is even. The only even choice is 24.

**2. A:** If $520 \div x = 40n$, then

$(40n)(x) = 520$ or

$40nx = 520$

$nx = 13.$

**3. B:** If 12 books remain, 76 – 12 = 64 were purchased.

Average = <u>Sum of the terms</u>

           Number of terms

So the average number of books purchased by the customers is 64 ÷ 16 = 4

**4. D:** If class starts at 9:00 a.m. and John arrives 26 minutes early, then he arrives at 9:00 – 26 minutes, or at 8:34 a.m. If his teacher arrives 30 minutes later, the teacher arrives at 8:34 + 30 minutes, or 9:04 a.m.

**5. D:** .33 is equal to roughly $1/3$, so find which choice is NOT less (i.e. greater) than $1/3$. Since the "3" in the denominator of $1/3$ is a factor of the denominators of all the answer choices, you can compare the fractions with relative ease.

**6. D:** Isolate $a$: $a = 8b + 6 + 16$. Thus, $a = 8b + 22$. Next, add 3 to both side of the equation: $a + 3 = 8b + 22 + 3 = 8b + 25$.

**7. D:** Angles around a point add up to 360 degrees. Add the degrees of the given angles: 72° + 110° + 58° = 240°. Then subtract from 360° - 240° = 120°. Remember to divide 120° in half, since the question is asking for the degree measure of one angle, angle $d$.

**8. A:** To answer this question, use this formula for rate: distance = rate X time. You need to calculate the time he walked by converting the days the into hours because the rate is given in terms of hours. There are 24 hours in a day X 3 days = 72 hours. Thus, 2.5 X 72 = 180 miles, the distance

**9. B:** Translate this word problem into a mathematical equation. Let Janice's weight = $x$. Let Elaina's weight = $x + 23$. Let June's weight = $x + 14$. Add their weights together and subtract 25 pounds:

$= x + x + 23 + x + 14 - 25$

$= 3x + 37 - 25$

$= 3x + 12.$

**10. B:** Add the 14 blue, 6 red, 12 green and 8 purple buttons to get a total of 40 buttons. If 25 buttons are removed, there are 15 buttons remaining in the bag. If the chance of drawing a red button is now $1/3$, divide 15 into thirds to get 5 red buttons remaining in the bag. The original total of red buttons was 6; so 6 – 5 = 1: one red button was removed, choice (B).

**11. D:** First, determine how many revolutions the washer makes in one wash by multiplying 85 X 15 = 1,275. Then divide 100,000 by 1,275 to determine how many washes it will take to reach

**228**

Copyright © Mometrix Media. You have been licensed one copy of this document for personal use only. Any other reproduction or redistribution is strictly prohibited. All rights reserved. This content is provided for test preparation purposes only and does not imply an endorsement by Mometrix of any particular political, scientific, or religious point of view.

100,000 revolutions 100,000 ÷ 1,275 = 78.431373. Round this number to 78, the nearest whole number. You may not be able to determine the precise answer, but you may be able to solve at least to the tenths decimal place and see that the answer is roughly 78.

**12. C:** This equation is asking you to multiply three algebraic expressions. When multiplying more than two expressions, multiply any two expressions (using the FOIL method), then multiply the result by the third expression. Start by multiplying:

$(y + 1)(y + 2) = (y \times y) + (y \times 2) + (1 \times y) + (1 \times 2)$

$= y^2 + 2y + y + 2$

$= y^2 + 3y + 2$

Then multiply the result by the third expression:

$(y^2 + 3y + 2)(y + 3) = (y^2 + 3y +2)(y) + (y^2 + 3y +2)(3)$

$= (y^3 + 3y^2 + 2y) + (3y^2 + 9y + 6)$

$= y^3 + 3y^2 + 2y + 3y^2 + 9y + 6$

$= y^3 + 3y^2 + 3y^2 + 9y + 2y + 6$

$= y^3 + 6y^2 + 11y + 6$

**13. D:** The area of a parallelogram is base X height or $A = bh$, where $b$ is the length of a side and $h$ is the length of an altitude to that side. In this problem, $A = 6 \times 4$; $A = 24$. Remember, use the length of $BE$, not the length of $CD$ for the height.

**14. A:** There are a total of 90 students that take Math, English, or both. You must avoid counting any student twice, and you may find it helpful to create a Venn diagram or some sort of chart to keep the different types of students separate.

| Total students | 90 |
| --- | --- |
| Students taking both courses: | -50 |
| Students taking just English: | -25 |
| Students taking just Math: | 15 |

**15. A:** To find the interest earned, multiply the interest rate by the deposit amount. Because this account uses simple interest, you do not need to worry about compounding the interest. Remember to convert the interest rate to a percentage.

0.0375 X 2,500 = 93.75.

Choice (D) might be a tempting answer, since it is the deposit amount added to the interest earned, but the question asks how much interest will be earned, not the total amount of the deposit after earning interest.

**16. B:** Use the Pythagorean Theorem to solve this problem: $a^2 + b^2 = c^2$ where c is the hypotenuse while $a$ and $b$ are the legs of the triangle.

$5^2 + 12^2 = c^2$

Copyright © Mometrix Media. You have been licensed one copy of this document for personal use only. Any other reproduction or redistribution is strictly prohibited. All rights reserved. This content is provided for test preparation purposes only and does not imply an endorsement by Mometrix of any particular political, scientific, or religious point of view.

25 + 144 = 169

$\sqrt{169}$ = 13.

**17. B:** A percentage is changed into a fraction by first converting the percentage into a decimal, and then changing the decimal to a fraction.

To convert a percentage into a decimal, divide the percentage by 100 by moving the decimal point two places to the left:

12.5% = .125

To convert this decimal into a fraction, the numbers to the right of the decimal point become the numerator. Because the last decimal place is the thousandths place, the numerator of the faction is 1000. Reduce the fraction to the lowest terms:

$^{125}/_{1000}$= $^1/_8$

Remember that you can reduce the fraction into progressively lower terms until you find the most reduced fraction (ex: $^{25}/_{200}$ → $^5/_{40}$ → $^1/_8$).

**18. D:** The average of a group of terms is the sum of the terms divided by the number of terms. In this problem, the teacher disregards Rick's highest and lowest scores, so do not use 95% or 64% in your calculation. Add the remaining scores:

68 + 86 + 83 + 92 + 79 = 408

Divide by the number of scores:

408 ÷ 5 = 81.6.

**19. D:** Use the formula for probability to solve this problem:

Probability = <u>Number of Desirable Outcomes</u>

Number of Possible Outcomes

Because there are effectively multiple events – the roll of each die is its own event – you must multiply all the possible outcomes for each die. Thus, to determine the number of possible outcomes, multiply the number of sides on dice exponentially by the number dice:

$6^5$ = (6 x 6 x 6 x 6 x 6) = 7,776

There is one desirable outcome: rolling all sixes. Probability = $^1/_{7,776}$

**20. B:** Remember to use the order of operations when simplifying this equation. The acronym *PEMDAS* will help you remember the correct order: Parenthesis, Exponentiation, Multiplication/Division, Addition/Subtraction.

$4(6 – 3)^2 – (-2)$

First, simplify the parentheses: $4 \times 3^2 – (-2)$

Next, simplify the exponent: $4 \times 9 – (-2)$

Copyright © Mometrix Media. You have been licensed one copy of this document for personal use only. Any other reproduction or redistribution is strictly prohibited. All rights reserved. This content is provided for test preparation purposes only and does not imply an endorsement by Mometrix of any particular political, scientific, or religious point of view.

Then multiply:  36 – (-2)

Finally, subtract:  36 – (-2) = 36 + 2 = 38

The PEMDAS method is used to simplify multiple equations in this practice test.

**21. D:** Use the following proportion:   $\dfrac{1 \text{ in.}}{45 \text{ miles}} = \dfrac{3.2 \text{ inches}}{x \text{ miles}}$

Cross multiply:  x = (45)(3.2) = 144 miles

**22. B:** Angles that form a straight line add up to 180 degrees.  Such angles are sometimes referred to as being "supplementary."

60 + 2x = 180

2x = 120

x = 60

**23. A:** You can eliminate choices (B) and (C) since they are to the left of the decimal point.  This problem asks for the number in the thousandths place, and the "ths" indicate digits to the right of the decimal point. Of those digits:

- 9 is in the tenths place.
- 7 is in the hundredths place.
- 3 is in the thousandths place.
- 8 is in the ten thousandths place.

**24. B:** Use the following proportion:   $\dfrac{5 \, pies}{2 \, lbs \, flour} = \dfrac{7}{x}$

5x = 14

x = $^{14}/_5$ = 2 $^4/_5$

**25. D:** To solve for *n*, you have to isolate that variable by putting all of the other terms of the equation, including coefficients, integers, and variables on the other side of the equal sign.

Add *p* to each side of the equation:

4n – p = 3r

4n – p (+ p) = 3r (+ p)

4n = 3r + p

Divide each term by 4:

$$\frac{4n}{4} = \frac{3r}{4} + \frac{p}{4}$$

$$n = \frac{3r}{4} + \frac{p}{4}$$

Copyright © Mometrix Media. You have been licensed one copy of this document for personal use only. Any other reproduction or redistribution is strictly prohibited. All rights reserved.
This content is provided for test preparation purposes only and does not imply an endorsement by Mometrix of any particular political, scientific, or religious point of view.

**26. D:** An equilateral triangle has three sides of equal length. If each side is 4 inches long, the perimeter of the triangle is 12 inches. A square has four sides of equal length. Since its perimeter also must equal 12 inches, divide 12 by 4: $12 \div 4 = 3$,

**27. C:** Find the common denominator of $^3/_8$ and $^{13}/_{24}$.

$^3/_8 \times {}^3/_3 = {}^9/_{24}$

$^{13}/_{24} \times {}^1/_1 = {}^{13}/_{24}$

The value in the triangle must be greater than $^9/_{24}$ and less than $^{13}/_{24}$. Choice (C), $^5/_{12}$, when expressed as the equivalent fraction $^{10}/_{24}$, is correct.

**28. A:** The sum of the measures of the angles in a triangle equals 180°. Use the numbers given in the figure to make the following equation:

$6x + 8x + 4x = 180$

$18x = 180$

$x = 10$

**29. C:** To solve this word problem, first find Susan's current weekly pay by multiplying her weekly hours worked by her hourly wage:

$24 \times \$9.75 = \$234.00$

Subtract her current weekly pay from her future weekly pay:

$\$244.80 - \$234.00 = \$10.80$

Divide the difference by 24, the number of hours Susan works each week:

$\$10.80 \div 24 = \$.45$

**30. D:** Use this ratio for probability:

Probability = <u>Number of Desirable Outcomes</u>

Number of Possible Outcomes

There are 6 blue marbles and 3 red marbles for a total of 9 desirable outcomes. Add the total number of marbles to get the total number of possibilities, 14. The probability that a red or blue marble will be selected is $^9/_{14}$.

**31. D:** Use the formula for circumference:

Circumference = $\pi \times$ diameter ($\pi$ is approximately equal to 3.14).

To give the best estimate, round to the nearest whole number:

3.14 rounds to 3

12.2, the diameter, rounds to 12

Copyright © Mometrix Media. You have been licensed one copy of this document for personal use only. Any other reproduction or redistribution is strictly prohibited. All rights reserved. This content is provided for test preparation purposes only and does not imply an endorsement by Mometrix of any particular political, scientific, or religious point of view.

3 x 12 = 36

**32. B:** The chart indicates that each $x$ value must be tripled to equal the corresponding $y$ value, so $y = 3x$. One way you can determine this is by plugging corresponding pairs of $x$ and $y$ into the answer choices.

**33. D:** Turn the word problem into an equation. Remember that product means multiplication: $4^2$ X $6 = 96$.

**34. A:** Use the following ratio:  $\dfrac{\text{weight on moon}}{\text{weight on Earth}}$

$$\frac{30}{180} = \frac{200}{x}$$

$$30x = 36{,}000$$

$x = 1{,}200$ pounds. Note that 30/180 can be reduced to 1/6, which simplifies your cross-multiplication and eliminates the need for division.

**35. C:** This equation is asking you to multiply three algebraic expressions. When multiplying more than two expressions, multiply any two expressions, (using the FOIL method) then multiply the result by the third expression. Start by multiplying:

$(y + 2)(y + 3) = (y \times y) + (y \times 3) + (2 \times y) + (2 \times 3)$

$= y^2 + 3y + 2y + 6$

$= y^2 + 5y + 6$

Then multiply the result by the third expression:

$(y^2 + 5y + 6)(y + 4) = (y^2 + 5y + 6)(y) + (y^2 + 5y + 6)(4)$

$= (y^3 + 5y^2 + 6y) + (4y^2 + 20y + 24)$

$= y^3 + 5y^2 + 6y + 4y^2 + 20y + 24$

$= y^3 + 9y^2 + 26y + 24$

**36. D:** Let $x$ = the capacity of the tank. Use the following proportion to solve for $x$:

$$\frac{15}{x} = \frac{3}{4}$$

$$3x = 60$$

$$x = 20 \text{ gallons}$$

Copyright © Mometrix Media. You have been licensed one copy of this document for personal use only. Any other reproduction or redistribution is strictly prohibited. All rights reserved.
This content is provided for test preparation purposes only and does not imply an endorsement by Mometrix of any particular political, scientific, or religious point of view.

**37. B:** To solve this problem, you need to find the time needed to drive 275 miles at a speed of 55 miles per hour. If rate X time = distance, then time = distance ÷ rate:

$r X t = d$

$$\frac{r X t}{r} = \frac{d}{r}$$
$$t = \frac{d}{r}$$

$275 \div 55 = 5$ hours

The truck driver needs to arrive at 9:30 p.m., so subtract 5 hours from 9:30. The truck driver needs to leave at 4:30 p.m. to arrive on time.

**38. D:** The sum of the measures of the angles in a triangle equals 180°.

$x + 84 + 37 = 180$

$x + 121 = 180$

$x = 59$

**39. B:** Since $\frac{4}{5}$ of $\frac{5}{7}$ of 35 boys were at the practice, this is $35 \times \frac{5}{7} \times \frac{4}{5} = 35 \times \frac{4}{7} = 5 \times 4 = 20$.

**40. B:** Substitute each of the given values for $x$ and $y$ into the equation. This yields,

$(4)^2 - (2 \times 3 - 3) = 16 - 3 = 13$.

**41. C:** Write two equations to express the problem. Since the entertainment portion ($E$) lasted 15 minutes less than 4 times the advertising portion ($A$), the first equation is $E = 4A - 15$. Since both sections add up to the total show length, 60 minutes, the second equation is $E + A = 60$. Substituting the first equation into the second yields $4A - 15 + A = 60$, which is equivalent to $5A = 75$. Dividing both sides of this equation by 5 shows that $A = 15$ minutes. Now, since $E + A = 60$, it follows that $E = 60 - 15 = 45$ minutes.

**42. A:** This is an arithmetic sequence in which each term is equal to the preceding term plus (-3). To find the missing term, add (-3) to the preceding term: $15 + (-3) = 15 - 3 = 12$. To verify this result, add (-3) to this term: this results in the following term: $12 + (- 3) = 12 - 3 = 9$.

**43. A:** Since 12 inches equals 1 foot, each tile is 1 square foot in area. The area of the bedroom floor is 15 x 18 = 270 square feet. Therefore, the number of tiles that must be laid is 270. Since Morgan can lay 9 tiles per hour, the time required will be $\frac{270}{9} = 30$ hours.

**44. B:** The average is the total number of seconds divided by the total number of events. If there are four events (four swimmers), the average will be $22 = \frac{\text{Total}}{4}$. Solving for the total yields $Total = 88$ seconds. The total for the first three swimmers is 22.4 + 23.8 + 21.9 = 68.1 seconds. Therefore, the last swimmer must swim his lap in 88.0 – 68.1 = 19.9 seconds.

**45. D:** Substitute the given values into the expression, yielding $\frac{1}{3}(3)^2 + \frac{3 \times 4}{4} = 3 + 3$.

Copyright © Mometrix Media. You have been licensed one copy of this document for personal use only. Any other reproduction or redistribution is strictly prohibited. All rights reserved. This content is provided for test preparation purposes only and does not imply an endorsement by Mometrix of any particular political, scientific, or religious point of view.

# How to Overcome Test Anxiety

Just the thought of taking a test is enough to make most people a little nervous. A test is an important event that can have a long-term impact on your future, so it's important to take it seriously and it's natural to feel anxious about performing well. But just because anxiety is normal, that doesn't mean that it's helpful in test taking, or that you should simply accept it as part of your life. Anxiety can have a variety of effects. These effects can be mild, like making you feel slightly nervous, or severe, like blocking your ability to focus or remember even a simple detail.

If you experience test anxiety—whether severe or mild—it's important to know how to beat it. To discover this, first you need to understand what causes test anxiety.

## Causes of Test Anxiety

While we often think of anxiety as an uncontrollable emotional state, it can actually be caused by simple, practical things. One of the most common causes of test anxiety is that a person does not feel adequately prepared for their test. This feeling can be the result of many different issues such as poor study habits or lack of organization, but the most common culprit is time management. Starting to study too late, failing to organize your study time to cover all of the material, or being distracted while you study will mean that you're not well prepared for the test. This may lead to cramming the night before, which will cause you to be physically and mentally exhausted for the test. Poor time management also contributes to feelings of stress, fear, and hopelessness as you realize you are not well prepared but don't know what to do about it.

Other times, test anxiety is not related to your preparation for the test but comes from unresolved fear. This may be a past failure on a test, or poor performance on tests in general. It may come from comparing yourself to others who seem to be performing better or from the stress of living up to expectations. Anxiety may be driven by fears of the future—how failure on this test would affect your educational and career goals. These fears are often completely irrational, but they can still negatively impact your test performance.

> **Review Video: <u>3 Reasons You Have Test Anxiety</u>**
> Visit mometrix.com/academy and enter code: 428468

235

Copyright © Mometrix Media. You have been licensed one copy of this document for personal use only. Any other reproduction or redistribution is strictly prohibited. All rights reserved.
This content is provided for test preparation purposes only and does not imply an endorsement by Mometrix of any particular political, scientific, or religious point of view.

# Elements of Test Anxiety

As mentioned earlier, test anxiety is considered to be an emotional state, but it has physical and mental components as well. Sometimes you may not even realize that you are suffering from test anxiety until you notice the physical symptoms. These can include trembling hands, rapid heartbeat, sweating, nausea, and tense muscles. Extreme anxiety may lead to fainting or vomiting. Obviously, any of these symptoms can have a negative impact on testing. It is important to recognize them as soon as they begin to occur so that you can address the problem before it damages your performance.

> **Review Video: 3 Ways to Tell You Have Test Anxiety**
> Visit mometrix.com/academy and enter code: 927847

The mental components of test anxiety include trouble focusing and inability to remember learned information. During a test, your mind is on high alert, which can help you recall information and stay focused for an extended period of time. However, anxiety interferes with your mind's natural processes, causing you to blank out, even on the questions you know well. The strain of testing during anxiety makes it difficult to stay focused, especially on a test that may take several hours. Extreme anxiety can take a huge mental toll, making it difficult not only to recall test information but even to understand the test questions or pull your thoughts together.

> **Review Video: How Test Anxiety Affects Memory**
> Visit mometrix.com/academy and enter code: 609003

# Effects of Test Anxiety

Test anxiety is like a disease—if left untreated, it will get progressively worse. Anxiety leads to poor performance, and this reinforces the feelings of fear and failure, which in turn lead to poor performances on subsequent tests. It can grow from a mild nervousness to a crippling condition. If allowed to progress, test anxiety can have a big impact on your schooling, and consequently on your future.

Test anxiety can spread to other parts of your life. Anxiety on tests can become anxiety in any stressful situation, and blanking on a test can turn into panicking in a job situation. But fortunately, you don't have to let anxiety rule your testing and determine your grades. There are a number of relatively simple steps you can take to move past anxiety and function normally on a test and in the rest of life.

> **Review Video: How Test Anxiety Impacts Your Grades**
> Visit mometrix.com/academy and enter code: 939819

Copyright © Mometrix Media. You have been licensed one copy of this document for personal use only. Any other reproduction or redistribution is strictly prohibited. All rights reserved.
This content is provided for test preparation purposes only and does not imply an endorsement by Mometrix of any particular political, scientific, or religious point of view.

# Physical Steps for Beating Test Anxiety

While test anxiety is a serious problem, the good news is that it can be overcome. It doesn't have to control your ability to think and remember information. While it may take time, you can begin taking steps today to beat anxiety.

Just as your first hint that you may be struggling with anxiety comes from the physical symptoms, the first step to treating it is also physical. Rest is crucial for having a clear, strong mind. If you are tired, it is much easier to give in to anxiety. But if you establish good sleep habits, your body and mind will be ready to perform optimally, without the strain of exhaustion. Additionally, sleeping well helps you to retain information better, so you're more likely to recall the answers when you see the test questions.

Getting good sleep means more than going to bed on time. It's important to allow your brain time to relax. Take study breaks from time to time so it doesn't get overworked, and don't study right before bed. Take time to rest your mind before trying to rest your body, or you may find it difficult to fall asleep.

> **Review Video: The Importance of Sleep for Your Brain**
> Visit mometrix.com/academy and enter code: 319338

Along with sleep, other aspects of physical health are important in preparing for a test. Good nutrition is vital for good brain function. Sugary foods and drinks may give a burst of energy but this burst is followed by a crash, both physically and emotionally. Instead, fuel your body with protein and vitamin-rich foods.

Also, drink plenty of water. Dehydration can lead to headaches and exhaustion, especially if your brain is already under stress from the rigors of the test. Particularly if your test is a long one, drink water during the breaks. And if possible, take an energy-boosting snack to eat between sections.

> **Review Video: How Diet Can Affect your Mood**
> Visit mometrix.com/academy and enter code: 624317

Along with sleep and diet, a third important part of physical health is exercise. Maintaining a steady workout schedule is helpful, but even taking 5-minute study breaks to walk can help get your blood pumping faster and clear your head. Exercise also releases endorphins, which contribute to a positive feeling and can help combat test anxiety.

When you nurture your physical health, you are also contributing to your mental health. If your body is healthy, your mind is much more likely to be healthy as well. So take time to rest, nourish your body with healthy food and water, and get moving as much as possible. Taking these physical steps will make you stronger and more able to take the mental steps necessary to overcome test anxiety.

Copyright © Mometrix Media. You have been licensed one copy of this document for personal use only. Any other reproduction or redistribution is strictly prohibited. All rights reserved. This content is provided for test preparation purposes only and does not imply an endorsement by Mometrix of any particular political, scientific, or religious point of view.

# Mental Steps for Beating Test Anxiety

Working on the mental side of test anxiety can be more challenging, but as with the physical side, there are clear steps you can take to overcome it. As mentioned earlier, test anxiety often stems from lack of preparation, so the obvious solution is to prepare for the test. Effective studying may be the most important weapon you have for beating test anxiety, but you can and should employ several other mental tools to combat fear.

First, boost your confidence by reminding yourself of past success—tests or projects that you aced. If you're putting as much effort into preparing for this test as you did for those, there's no reason you should expect to fail here. Work hard to prepare; then trust your preparation.

Second, surround yourself with encouraging people. It can be helpful to find a study group, but be sure that the people you're around will encourage a positive attitude. If you spend time with others who are anxious or cynical, this will only contribute to your own anxiety. Look for others who are motivated to study hard from a desire to succeed, not from a fear of failure.

Third, reward yourself. A test is physically and mentally tiring, even without anxiety, and it can be helpful to have something to look forward to. Plan an activity following the test, regardless of the outcome, such as going to a movie or getting ice cream.

When you are taking the test, if you find yourself beginning to feel anxious, remind yourself that you know the material. Visualize successfully completing the test. Then take a few deep, relaxing breaths and return to it. Work through the questions carefully but with confidence, knowing that you are capable of succeeding.

Developing a healthy mental approach to test taking will also aid in other areas of life. Test anxiety affects more than just the actual test—it can be damaging to your mental health and even contribute to depression. It's important to beat test anxiety before it becomes a problem for more than testing.

> **Review Video: Test Anxiety and Depression**
> Visit mometrix.com/academy and enter code: 904704

Copyright © Mometrix Media. You have been licensed one copy of this document for personal use only. Any other reproduction or redistribution is strictly prohibited. All rights reserved.
This content is provided for test preparation purposes only and does not imply an endorsement by Mometrix of any particular political, scientific, or religious point of view.

# Study Strategy

Being prepared for the test is necessary to combat anxiety, but what does being prepared look like? You may study for hours on end and still not feel prepared. What you need is a strategy for test prep. The next few pages outline our recommended steps to help you plan out and conquer the challenge of preparation.

## STEP 1: SCOPE OUT THE TEST

Learn everything you can about the format (multiple choice, essay, etc.) and what will be on the test. Gather any study materials, course outlines, or sample exams that may be available. Not only will this help you to prepare, but knowing what to expect can help to alleviate test anxiety.

## STEP 2: MAP OUT THE MATERIAL

Look through the textbook or study guide and make note of how many chapters or sections it has. Then divide these over the time you have. For example, if a book has 15 chapters and you have five days to study, you need to cover three chapters each day. Even better, if you have the time, leave an extra day at the end for overall review after you have gone through the material in depth.

If time is limited, you may need to prioritize the material. Look through it and make note of which sections you think you already have a good grasp on, and which need review. While you are studying, skim quickly through the familiar sections and take more time on the challenging parts. Write out your plan so you don't get lost as you go. Having a written plan also helps you feel more in control of the study, so anxiety is less likely to arise from feeling overwhelmed at the amount to cover.

## STEP 3: GATHER YOUR TOOLS

Decide what study method works best for you. Do you prefer to highlight in the book as you study and then go back over the highlighted portions? Or do you type out notes of the important information? Or is it helpful to make flashcards that you can carry with you? Assemble the pens, index cards, highlighters, post-it notes, and any other materials you may need so you won't be distracted by getting up to find things while you study.

If you're having a hard time retaining the information or organizing your notes, experiment with different methods. For example, try color-coding by subject with colored pens, highlighters, or post-it notes. If you learn better by hearing, try recording yourself reading your notes so you can listen while in the car, working out, or simply sitting at your desk. Ask a friend to quiz you from your flashcards, or try teaching someone the material to solidify it in your mind.

## STEP 4: CREATE YOUR ENVIRONMENT

It's important to avoid distractions while you study. This includes both the obvious distractions like visitors and the subtle distractions like an uncomfortable chair (or a too-comfortable couch that makes you want to fall asleep). Set up the best study environment possible: good lighting and a comfortable work area. If background music helps you focus, you may want to turn it on, but otherwise keep the room quiet. If you are using a computer to take notes, be sure you don't have any other windows open, especially applications like social media, games, or anything else that could distract you. Silence your phone and turn off notifications. Be sure to keep water close by so you stay hydrated while you study (but avoid unhealthy drinks and snacks).

Also, take into account the best time of day to study. Are you freshest first thing in the morning? Try to set aside some time then to work through the material. Is your mind clearer in the afternoon or evening? Schedule your study session then. Another method is to study at the same time of day that

Copyright © Mometrix Media. You have been licensed one copy of this document for personal use only. Any other reproduction or redistribution is strictly prohibited. All rights reserved. This content is provided for test preparation purposes only and does not imply an endorsement by Mometrix of any particular political, scientific, or religious point of view.

you will take the test, so that your brain gets used to working on the material at that time and will be ready to focus at test time.

## Step 5: Study!

Once you have done all the study preparation, it's time to settle into the actual studying. Sit down, take a few moments to settle your mind so you can focus, and begin to follow your study plan. Don't give in to distractions or let yourself procrastinate. This is your time to prepare so you'll be ready to fearlessly approach the test. Make the most of the time and stay focused.

Of course, you don't want to burn out. If you study too long you may find that you're not retaining the information very well. Take regular study breaks. For example, taking five minutes out of every hour to walk briskly, breathing deeply and swinging your arms, can help your mind stay fresh.

As you get to the end of each chapter or section, it's a good idea to do a quick review. Remind yourself of what you learned and work on any difficult parts. When you feel that you've mastered the material, move on to the next part. At the end of your study session, briefly skim through your notes again.

But while review is helpful, cramming last minute is NOT. If at all possible, work ahead so that you won't need to fit all your study into the last day. Cramming overloads your brain with more information than it can process and retain, and your tired mind may struggle to recall even previously learned information when it is overwhelmed with last-minute study. Also, the urgent nature of cramming and the stress placed on your brain contribute to anxiety. You'll be more likely to go to the test feeling unprepared and having trouble thinking clearly.

So don't cram, and don't stay up late before the test, even just to review your notes at a leisurely pace. Your brain needs rest more than it needs to go over the information again. In fact, plan to finish your studies by noon or early afternoon the day before the test. Give your brain the rest of the day to relax or focus on other things, and get a good night's sleep. Then you will be fresh for the test and better able to recall what you've studied.

## Step 6: Take a Practice Test

Many courses offer sample tests, either online or in the study materials. This is an excellent resource to check whether you have mastered the material, as well as to prepare for the test format and environment.

Check the test format ahead of time: the number of questions, the type (multiple choice, free response, etc.), and the time limit. Then create a plan for working through them. For example, if you have 30 minutes to take a 60-question test, your limit is 30 seconds per question. Spend less time on the questions you know well so that you can take more time on the difficult ones.

If you have time to take several practice tests, take the first one open book, with no time limit. Work through the questions at your own pace and make sure you fully understand them. Gradually work up to taking a test under test conditions: sit at a desk with all study materials put away and set a timer. Pace yourself to make sure you finish the test with time to spare and go back to check your answers if you have time.

After each test, check your answers. On the questions you missed, be sure you understand why you missed them. Did you misread the question (tests can use tricky wording)? Did you forget the information? Or was it something you hadn't learned? Go back and study any shaky areas that the practice tests reveal.

Copyright © Mometrix Media. You have been licensed one copy of this document for personal use only. Any other reproduction or redistribution is strictly prohibited. All rights reserved.
This content is provided for test preparation purposes only and does not imply an endorsement by Mometrix of any particular political, scientific, or religious point of view.

Taking these tests not only helps with your grade, but also aids in combating test anxiety. If you're already used to the test conditions, you're less likely to worry about it, and working through tests until you're scoring well gives you a confidence boost. Go through the practice tests until you feel comfortable, and then you can go into the test knowing that you're ready for it.

## Test Tips

On test day, you should be confident, knowing that you've prepared well and are ready to answer the questions. But aside from preparation, there are several test day strategies you can employ to maximize your performance.

First, as stated before, get a good night's sleep the night before the test (and for several nights before that, if possible). Go into the test with a fresh, alert mind rather than staying up late to study.

Try not to change too much about your normal routine on the day of the test. It's important to eat a nutritious breakfast, but if you normally don't eat breakfast at all, consider eating just a protein bar. If you're a coffee drinker, go ahead and have your normal coffee. Just make sure you time it so that the caffeine doesn't wear off right in the middle of your test. Avoid sugary beverages, and drink enough water to stay hydrated but not so much that you need a restroom break 10 minutes into the test. If your test isn't first thing in the morning, consider going for a walk or doing a light workout before the test to get your blood flowing.

Allow yourself enough time to get ready, and leave for the test with plenty of time to spare so you won't have the anxiety of scrambling to arrive in time. Another reason to be early is to select a good seat. It's helpful to sit away from doors and windows, which can be distracting. Find a good seat, get out your supplies, and settle your mind before the test begins.

When the test begins, start by going over the instructions carefully, even if you already know what to expect. Make sure you avoid any careless mistakes by following the directions.

Then begin working through the questions, pacing yourself as you've practiced. If you're not sure on an answer, don't spend too much time on it, and don't let it shake your confidence. Either skip it and come back later, or eliminate as many wrong answers as possible and guess among the remaining ones. Don't dwell on these questions as you continue—put them out of your mind and focus on what lies ahead.

Be sure to read all of the answer choices, even if you're sure the first one is the right answer. Sometimes you'll find a better one if you keep reading. But don't second-guess yourself if you do immediately know the answer. Your gut instinct is usually right. Don't let test anxiety rob you of the information you know.

If you have time at the end of the test (and if the test format allows), go back and review your answers. Be cautious about changing any, since your first instinct tends to be correct, but make sure you didn't misread any of the questions or accidentally mark the wrong answer choice. Look over any you skipped and make an educated guess.

At the end, leave the test feeling confident. You've done your best, so don't waste time worrying about your performance or wishing you could change anything. Instead, celebrate the successful

Copyright © Mometrix Media. You have been licensed one copy of this document for personal use only. Any other reproduction or redistribution is strictly prohibited. All rights reserved.
This content is provided for test preparation purposes only and does not imply an endorsement by Mometrix of any particular political, scientific, or religious point of view.

completion of this test. And finally, use this test to learn how to deal with anxiety even better next time.

**Review Video: <u>5 Tips to Beat Test Anxiety</u>**
Visit mometrix.com/academy and enter code: 570656

## Important Qualification

Not all anxiety is created equal. If your test anxiety is causing major issues in your life beyond the classroom or testing center, or if you are experiencing troubling physical symptoms related to your anxiety, it may be a sign of a serious physiological or psychological condition. If this sounds like your situation, we strongly encourage you to seek professional help.

Copyright © Mometrix Media. You have been licensed one copy of this document for personal use only. Any other reproduction or redistribution is strictly prohibited. All rights reserved.
This content is provided for test preparation purposes only and does not imply an endorsement by Mometrix of any particular political, scientific, or religious point of view.

# How to Overcome Your Fear of Math

Not again. You're sitting in math class, look down at your test, and immediately start to panic. Your stomach is in knots, your heart is racing, and you break out in a cold sweat. You're staring at the paper, but everything looks like it's written in a foreign language. Even though you studied, you're blanking out on how to begin solving these problems.

Does this sound familiar? If so, then you're not alone! You may be like millions of other people who experience math anxiety. Anxiety about performing well in math is a common experience for students of all ages. In this article, we'll discuss what math anxiety is, common misconceptions about learning math, and tips and strategies for overcoming math anxiety.

## What Is Math Anxiety?

Psychologist Mark H. Ashcraft explains math anxiety as a feeling of tension, apprehension, or fear that interferes with math performance. Having math anxiety negatively impacts people's beliefs about themselves and what they can achieve. It hinders achievement within the math classroom and affects the successful application of mathematics in the real world.

### SYMPTOMS AND SIGNS OF MATH ANXIETY

To overcome math anxiety, you must recognize its symptoms. Becoming aware of the signs of math anxiety is the first step in addressing and resolving these fears.

### NEGATIVE SELF-TALK

If you have math anxiety, you've most likely said at least one of these statements to yourself:

- "I hate math."
- "I'm not good at math."
- "I'm not a math person."

The way we speak to ourselves and think about ourselves matters. Our thoughts become our words, our words become our actions, and our actions become our habits. Thinking negatively about math creates a self-fulfilling prophecy. In other words, if you take an idea as a fact, then it will come true because your behaviors will align to match it.

### AVOIDANCE

Some people who are fearful or anxious about math will tend to avoid it altogether. Avoidance can manifest in the following ways:

- Lack of engagement with math content
- Not completing homework and other assignments
- Not asking for help when needed
- Skipping class
- Avoiding math-related courses and activities

Avoidance is one of the most harmful impacts of math anxiety. If you steer clear of math at all costs, then you can't set yourself up for the success you deserve.

243

Copyright © Mometrix Media. You have been licensed one copy of this document for personal use only. Any other reproduction or redistribution is strictly prohibited. All rights reserved.
This content is provided for test preparation purposes only and does not imply an endorsement by Mometrix of any particular political, scientific, or religious point of view.

## LACK OF MOTIVATION

Students with math anxiety may experience a lack of motivation. They may struggle to find the incentive to get engaged with what they view as a frightening subject. These students are often overwhelmed, making it difficult for them to complete or even start math assignments.

## PROCRASTINATION

Another symptom of math anxiety is procrastination. Students may voluntarily delay or postpone their classwork and assignments, even if they know there will be a negative consequence for doing so. Additionally, they may choose to wait until the last minute to start projects and homework, even when they know they need more time to put forth their best effort.

## PHYSIOLOGICAL REACTIONS

Many people with a fear of math experience physiological side effects. These may include an increase in heart rate, sweatiness, shakiness, nausea, and irregular breathing. These symptoms make it difficult to focus on the math content, causing the student even more stress and fear.

## STRONG EMOTIONAL RESPONSES

Math anxiety also affects people on an emotional level. Responding to math content with strong emotions such as panic, anger, or despair can be a sign of math anxiety.

## LOW TEST SCORES AND PERFORMANCE

Low achievement can be both a symptom and a cause of math anxiety. When someone does not take the steps needed to perform well on tests and assessments, they are less likely to pass. The more they perform poorly, the more they accept this poor performance as a fact that can't be changed.

## FEELING ALONE

People who experience math anxiety feel like they are the only ones struggling, even if the math they are working on is challenging to many people. Feeling isolated in what they perceive as failure can trigger tension or nervousness.

## FEELING OF PERMANENCY

Math anxiety can feel very permanent. You may assume that you are naturally bad at math and always will be. Viewing math as a natural ability rather than a skill that can be learned causes people to believe that nothing will help them improve. They take their current math abilities as fact and assume that they can't be changed. As a result, they give up, stop trying to improve, and avoid engaging with math altogether.

## LACK OF CONFIDENCE

People with low self-confidence in math tend to feel awkward and incompetent when asked to solve a math problem. They don't feel comfortable taking chances or risks when problem-solving because they second-guess themselves and assume they are incorrect. They don't trust in their ability to learn the content and solve problems correctly.

## PANIC

A general sense of unexplained panic is also a sign of math anxiety. You may feel a sudden sense of fear that triggers physical reactions, even when there is no apparent reason for such a response.

Copyright © Mometrix Media. You have been licensed one copy of this document for personal use only. Any other reproduction or redistribution is strictly prohibited. All rights reserved.
This content is provided for test preparation purposes only and does not imply an endorsement by Mometrix of any particular political, scientific, or religious point of view.

## CAUSES OF MATH ANXIETY

Math anxiety can start at a young age and may have one or more underlying causes. Common causes of math anxiety include the following:

### THE ATTITUDE OF PARENTS OR GUARDIANS

Parents often put pressure on their children to perform well in school. Although their intentions are usually good, this pressure can lead to anxiety, especially if the student is struggling with a subject or class.

Perhaps your parents or others in your life hold negative predispositions about math based on their own experiences. For instance, if your mother once claimed she was not good at math, then you might have incorrectly interpreted this as a predisposed trait that was passed down to you.

### TEACHER INFLUENCE

Students often pick up on their teachers' attitudes about the content being taught. If a teacher is happy and excited about math, students are more likely to mirror these emotions. However, if a teacher lacks enthusiasm or genuine interest, then students are more inclined to disengage.

Teachers have a responsibility to cultivate a welcoming classroom culture that is accepting of mistakes. When teachers blame students for not understanding a concept, they create a hostile classroom environment where mistakes are not tolerated. This tension increases student stress and anxiety, creating conditions that are not conducive to inquiry and learning. Instead, when teachers normalize mistakes as a natural part of the problem-solving process, they give their students the freedom to explore and grapple with the math content. In such an environment, students feel comfortable taking chances because they are not afraid of being wrong.

Students need teachers that can help when they're having problems understanding difficult concepts. In doing so, educators may need to change how they teach the content. Since different people have unique learning styles, it's the job of the teacher to adapt to the needs of each student. Additionally, teachers should encourage students to explore alternate problem-solving strategies, even if it's not the preferred method of the educator.

### FEAR OF BEING WRONG

Embarrassing situations can be traumatic, especially for young children and adolescents. These experiences can stay with people through their adult lives. Those with math anxiety may experience a fear of being wrong, especially in front of a group of peers. This fear can be paralyzing, interfering with the student's concentration and ability to focus on the problem at hand.

### TIMED ASSESSMENTS

Timed assessments can help improve math fluency, but they often create unnecessary pressure for students to complete an unrealistic number of problems within a specified timeframe. Many studies have shown that timed assessments often result in increased levels of anxiety, reducing a student's overall competence and ability to problem-solve.

Copyright © Mometrix Media. You have been licensed one copy of this document for personal use only. Any other reproduction or redistribution is strictly prohibited. All rights reserved. This content is provided for test preparation purposes only and does not imply an endorsement by Mometrix of any particular political, scientific, or religious point of view.

# Debunking Math Myths

There are lots of myths about math that are related to the causes and development of math-related anxiety. Although these myths have been proven to be false, many people take them as fact. Let's go over a few of the most common myths about learning math.

## MYTH: MEN ARE BETTER AT MATH THAN WOMEN

Math has a reputation for being a male-dominant subject, but this doesn't mean that men are inherently better at math than women. Many famous mathematical discoveries have been made by women. Katherine Johnson, Dame Mary Lucy Cartwright, and Marjorie Lee Brown are just a few of the many famous women mathematicians. Expecting to be good or bad at math because of your gender sets you up for stress and confusion. Math is a skill that can be learned, just like cooking or riding a bike.

## MYTH: THERE IS ONLY ONE GOOD WAY TO SOLVE MATH PROBLEMS

There are many ways to get the correct answer when it comes to math. No two people have the same brain, so everyone takes a slightly different approach to problem-solving. Moreover, there isn't one way of problem-solving that's superior to another. Your way of working through a problem might differ from someone else's, and that is okay. Math can be a highly individualized process, so the best method for you should be the one that makes you feel the most comfortable and makes the most sense to you.

## MYTH: MATH REQUIRES A GOOD MEMORY

For many years, mathematics was taught through memorization. However, learning in such a way hinders the development of critical thinking and conceptual understanding. These skill sets are much more valuable than basic memorization. For instance, you might be great at memorizing mathematical formulas, but if you don't understand what they mean, then you can't apply them to different scenarios in the real world. When a student is working from memory, they are limited in the strategies available to them to problem-solve. In other words, they assume there is only one correct way to do the math, which is the method they memorized. Having a variety of problem-solving options can help students figure out which method works best for them. Additionally, it provides students with a better understanding of how and why certain mathematical strategies work. While memorization can be helpful in some instances, it is not an absolute requirement for mathematicians.

## MYTH: MATH IS NOT CREATIVE

Math requires imagination and intuition. Contrary to popular belief, it is a highly creative field. Mathematical creativity can help in developing new ways to think about and solve problems. Many people incorrectly assume that all things are either creative or analytical. However, this black-and-white view is limiting because the field of mathematics involves both creativity and logic.

## MYTH: MATH ISN'T SUPPOSED TO BE FUN

Whoever told you that math isn't supposed to be fun is a liar. There are tons of math-based activities and games that foster friendly competition and engagement. Math is often best learned through play, and lots of mobile apps and computer games exemplify this.

Additionally, math can be an exceptionally collaborative and social experience. Studying or working through problems with a friend often makes the process a lot more fun. The excitement and satisfaction of solving a difficult problem with others is quite rewarding. Math can be fun if you look for ways to make it more collaborative and enjoyable.

Copyright © Mometrix Media. You have been licensed one copy of this document for personal use only. Any other reproduction or redistribution is strictly prohibited. All rights reserved. This content is provided for test preparation purposes only and does not imply an endorsement by Mometrix of any particular political, scientific, or religious point of view.

## MYTH: NOT EVERYONE IS CAPABLE OF LEARNING MATH

There's no such thing as a "math person." Although many people think that you're either good at math or you're not, this is simply not true. Everyone is capable of learning and applying mathematics. However, not everyone learns the same way. Since each person has a different learning style, the trick is to find the strategies and learning tools that work best for you. Some people learn best through hands-on experiences, and others find success through the use of visual aids. Others are auditory learners and learn best by hearing and listening. When people are overwhelmed or feel that math is too hard, it's often because they haven't found the learning strategy that works best for them.

## MYTH: GOOD MATHEMATICIANS WORK QUICKLY AND NEVER MAKE MISTAKES

There is no prize for finishing first in math. It's not a race, and speed isn't a measure of your ability. Good mathematicians take their time to ensure their work is accurate. As you gain more experience and practice, you will naturally become faster and more confident.

Additionally, everyone makes mistakes, including good mathematicians. Mistakes are a normal part of the problem-solving process, and they're not a bad thing. The important thing is that we take the time to learn from our mistakes, understand where our misconceptions are, and move forward.

## MYTH: YOU DON'T NEED MATH IN THE REAL WORLD

Our day-to-day lives are so infused with mathematical concepts that we often don't even realize when we're using math in the real world. In fact, most people tend to underestimate how much we do math in our everyday lives. It's involved in an enormous variety of daily activities such as shopping, baking, finances, and gardening, as well as in many careers, including architecture, nursing, design, and sales.

# Tips and Strategies for Overcoming Math Anxiety

If your anxiety is getting in the way of your level of mathematical engagement, then there are lots of steps you can take. Check out the strategies below to start building confidence in math today.

## FOCUS ON UNDERSTANDING, NOT MEMORIZATION

Don't drive yourself crazy trying to memorize every single formula or mathematical process. Instead, shift your attention to understanding concepts. Those who prioritize memorization over conceptual understanding tend to have lower achievement levels in math. Students who memorize may be able to complete some math, but they don't understand the process well enough to apply it to different situations. Memorization comes with time and practice, but it won't help alleviate math anxiety. On the other hand, conceptual understanding will give you the building blocks of knowledge you need to build up your confidence.

Copyright © Mometrix Media. You have been licensed one copy of this document for personal use only. Any other reproduction or redistribution is strictly prohibited. All rights reserved. This content is provided for test preparation purposes only and does not imply an endorsement by Mometrix of any particular political, scientific, or religious point of view.

## REPLACE NEGATIVE SELF-TALK WITH POSITIVE SELF-TALK

Start to notice how you think about yourself. Whenever you catch yourself thinking something negative, try replacing that thought with a positive affirmation. Instead of continuing the negative thought, pause to reframe the situation. For ideas on how to get started, take a look at the table below:

| Instead of thinking... | Try thinking... |
|---|---|
| "I can't do this math." "I'm not a math person." | "I'm up for the challenge, and I'm training my brain in math." |
| "This problem is too hard." | "This problem is hard, so this might take some time and effort. I know I can do this." |
| "I give up." | "What strategies can help me solve this problem?" |
| "I made a mistake, so I'm not good at this." | "Everyone makes mistakes. Mistakes help me to grow and understand." |
| "I'll never be smart enough." | "I can figure this out, and I am smart enough." |

## PRACTICE MINDFULNESS

Practicing mindfulness and focusing on your breathing can help alleviate some of the physical symptoms of math anxiety. By taking deep breaths, you can remind your nervous system that you are not in immediate danger. Doing so will reduce your heart rate and help with any irregular breathing or shakiness. Taking the edge off of the physiological effects of anxiety will clear your mind, allowing your brain to focus its energy on problem-solving.

## DO SOME MATH EVERY DAY

Think about learning math as if you were learning a foreign language. If you don't use it, you lose it. If you don't practice your math skills regularly, you'll have a harder time achieving comprehension and fluency. Set some amount of time aside each day, even if it's just for a few minutes, to practice. It might take some discipline to build a habit around this, but doing so will help increase your mathematical self-assurance.

## USE ALL OF YOUR RESOURCES

Everyone has a different learning style, and there are plenty of resources out there to support all learners. When you get stuck on a math problem, think about the tools you have access to, and use them when applicable. Such resources may include flashcards, graphic organizers, study guides, interactive notebooks, and peer study groups. All of these are great tools to accommodate your individual learning style. Finding the tools and resources that work for your learning style will give you the confidence you need to succeed.

## REALIZE THAT YOU AREN'T ALONE

Remind yourself that lots of other people struggle with math anxiety, including teachers, nurses, and even successful mathematicians. You aren't the only one who panics when faced with a new or challenging problem. It's probably much more common than you think. Realizing that you aren't alone in your experience can help put some distance between yourself and the emotions you feel about math. It also helps to normalize the anxiety and shift your perspective.

Copyright © Mometrix Media. You have been licensed one copy of this document for personal use only. Any other reproduction or redistribution is strictly prohibited. All rights reserved. This content is provided for test preparation purposes only and does not imply an endorsement by Mometrix of any particular political, scientific, or religious point of view.

## ASK QUESTIONS

If there's a concept you don't understand and you've tried everything you can, then it's okay to ask for help! You can always ask your teacher or professor for help. If you're not learning math in a traditional classroom, you may want to join a study group, work with a tutor, or talk to your friends. More often than not, you aren't the only one of your peers who needs clarity on a mathematical concept. Seeking understanding is a great way to increase self-confidence in math.

## REMEMBER THAT THERE'S MORE THAN ONE WAY TO SOLVE A PROBLEM

Since everyone learns differently, it's best to focus on understanding a math problem with an approach that makes sense to you. If the way it's being taught is confusing to you, don't give up. Instead, work to understand the problem using a different technique. There's almost always more than one problem-solving method when it comes to math. Don't get stressed if one of them doesn't make sense to you. Instead, shift your focus to what does make sense. Chances are high that you know more than you think you do.

## VISUALIZATION

Visualization is the process of creating images in your mind's eye. Picture yourself as a successful, confident mathematician. Think about how you would feel and how you would behave. What would your work area look like? How would you organize your belongings? The more you focus on something, the more likely you are to achieve it. Visualizing teaches your brain that you can achieve whatever it is that you want. Thinking about success in mathematics will lead to acting like a successful mathematician. This, in turn, leads to actual success.

## FOCUS ON THE EASIEST PROBLEMS FIRST

To increase your confidence when working on a math test or assignment, try solving the easiest problems first. Doing so will remind you that you are successful in math and that you do have what it takes. This process will increase your belief in yourself, giving you the confidence you need to tackle more complex problems.

## FIND A SUPPORT GROUP

A study buddy, tutor, or peer group can go a long way in decreasing math-related anxiety. Such support systems offer lots of benefits, including a safe place to ask questions, additional practice with mathematical concepts, and an understanding of other problem-solving explanations that may work better for you. Equipping yourself with a support group is one of the fastest ways to eliminate math anxiety.

## REWARD YOURSELF FOR WORKING HARD

Recognize the amount of effort you're putting in to overcome your math anxiety. It's not an easy task, so you deserve acknowledgement. Surround yourself with people who will provide you with the positive reinforcement you deserve.

# Remember, You Can Do This!

Conquering a fear of math can be challenging, but there are lots of strategies that can help you out. Your own beliefs about your mathematical capabilities can limit your potential. Working toward a growth mindset can have a tremendous impact on decreasing math-related anxiety and building confidence. By knowing the symptoms of math anxiety and recognizing common misconceptions about learning math, you can develop a plan to address your fear of math. Utilizing the strategies discussed can help you overcome this anxiety and build the confidence you need to succeed.

Copyright © Mometrix Media. You have been licensed one copy of this document for personal use only. Any other reproduction or redistribution is strictly prohibited. All rights reserved.
This content is provided for test preparation purposes only and does not imply an endorsement by Mometrix of any particular political, scientific, or religious point of view.

# Thank You

We at Mometrix would like to extend our heartfelt thanks to you, our friend and patron, for allowing us to play a part in your journey. It is a privilege to serve people from all walks of life who are unified in their commitment to building the best future they can for themselves.

The preparation you devote to these important testing milestones may be the most valuable educational opportunity you have for making a real difference in your life. We encourage you to put your heart into it—that feeling of succeeding, overcoming, and yes, conquering will be well worth the hours you've invested.

We want to hear your story, your struggles and your successes, and if you see any opportunities for us to improve our materials so we can help others even more effectively in the future, please share that with us as well. **The team at Mometrix would be absolutely thrilled to hear from you!** So please, send us an email (support@mometrix.com) and let's stay in touch.

Copyright © Mometrix Media. You have been licensed one copy of this document for personal use only. Any other reproduction or redistribution is strictly prohibited. All rights reserved.
This content is provided for test preparation purposes only and does not imply an endorsement by Mometrix of any particular political, scientific, or religious point of view.

# Additional Bonus Material

Due to our efforts to try to keep this book to a manageable length, we've created a link that will give you access to all of your additional bonus material:

**mometrix.com/bonus948/iseeupper**

Copyright © Mometrix Media. You have been licensed one copy of this document for personal use only. Any other reproduction or redistribution is strictly prohibited. All rights reserved.
This content is provided for test preparation purposes only and does not imply an endorsement by Mometrix of any particular political, scientific, or religious point of view.

Made in the USA
Middletown, DE
25 August 2023

37373238R00146